To: Keith

Best Regards

One &

Forest L

~The Blue WARRIOR

MICL BURNS

From OJ Mancha

The Blue Warrior

Above the Line of Duty

O.J. Moravek

A Hearthstone Book

Carlton Press Corp. ❖ **New York, NY**

Victims and witnesses names have been changed to protect the innocent!

IN MEMORY OF
Det. JOHN W. SCZYREK JR. (N.P.D.)
1963–1993
Killed in the Line of Duty
June 3rd, 1993

IN MEMORY OF
Officer SEAN McDONALD (N.Y.P.D.)
1968–1994
Killed in the Line of Duty
March 15, 1994

Contents

The Police Officer's Role

By O.J. Moravek

The life and death of a police officer cannot be distinguished,
for he represents the law and justice with pride and integrity.
The career he leads is dangerous and he lives in fear all of the time.
His reaction to a situation must be quick and justified without a doubt in his mind.
The police officer's role is important to the citizens who rely on him,
but his chances of gaining respect today are slim.
Police are known as the fuzz, flatfoot, dick, bull, cop, heat, and pigs across the nation,
but these same name-callers rely on the police to assist them for help and salvation.
The role of an officer is a doctor, lawyer, plumber, mechanic, counselor.
He tries to do all to the best of his ability with knowledge and helpfulness alike.
Officers accept the role with the hope that people realize we have pride and integrity.
We are here to protect the lives and property of the citizens. This is a reality.
The death of an officer killed in action brings sadness to his family and friends.
The sacrifice that he offers is a never-ending quest for justice along every bend.
The fear and anxiety police officers face is a reality everyday of their lives.
Officers always bear in mind the reality of death as a possibility.
The police officer takes quite a bit of abuse, but he still always respects his badge and performs his role to the best of his ability.
His way of earning a living is by trying to protect our city and citizens.

They can count on our reliability.

Overshadowing the police officer is his willingness to serve the public twenty-four hours a day.

He works three shifts a month, which includes weekends and holidays.

His reward for his perilous efforts could never be matched in gold.

This is the life and career we chose and this is a police officer's role.

Acknowledgements

A special and sincere thank you to my father, Otto Moravek, Sr., to his secretary of forty years, Marie Tutela, and, most importantly, to my brother, Edward Moravek, and my wife, Aida Moravek. Each has contributed to inspire me to write this book.

My entire family have dedicated their lives to law enforcement. My father recently retired from the Essex County Deputy Sheriff's Department, where he served as Chief for thirty-eight years. My older brother Edward Moravek is a Detective in the Youth Aid Bureau who has served with the Newark Police Department for thirty years, has been selected as one of the Veteran Blue Warriors, and who inspired me to always wear the uniform proudly. My younger brother, John Moravek, has served with the Essex County Deputy Sheriffs for twenty-six years, and was recently promoted to Deputy Chief. My sister, Alina Moravek, has served as a liaison officer with the Deputy Sheriff's Department for twenty-two years. Thank you all so very much for your love and support.

I would also like to thank all of the staff at Carlton Press who have been in direct contact with me throughout the process of producing this book, and for their painstaking and excellent efforts in re-editing and producing what, for me, started out as a dream and a goal and has now become a reality.

The Blue Warrior

1 Change of Uniform

I remember receiving a letter from the induction board on October 12, 1968. It was my draft notice; the letter went like this: "Greetings Sir, you have been officially inducted into the United States Marine Corps. You will report to the draft board on Nye Avenue and Lincoln Street in Irvington, New Jersey at 0700 hours December 3, 1968." My father drove me down to the induction center. I was given assignment papers and my father and I drove down to the induction ceremony at Penn Railroad Station in Newark, New Jersey. At 0800 hours I said good-bye to my father. He had tears in his eyes and wished me good luck.

The train transported all of us recruits to the Marine Corps Depot Station, Parris Island, South Carolina. The train ride was long, taking twenty-two hours. We stopped once between Newark and Washington, D.C. The train stopped in Washington, D.C. for a few hours. We got off the train and had a bite to eat, and soon we were on our way to Parris Island, South Carolina. We arrived at the bus depot in Savanah, Georgia at 0500 hours. The bus trip from Savanah, Georgia to Parris Island took one and a half hours. We arrived at Parris Island at 0630 hours, and were greeted by a Sergeant Kiss.

The Marine Corps Drill Instructor, Sergeant Kiss, boarded the bus and he had a warm greeting for us.

"Good morning, maggots," he said. "My name is Sergeant Robert Kiss, and you scumbags will quickly get off the bus, line up and stand at attention for roll call. I want to make this perfectly clear, if any of you maggots think that you are here for a party forget it. Now get your gear together and prepare for the nightmare of your life. You scummy worms will report to Company C barracks, third platoon, Second Marine Division, Second Battalion.

"I along with Staff Sergeant Tom Branson and Gunnery Sergeant Ray Taylor will be your on-base drill instructors. We will train you boys to become the finest working machine in the armed forces. We will turn you scummy mice into fine men, you will be proud of your accomplishments, but you will have to earn every ounce of blood that represents the United States Marine Corps.

"By the time you maggots complete your eighteen weeks of training, we will transform you mice into men. We will make you or we will break you. You will have to earn the title of United States Marine."

Sergeant Kiss introduced us to drill instructor Staff Sergeant Branson.

The following morning Staff Sergeant Tom Branson entered the recruit barracks.

"Good morning, marine recruits," he said. "During the next eighteen weeks I will be your drill instructor in physical fitness. When I am done training you recruits, you will be in the finest physical and mental condition of your life. Your physical fitness training will consist of a daily three mile endurance run. You will be required to do twenty-five push-ups, twenty-five sit-ups, and one hundred jumping jacks. Your endurance run will increase by one mile every other week. When you complete eighteen weeks of training you will be required to endure a ten mile run. All other exercises will increase by ten in each category. One week before you graduate, you will take a physical fitness endurance test. The test will consist of a ten mile endurance run, one hundred push-ups, one hundred sit-ups, and 500 jumping jacks. You will have to successfully climb a one hundred foot rope to the platform of the slide for life. The last course is the slide for life. This rope extends 600 feet across and one hundred feet above a lake. You will use your hand strength to slide across the lake elevating your feet and legs to maneuver across to the other side of the lake."

I remember in the early afternoon on the second day of our training, Staff Sergeant Branson introduced Gunner Sergeant Ray Taylor.

"Good afternoon marine recruits," he said. "After surviving your eighteen weeks of training we will be proud to call all of you men United States Marines. You will be honored to carry that title. However you will have to earn the right to be called a graduate of the United States Marine Corps Recruit Depot. Among you in this Battalion we have 162 recruits, less than half of you will graduate. Not everyone here is cut out to be a Marine. Everyone here will not be able to take the physical and mental ordeal that all of you will have to deal with. When you successfully complete your training the title United States Marine will be with you the rest of your life. Ten, twenty, thirty years from now you will always remember your three drill instructors. Our names will remain in your minds for the rest of your life.

"I will be training you on the parade deck. You will learn how to march to perfection as one unit. You will learn how to position your rifle at port arms for inspections. You will learn how to in unison flawlessly switch your rifle to many different positions. You will go to sleep at 1830 hours every night and reveille will be at 0430 hours. Breakfast will be served at 0630 hours, lunch will be at 1300 hours and dinner will be at 1800 hours. The recruits who are overweight will be served in a special diet line. The underweight recruits will be in a special protein diet line. Most of you Marines will graduate at a weight of approximately 175 pounds of solid muscle. The physical fitness conditioning you will endure will have your body in the best shape that you will ever be in for the remainder of your life.

"When you complete your training you will know why the United States Marine Corps has the finest soldiers assembled anywhere on earth. I wish everyone here good luck and I will see you tomorrow morning at 0430 hours."

The drill instructors were right. The eighteen weeks of boot camp training was a challenge for all of us to bear and reckon with. The recruits that were smokers, heavy drinkers and or were overweight had a greater burden in comparison to recruits who were in fair condition and did not smoke and drink. I was in top physical condition. I did not smoke or drink. We were prohibited from those bad habits when I was playing on a semi-pro baseball team, and yet I was physically and mentally drained from the eighteen weeks of continuous physical conditioning. My muscles were all very sore. My skin felt as if it were being peeled off. My body felt as if it were being reborn or recycled again. It was as if I were given a new body. Twenty-five years later I can only wish that I could be in that body.

Our first week of training we learned how to take apart our M-16 rifle. We learned how to shoot our rifle proficiently and we learned how to take apart our rifle blind folded. Our second week of training was platoon formations in combat situations. Our third week of training dealt with survival in a combat zone. Our fourth week of training dealt with defensive combat tactic maneuvers and defensive bayonet training.

Our fifth and sixth week of training dealt with vigorous physical fitness. Our seventh and eighth week of training dealt with chemical warfare procedures. The training focused on how to use a gas mask properly for breathing during a chemical gas attack. We all went into a building that was filled with simulated deadly gas. In numerous practice sessions we all learned how to use a gas mask properly. We were all told the reality that a failure to use a gas mask properly would cause instant death during a chemical warfare attack.

Our ninth and tenth week of training dealt with the slide for life course. This particular course was a challenge to every Marine; we were prepared for the course. We were in top physical shape and the rigorous training only made us stronger and more confident. The course consisted of rope climbing, crawling under a wired field with a twelve-inch clearing, scaling a twenty foot wall, scaling a one hundred foot ladder on a horizontal bar that requires each Marine carrying his rifle and a twenty-pound ammunition pack.

With the equipment on each shoulder we ran a four-mile course. The course had us crawling thorough a barbed wire field. The course continued with a one-mile stretch of muddy, murky water with a man-made stream that each Marine had to drag his body through. When the course was over we had to run two miles with approximately 150 pounds of mud clinging onto our uniforms. The day ended with the ultimate challenge, the slide for life. This was an incredible course to conquer and in the dead of winter this was not an easy accomplishment. To attain success in this course each Marine was required to climb a 100 foot rope to the top of the slide for life platform. From the platform you would extend your feet and hug the rope and using your hands and feet you would slowly descend across the lake. No one fell into the water, the extensive and vigorous training paid off. We all successfully completed the slide for life.

Our eleventh, twelth and thirteeth week of training dealt with defensive combat training. This training had courses in poco stick fighting. The poco sticks were simulated as if you had a bayonet. Each Marine fought an opponent in a circled area.

During the defensive combat training I remember getting knocked in the head a few times. Every Marine had a competitive opponent. After one week of extensive bayonet training, the opponents were well prepared for each other. During the afternoon Staff Sergeant Branson and Gunnery Sergeant Taylor instructed us on platoon formations. On the parade deck we had extensive training that focused on flank positions.

Our fourteeth, fifteeth and sixteeth week of training dealt with learning the various arsenals of weapons that were issued to marines in a combat zone. Some of the many weapons we were trained to operate were, hand grenades, .45 colt automatic, semi-automatic machine guns, rocket launchers and rocket flares.

Our seventeeth week of training focused on a review of the combat maneuvers and flank formations. We also reviewed our marching formations on the parade deck. The week ended with a physical fitness course and additional training on the rifle range.

During our eighteenth week of training our drill instructors gave us orientation on all the reasons why they stressed discipline and physical endurance. The last three days were focused on qualifying and passing the following tests: On Wednesday we had our physical fitness test. On Thursday we had our slide for life endurance test. On Friday we were on the rifle range for qualification. Saturday was a day for rest. Sunday was graduation day for the Marines who passed the courses.

The proudest day of my life was graduation day April 29, 1968. My father and two brothers came down from New Jersey to congratulate me on this very special day. Our battalion graduated with a class of seventy-nine Marines. We started out with one hundred and sixty-two recruits, but unfortunately only about half graduated.

The Marine Corps is tough and not everyone survives that kind of training. Gunnery Sergeant Taylor informed us from the beginning that all of us would not graduate from this training course. The Marine Corps will keep a Marine recruit for six months in boot camp. If he does not pass the physical fitness and slide for life course within the six month leniency period, he will be given a general discharge.

I was proud to have my father and brothers at Parris Island, South Carolina, on graduation day. It is a day I will always remember. I know "Marine" was not an easy title to attain and I know I will always be proud that I served two years in the United States Marine Corps. The physical condition you attain can never be matched. This is a once in a lifetime experience.

We were transferred to Camp Geiger, North Carolina for ten weeks of extensive Combat Training. During the ten week training period we learned how to operate a M-60 rocket launcher, a M-60 machine gun, M-16 rifle, colt 45 automatic, hand grenades, and a 3.5 rocket launcher. We also learned basic hand to hand combat fighting. We had special classes on platoon formations. We were trained on how to safely get through mine fields. After graduating from the Camp Geiger Combat School we were all given a three-week leave to go wherever we wanted. I went home for three weeks. I had a nice welcome home party and received a terrific gift from my father—a brand new olds-mobile, which I took back to base.

I returned to Camp LeJuene, North Carolina where I was stationed for fourteen months. I subsequently was stationed at Vieques, Puerto Rico for four months. I enjoyed my stay on that small island. I remember one afternoon in Vieques. I was pumping water from a spring when suddenly a bolt of lighting struck five feet in front of me. It had a bright flash and a loud crackling sound. It was the closest I came to death in my two-year stint.

I was released from the Marines on December 7, 1970, with a rank of Corporal and an honorable discharge.

As a little boy growing up, I remember always being afraid of the police. I could never understand why, but I always had a fear when it came to the police. I wanted to be a professional baseball player. My friends Rudy Skoczynski, Rich Skoszynski, and Mike Mann, played baseball games five games a week. We played guys from the neighborhood like Bobby Mazza, Steve Mann, Clem Restine, Bobby Rydele and Robert Paschick. We played for twenty-one years. We played well over twelve hundred games. On weekends I played semi-pro baseball. Unfortunately, when I was twenty-three years old I tore the ligaments in my right shoulder leaping two feet over the fence to rob a player of a home run in a championship game. It was a great disappointment that I had to give up my goal of becoming a professional baseball player.

It was time to change uniforms once again. I turned in my Marine uniform, I had to hang up my baseball uniform. Now it was time to change into a blue uniform. I was continuing a family tradition. My father is a retired Chief of the Essex County Deputy Sheriffs Department. My older brother is employed by the Newark Police Department as a Detective for the Youth Aid Bureau and his son-in-law is a Newark Police Officer. My younger brother is a Deputy Chief in the Essex County Deputy Sheriffs Department. A cousin, Gene Olson, is a Sergeant on the Irvington Police Department.

While I was in the United States Marine Corps, I decided that I wanted to be a police officer. I remember taking a weekend pass from Camp LeJeune, North Carolina and going on a Saturday morning to Barringer High School to take the Newark Police Civil Service Exam. I passed the test and was notified by Civil Service that as soon as my military time was completed I would be going into the first class available at the Newark Police Academy.

I started classes at the Police Academy five weeks after being discharged from the Marine Corps. We had a class of twenty two cadets, our first day commenced on January 11, 1971. I remember my first police instructor, Sergeant Eames.

Sergeant Eames addressed us by saying to us. "Good morning, police cadets.

"During the next fourteen weeks you will have classes in criminal law, state and municipal statutes, report writing, use of deadly force, self-defense classes, pistol range shooting and physical fitness class.

"Gentlemen, he said, I want to stress to you that most of what you learn will be done when you have your on the job training in the streets."

At the Police Academy we were taught the basic laws. We were told by our instructors to judge each assignment differently and to deal with each situation uniquely and individually. Every one of our assignments would bring a new challenge. Our personality and discretion would be a big factor on how each officer reacts to a situation. We had four weeks of training at the pistol range with a colt .38 service revolver. We were trained to fire our guns in 1.5 seconds. You will have situations where you will only have a split second to react. When a police officer is confronted with a suspect, it is a tough decision to make. We were all given extensive classes on the proper use of deadly force.

Lieutenant Adubato told us that during our career in law enforcement we would be confronted with taking a life, giving a life, and saving a life. All three are challenging situations and quick thinking would decide our fate.

We graduated on May 12, 1971. Twenty-four years later on May 12, we have thirteen officers remaining from our class. Five are dead: Officer Fultz, Officer Kurtz, Officer Friday, Officer Patuto, and Officer Sprull. Six other officers left the police department for personal reasons. We have eleven officers presently assigned to precincts. Officer Richard L. Allen, South District; George T. Brodo, West District; Robert D'Angelo, West Squad Detective Bureau; Gerard V.

Fillipone, Mounted Squad, East District; Otto J. Moravek, Police Headquarters, Detective Division; Raymond J. Nesto, North District; Michael Petrillo, Narcotics Division; Fred R. Robson, South District; Vincent I. Servis, Jr., Auto Squad, Hit and Run Division; and Officer Lawrence J. Lewis, South District; Lieutenant Kenneth Rox, Directors Office; and Lieutenant Phillip Aquino. Internal Affairs Division. In one year we are eligible to retire.

2 The Explosion at P.S.E.&G.

Officer William Magaletta and I were given an assignment by the police dispatcher. Unit 316 respond on a code 580 explosion at 821 Raymond Boulevard. Unit 316, your time is 0210 hours. Lieutenant Carne, Emergency Unit 87, and EMS Unit 102 are responding to the scene. We have possible injuries and a deceased worker. Please advise us of the situation when you arrive at the scene.

I was driving the police car and I had my emergency lights and siren wailing. It took us approximately four minutes to arrive at the scene. There was an explosion at the Public Service, Electric, and Gas Building. Officer William Magaletta and I ran up the stairs to the second floor where the explosion occurred. You could smell the terrible stench of a human body that had been severely burned by the intense heat of the explosion. I remember the thick greyish black smoke flowing out of the huge generator. It was choking everyone in the building. It was a horrible sight. A PSE and G technician had been killed by the explosion. The tragedy that occured that night is a part of life that is hard to accept.

As experienced police officers, we are trained to accept tragedy as a part of life. We cannot overreact. We have to find a way to show no emotion. We have to be strong for the people who have to endure the tragedy. The victim was a middle-aged white male who was lying motionless below the giant generator door. The body of the deceased was mangled. It looked like a dead steer that was hit by a train. The victim's head and left shoulder were completely dismembered and torn off the body. This was caused when the generator door blew up in front of him. The generator was smouldering. A thick greyish black smoke continued to blow out of the generator. The heat coming out from the generator was very intense. It had to be well over one hundred degrees in the building. Six police officers searched for well over an hour looking for the victim's head and shoulder. Unfortunately no one could find his remains. EMS technicians placed the victim's body in a green plastic body bag.

We found the victim's wallet and homicide detectives notified his next of kin. When a love one is killed in a terrible tragedy, it is never an easy task for a detective to contact the family.

Lieutenant Carne asked me if I had any success in finding Mr. Lewson's remains. I advised Lieutenant Carne that it was very difficult to see. The thick black smoke and the poor lighting hampered our search. I asked Lieutenant Carne if I could continue the search. I advised him that if I checked the area closer to the walls I could find the remains. Lieutenant Carne gave me fifteen minutes to canvass the area. He told me to leave the area if I failed to find the remains.

After sweating profusely for ten minutes I found a trail of blood along the walls by the staircase. I found the victims head and shoulder wedged behind a radiator approximately 150 feet from the generator. The radio dispatcher notified the EMS technicians to respond. The victims remains were placed in a green bag and taken to the City Morgue.

This was a very tense situation that caused a great deal

of stress and anxiety. This assignment was the first of many stressful jobs that I experienced in my twenty-three years of law enforcement. We were all very fortunate that we were not seriously injured. The thick smoke caused most of us to suffer from skin irritation and shortness of breathe.

Emergency Unit 84, Officer Michael LaMotta and his partner, Officer John Malanga, was the first unit on the scene. Officer LaMotta assisted me in finding the victim's remains. Special thanks to Officers LaMotta and Malanga who have been partners for twenty years. They have both displayed exemplary courage in the field.

3 Premature Last Rights

I was working the midnight shift. We call it the graveyard shift. The first three hours were quiet. We only had
one assignment. That job was a minor two car accident.
At 0300 hours, we asked the radio dispatcher for a twenty
minute breakfast break. We went to Andros restaurant, and
had a nice quiet breakfast. I was working with a rookie
police officer on this night. My partner's name was Officer
Jose Valez. He told me this was his third week in a police
car.

The radio dispatcher gave us an assignment when we
called back after our twenty minute break. We were assigned to motor patrol unit number 311. The police dispatcher gave us a code 500 explosion at Orange Street and
Broad Street. Residents were trapped in the building. Officer Valez acknowledged the transmission and advised the
dispatcher that we were responding. We were advised that
two EMS Units were responding along with Newark Fire
Units. The radio dispatcher asked us to give him a detailed
account of the situation when we arrived at the scene.

I was driving the police car that night, the fateful night of October 23, 1973. It will always remain a terrible nightmare. The radio dispatcher requested backup units to respond to the scene.

I was driving the car at a speed of approximately forty miles an hour. I was heading west of Ferry Street. I had the emergency red lights flashing and the siren wailing. The streets were clear. There was very little traffic. When I got to the corner of Broad and Market I made a quick right turn and headed north on Broad Street. My entire body was very tense. I wanted to get to the scene as soon as possible. Minutes would make the difference between life and death for the fire victims trapped in the building. I suddenly accelerated the speed of the police car to sixty miles per hour. I had all green lights ahead of me so I maintained the speed I was doing. When I got to the intersection of Broad Street and Raymond Boulevard, I looked to my right. Traffic was frozen in the westbound lanes of Raymond Boulevard. Suddenly I heard my partner Valez yell out "Jerry look out, look out!" In a split second my life passed right in front of me. I looked to my left and this big truck was barreling into our police cruiser. There was nothing I could do. I was helpless.

The impact of the truck knocked me flat out and I did not remember anything. Officer Jose Valez and I were both knocked unconscious. The police car was severely smashed and Officer Valez and I were trapped in the car. I never saw the truck hit the police car. The truck hit the driver's side of the police car. The impact turned the car into a "V" shape.

Officer Pete Steffens was detailed at Broad Street and Cedar Street. There had been a fire at that location earlier in the night. Officer Steffens observed the accident and he notified the dispatcher to clear the air. Officer Steffens told the radio dispatcher that unit 311 was involved in a code 550 car accident. Officer Steffens told the radio dispatcher that Unit 311 had been wiped out. It was involved in a serious collision with a bread truck at the intersection of Broad Street and Raymond Boulevard. Officer Steffens told the dispatcher that both officers were unconscious and trapped in the police car.

The radio dispatcher informed Officer Steffens who was

responding: Police emergency unit 80; EMS Emergency Unit 209; Unit 302 with Sergeant Ronald Tutela; and Unit 300 with Captain Robert Morris.

The dispatcher advised Unit 316 Officer Ed Moravek respond to Broad Street and Raymond Boulevard. Your brother, Officer Jerry Moravek, was involved in a serious accident and is in critical condition.

Sergeant Ronald Tutela arrived at the scene and Officer Steffens was asked to explain what occurred. Officers Steffens told Sergeant Tutela that he was detailed at the corner intersection of Broad Street and Cedar Street.

"I observed Unit 311 driving north on Broad Street. As Unit 311 approached Broad Street and Raymond Boulevard, a green bread truck (Iberia Inc.) was traveling at a high speed east on Raymond Boulevard. The truck passed through a red light and crashed into Unit 311. The initial impact of the crash was devastating. Unit 311 spun around in a circle twice. There was three teenagers in the bread truck. The impact sent all three teenagers crashing through the front windshield."

Sergeant Tutela advised Officer Steffens to execute an accident report, to issue the truck driver two summons, reckless driving and a failure to stop at a red light. The truck was also towed for investigation.

I remember when I was lying in a unconscious state. The grim reaper was hovering over my motionless body. You cannot come any closer to death than I was. If you have a strong will, you have a fighting chance to stay alive. However, all my vital signs were negative. I was bleeding profusely from the mouth. My eyes were wide open but I was in a state of shock and trauma. I had blood streaming down the brow of my forehead. The blood was oozing from my head, nose, neck, and mouth. Our police cars are designed so prisoners that are being transported cannot reach from the rear seat and attack us. The bars that are used to protect us are made from a brass alloy. When Officer Valez and I were struck by the truck the bars buckled and the thick wires snapped and penetrated parts of our body. Officer Valez had a wire penetrate his left hand and another penetrated his right shoulder. One of the wire penetrated my left upper arm.

The impact from the collision caused my forehead to hit

the steering wheel. My mouth and jaw had smashed into the steering wheel. This shattered eleven of my teeth, four lower teeth and seven upper teeth. Four of my bottom teeth ripped through my lower chin, causing extensive bleeding from my mouth. The officers and paramedics were very concerned. They all thought that I was bleeding internally.

My brother, Officer Ed Moravek, told me that he requested a priest be notified to come to the scene as soon as possible. My brother told me that everyone was concerned that I was going to die from the loss of so much blood. What made the odds of my survival diminish was the fact that I could not receive medical attention. Emergency Unit 80 was working frantically to free us from the mangled vehicle. Our police car was totally wiped out by the tremendous impact caused by the five-ton bread truck.

A priest arrived and he gave me my last rites and blessed me. The priest prayed that my life be spared but everyone thought I was running out of time. My brother Ed told me he was very depressed, angry, and frustrated that he was helpless, unable to help me. My brother said he was sitting on the hood of his police car in tears. He really thought he was going to lose his brother. It took the emergency unit almost two hours to get us out of the police car. Officer Valez and I were taken to University Hospital. After receiving emergency treatment at University Hospital I was admitted to St. James Hospital for observation. I woke up three days later and the first people I saw were my father, my brother Ed, and Captain Morris. I will never forget the first time I looked in the mirror. I looked worse than Frankenstein's monster.

I was out of work and on the injury list for almost a year. I had to go for therapy for my neck and back for three months. I had to see a dentist on a weekly basis for nine months. The oral surgery I went thorough was an ordeal.

My partner, Jose Valez, suffered a severe hand and neck injury. He returned to work four months later. Currently Jose Valez is a detective in the robbery squad. I returned to work eleven months later and had a walking post in the east district for the next three years.

4 Burglaries in Progress

I recall in my third year on the job in Newark's east district, my partner Officer Walter Reed and I encountered some intense burglaries in progress. Some were occurring without us responding to the crime scene in time to catch the thieves. However we did eventually catch up with the thieves. Our radio dispatcher gave us an assignment at 427 Halsey Street. He told us to respond to the scene on a signal 521 burglary in progress. The dispatcher advised us that the owner was responding to his business. We arrived at the scene of the Cave Bar at 0340 hours. Officer Walter Reed and I got out of the police car and observed that the front door was busted open. My partner Officer Reed said, "We have a burglary in progress and we have burglary suspects trapped in the building. Send us a backup unit." The radio dispatcher advised us that radio Units 312 and Sergeant Tutela Unit 302 were responding. All units in the field were advised to keep the air clear.

Officer Reed went into the building from the rear. I cautiously entered the building from the front of the tavern. I did not see any of the burglary suspects so I went out of the front door and into the rear alleyway. When I went to the rear of the building, a black male was hiding in the bushes. I had my gun drawn and I told the suspect to come out of the bushes with his hands above his head. I had my gun pointed directly at him. The suspect was ordered to lie face down on the ground. I than proceeded to handcuff the suspect. I placed him in the police car. I went back to the front of the tavern. I looked in the window and I observed two burglary suspects. One of the suspects had a gun. When he saw me, he quickly drew a gun from his waist. I told the suspect to freeze and lie on the floor. Suddenly the suspect made a move for his gun and I fired two shots in his direction. At the same time that I fired two shots at the burglary suspect, my partner, Officer Reed, burst through the kitchen door. He wrestled with the suspect and knocked him to the ground. Officer Reed managed to contain the suspect. Officer Reed grabbed the gun from the suspect. Fortunately the two shots I fired at the suspects missed hitting Officer Reed. It was close.

All three suspects were advised of their Miranda rights and they were slated at the East District Precinct.

Officer Reed said "Jerry you scared the livin' shit out of me. That was a close call. One of those bullets you fired at the suspect whizzed right by my ear. When I saw the gun in his hand I grabbed for it."

I told Officer Reed that I thought I might have shot him. I was petrified when he burst out of the kitchen. Officer Reed was directly in my line of fire. It really jolted my mind when I saw my partner at the last second. I had already fired the shots at the suspect. This job never has a dull moment. Our next intense situation occurred seven months later.

Our Unit 310 responded to 722 Broad Street on a signal 521 burglary in progress. the radio dispatcher advised us to use caution as there were possibly four burglary suspects in the building and they might be armed with guns. We arrived at the scene of Rich Jewelry Store at 0120 hours. Officer Reed and I got out of the police car along with Units 312, Officers Klenke and Petrillo, and Unit 314, Officers Caufield and Shaefer. We could not find any signs of a break-in in the building. We checked the entire building.

We found a van in the rear of the building, which made us all suspicious that the burglary suspects had to be on the roof. We received notification from the radio dispatcher that a second burglary alarm had been triggered. The alarm was called in from Wells Fargo Alarm Systems. The suspects were hiding somewhere in the building.

I advised the radio dispatcher that we believe that the burglary suspects have gained entry into the building from the roof. I asked the dispatcher to send us a hook and ladder fire truck. We had no access to check the roof area. The Newark Fire Department arrived at the scene. We went up the ladder to the roof. We found a break by the skyline. Officer Reed and I went down the stairs from the skyline entrance. We did a wall to wall search looking for the suspects. We were in an intense situation. It was dark and murky. We both had our guns drawn read to shoot at the burglary suspects. We sensed they were hiding and watching us. They were the prey. Yet we were at a disadvantage because they could see us and we could not see them. We were left with no alternatives. We cautiously searched the entire building. We knew the burglars did not escape. We knew we had them trapped somewhere in the building or on the roof. We did not know if the burglars were armed. We used extreme caution at all times. If these burglary suspects were armed we knew that we could get involved in a shootout. We discovered the safe was busted open. We asked the radio dispatcher to have Unit 312 assist us in the search of the store.

Unit 303 Sergeant Reilly responded to 722 Broad Street in the rear of Rich's Jewelry Store. We had four suspects trapped in the building. The radio dispatcher advised Sergeant Reilly that Officer Reed and I (Unit 310) had the assignment. Police Units 312 and 314 were on the scene as backup units. I told Sergeant Reilly that we did an extensive search of the building. We did not find any suspects. We all knew the burglary suspects did not escape. We also found the safe broken into. There was no money found in the safe. I asked Sergeant Reilly if I could check and search the adjacent roofs. I had a gut feeling that the suspects were hiding on the roof. There were three roofs to search. After searching for ten minutes, suddenly on an adjacent roof I found four white males all in their late twenties. They were lying flat on their stomachs and clinging close to a skyline window. They were hiding behind the skyline like four sly weasels. I had my gun drawn on all four burglary suspects. I ordered them to freeze and not make any foolish moves. I told the burglars that if anyone makes a move to draw a gun, I would have to shoot and kill them. I called the radio dispatcher.

"Unit 310 I am holding four burglary suspects at gunpoint. I need Units 312 and 314. I am on the third roof adjacent to the jewelry store." I ordered the suspects to keep their hands clasped together behind their heads. The suspects were ordered to stay in a sitting position. A few minutes passed as I patiently waited for officers to assist me. My partner, Officer Reed, along with Officers Klenke and Petrillo assisted me. All four burglary suspects were handcuffed. I searched the suspects. Thousands of dollars were stuffed in their shirt pockets. I searched the front and back pockets of their pants. Stuffed in their pockets were thousands of dollars worth of eighteen-karat gold jewelry. the burglars were advised of their rights to have a lawyer present. I told them, "You have a right to remain silent. However, anything that you say forth right will be prosecuted against you. If you cannot afford a lawyer the state will provide one for you." The burglary suspects were transported to the East District Precinct and slated. The money and jewelry was submitted on a property voucher by Sergeant Reilly.

Sergeant Reilly told Officer Reed and me that the owner of Rich's Jewelry store sent a letter to Captain Tenpenny. The letter was addressed to Captain Raymond Tenpenny, Commander of the East District. Captain Tenpenny gave all six Police Officers copies of the letter. He commended us on a job well done. Mr. Rich told us in his letter how appreciative he was for the excellent police work. Mr. Rich was advised by Sergeant Reilly that the money and jewelry recovered was submitted as evidence. All contents of their money and jewelry was secured at the police property room. Mr. Rich was advised that all his property would be returned after the trial. Sergeant Reilly told Officer Reed and me that he submitted a property voucher. The cash recovered from the suspects $18,120 dollars. The jewelry recovered was worth $22,600 in assorted diamond rings, gold watches and gold bracelets.

Command citations were issued to Officer Mike Klenke, Officer Carmine Petrillo, Officer Charles Shaefer, Officer Bill Caufield, Officer Walter Reed and me. The case went to trial ten months later. All four burglary suspects pleaded guilty. They were sentenced to four years in jail. Mr. Rich, the owner of Rich's Jewelry, had all his property returned to him by Sergeant Reilly.

5 Fort Apache (The Wild West Precinct)

I was transferred from the East District Command to the West District Command on June 4, 1977. I remember when I walked into the precinct. Behind the Lieutenant's desk on the wall there were two tomahawks with Indian feathers decorated around a sign. The words inscribed on a wood base were "Fort Apache" (The Wild West Command). I worked at the west district for six years. During my time there I was involved in three shoot-outs. I was presented three class "A" medal of honor awards. The class "A" award is selected by the police honor board committee. It is presented to police officers who have demonstrated courage and valor above the line of duty. The class "A" award is the highest commendation a police officer can receive from the Newark Police Department. My assignment in the west district was working in the safe streets program. I was detailed to a walking post on Springfield

Avenue. It covered a one mile radius from Boston Street to Seventeenth Street. I was assigned motor patrol police Unit 491. It became very useful to cover the extensive area. However, eighty percent of the time, I was out of the car and checking the ninety-three business stores on my post. The police car served two good purposes. It provided quick transportation to the post. It benefitted all the merchants by having me available to respond quickly. The police car also served as a decoy car. I parked the car on the avenue. I stopped and talked with each merchant within a four block area. During the spring and summer of 1978, I was confronted with numerous burglaries and robberies.

My first assignment was located at 10 Livington Street. Captain Joseph Rox was the Commander of the West District. Captain Rox called me into his office. He briefed me on my next assignment. He informed me that he has received thirty-seven police reports in the past two months. "Burglaries are occurring at 10 Livingston Street. The building is owned by Mr. Frank Sibert. He is the inventor of many different and useful gadgets," Captain Rox said.

"The perpetrators are breaking into Mr. Sibert's building during the early morning hours. The actors take the gadgets apart in a garage adjoining the building. The burglars take the medal and alloy parts to 108 Livingston Street. At this location is a melting factory. The customer is paid a substantial amount of money. The amount of weight determines how much he will be paid," Captain Rox said.

Captain Rox asked me if I wanted a partner to work with. I told Captain Rox, "I appreciate your concern for me. I appreciate the fact that you have the confidence in me to handle the assignment. I prefer to work alone at this time. I will do my best to catch the thieves who have been committing the burglaries at 10 Livingston Street." Lieutenant Barone changed my shift so that I would have a good chance of catching the thieves. My tour of duty was changed. I was working a day shift from nine A.M. to five P.M.

I was on a stake out at 10 Livingston street for two weeks. On the fourth day of the stake out, I observed the burglars breaking into the building. On two occasions I called for back up units to assist me in arresting the burglars. When the radio units responded to the scene, we went into the building to arrest the burglary suspects. Unfortunately, on both occasions, they were able to elude us. They escaped by jumping out of a second floor window. The fall was approximately twenty feet. They continued their escape onto an adjoining roof. They descended down a telephone pole in the parking lot.

I was frustrated that these weasels thought they were slick escape artists. I decided to play their game. I patiently waited for the suspects to break into the building. I climbed up the telephone located in the parking lot. The telephone pole had spikes, so it was easy to climb. I sat on the roof for four days from seven A.M. till one-thirty P.M. each morning. I had an excellent view of the building entrance. This is where the perpetrators were gaining entrance into Mr. Sibert's warehouse. On early Thursday afternoon at approximately twelve forty-five P.M. I was sitting on the roof. I sat on the roof for almost four hours. Suddenly I observed six black males break into the building at 10 Livingston Street. I stayed on the roof and waited to see how they were stealing the products. Once inside the building the burglars were transferring the products to an abandoned garage adjoining 10 Livingston St. The burglary suspects were inside the building for half an hour. Then I observed the burglars throwing aluminum shaped boxes out of the second and third floor windows. They continued to throw the boxes out of the windows for another hour.

At approximately three P.M. I observed all six burglary suspects carrying large cardboard boxes. Inside the boxes were aluminum pillow vibrators. They took the material to an abandoned garage adjoining the warehouse. The garage was located approximately fifty feet from the warehouse. It took the burglars about an hour to transfer the material to the garage.

I descended from the telephone pole. I drove the police car around the corner to 10 Livingston Street. I did not call for backup. The police cars would only hamper my chances of arresting the suspects. I felt that two failed attempts was enough for me. I was not going to blow two weeks of surveillance. I cautiously drove the police car to the abandoned garage. The garage door was wide open. I got out of the car and was surprised to observe all six burglary suspects. They were nonchalantly sitting inside the garage. They were taking apart the aluminum section of the pillow vibrators that Mr. Sibert invented. I quickly drew my service revolver and had it pointed at the burglary suspects. I was approximately fifteen feet from the suspects. I stated to the burglars: "You are all under arrest. Anyone that makes a move to draw a weapon will be shot and killed. Everyone will now slowly put your hands clasped together behind your head." The suspects obeyed my command. They were scared having a gun pointed at their faces. I was scared to death being that I was outnumbered six to one. I thought to myself, My God how can I contain six burglary suspects? I was petrified of the precarious position I was in. If these guys were armed with guns, chances were someone was going to get shot. My biggest mistake was leaving myself vulnerable. I realized too late that I should have taken cover behind the police car. I intently kept my sight on the suspects. It was an extremely intense situation. I had a gut wrenching feeling that I was going to have a shootout. The odds were not in my favor. I realized that if these guys were going to disobey my orders, it was going to be a bloody mess. I wished that I had more than six bullets in my gun.

In took out my walkie talkie unit with my left hand. I kept my gun pointed at the suspects with my right hand. I transmitted a call for help to the radio dispatcher.

"This is Unit 491, I need an assist officer back up at 10 Livingston Street." The radio dispatcher acknowledged my request for backup units. I advised the radio dispatcher that I was holding six burglars at gunpoint. The dispatcher in a clear distinct voice transmitted immediately.

"All available units in the field, respond on a code 555 assist officer at 10 Livingston Street. All units be advised Unit 491 is holding six burglars at gunpoint. All units in the field keep the air clear. First Unit at the scene please advise us of the situation." A few seconds after requesting for an assist officer, one of the burglary suspects came charging at me. The burglar attempted to take an object out of his jacket. I fired one shot at him from point blank range. He stumbled to the ground a few feet to my left side. I immediately got back on the airwaves. "Unit 491 I need that assist officer and an ambulance. I just shot one of the suspects." I was excited and asked the dispatcher to put a push on those back up units. The dispatcher broadcasted a second assist officer plea. He advised the units that a suspect has been shot. The suspect was lying on the ground for a few minutes. I did not know if he were dead or playing possum. Suddenly the suspect got up and fled.

I warned the five remaining suspects to immediately drop down to the ground. I stated to the suspects, "Anyone making a move for their pockets will be shot." A couple of the suspects reacted to my warning and shouted out, "Okay, Okay, please don't shoot us." The suspects dropped to the ground. Once again I got back on the radio waves with my portable police radio. "Unit 491 to radio dispatcher one of the burglars fled the scene." The burglar ran west on Springfield Avenue. I gave the radio dispatcher a partial description. It was very difficult to remember a clear-cut description. My main concern was staying focused on the burglars. My life was on the line. If I failed to watch the burglars, any distraction would give them a chance to reach for a gun. I know that in the blink of an eye if any of these guys had guns concealed in their pockets, I would be shot with two or three of them going down on me. It seemed like an eternity waiting for the police cars to arrive. I could hear the loud wailing of police sirens coming from all directions. Within three minutes after I requested an assist officer, four police car (Units 402, 410, 411, 415) arrived at the scene. In moments fourteen police cars were on the scene. I gave a sigh of relief when I saw those police cars. I was elated and thankful to the officers who made an effort to assist me.

Unit 410 was the first to respond to the radio dispatchers orders. Officer Kurtz advised the dispatcher that there were enough units at the scene. "Disregard any additional units responding. We have the situation under control." Radio car Units 410 and 411 assisted me in searching the suspects intently. All five suspects were handcuffed and advised of their rights. The squadroll (Unit 410) transported the prisoners to the precinct. All 226 of the stolen pillow vibrators were recovered. We put them in large cardboard boxes. They were transported to the precinct and submitted as evidence. When I arrived at the precinct, I was surprised to find six burglars in jail. The weasel that escaped from me was arrested by Detective Coley. I asked him where and how did you find him? Detective Coley told me that he observed the suspect running west on Springfield Avenue. The guy was slick; he quickly hid under a car. He was found under the car and arrested by Detective Coley. I thanked him for his excellent police work. I was surprised to discover that the burglar had no bullet wound. He was fortunate that the bullet I fired at him from point blank range missed him. The suspect told me he thought he was shot in the head.

I gratefully thanked the radio dispatcher for his professional excellence. The dispatcher expedited the backup units flawlessly. I asked the dispatcher to acknowledge my gratitude to all the officers who made an effort to assist me. I will never forget the feeling when all the police cars responded. I had goose bumps and a tingling sensation shot through my entire body.

The burglars were sentenced to four years in prison. Captain Rox presented me with the class "B" valor award. He thanked me for a job well done. Chief Charles Zizza saw me walking on Springfield Avenue the next day. He told me that during his twenty-nine years of law enforcement he could not recall one police officer apprehending six suspects by himself. He praised me for my composure during an extremely intense and dangerous situation. I replied that I was very fortunate that the suspects were not armed with guns. The Newark Star Ledger had an article in the paper the following day. The headline of the article read "One shot collars six burglary suspects." The article went on to say that an officer working on Springfield Avenue captured six burglary suspects. It told how they were arrested. The paper also listed the names of the arrested burglars.

The Police Benevolent Association named me Officer of the month. The PBA President presented me with the class "A" Medal of Valor Award.

ROBBERIES IN PROGRESS ON SPRINGFIELD AVENUE

A few weeks passed and quite a few robberies were being committed on our post. I submitted a report to Captain Rox requesting a partner. I felt that I needed a good partner to work with. I asked the Captain for Police Officer Robert D'Angelo. The day after I submitted my report, Captain Rox called Officer D'Angelo and me into his office. He told us that recently there were a rash of robberies occurring between the hours of five P.M. and eight P.M.

"The robberies are being perpetrated by five juveniles and one adult. They are armed with guns; use extreme caution. Your new tour of duty will be from two P.M. and ten P.M.," he said.

On the third day that we were working on our assignment the radio dispatcher had us respond to 702 Springfield Avenue. It was a code 510 robbery in progress. He told us to see the owner of the television repair shop. We were advised to use extreme caution. The robbery suspects were armed and dangerous. A minute later we were advised that the owner of the store was shot in the head. Backup Units 412 and 413 were responding along with emergency unit 218. Officer D'Angelo advised the dispatcher that we were across the street from 702 Springfield Avenue.

I asked Officer D'Angelo how these guys could have the audacity to rob and kill the owner. Our police car was parked directly across the street from the store.

Officer D'Angelo replied, "Jerry we are going to have a deadly confrontation with these guys someday soon."

I asked the radio dispatcher to clear the air.

"We need an ambulance immediately. We have a robbery victim shot twice in the head. We have no pulse and no signs of life. We need a homicide unit to respond to the scene."

Officer D'Angelo transmitted a partial description of the assailants. The radio dispatcher broadcasted a description of the suspects. "All units in the field be on the lookout for five black teenage males. They range in age from fourteen to sixteen years old. The sixth suspect is a black male adult. He is six feet one, one hundred and fifty pounds. He is in his mid-twenties. Use extreme caution he is armed with a .357 Magnum." "All six robbers are wanted for armed robbery and a homicide. They were last seen fleeing west on Springfield Avenue." We were advised to respond to Police Headquarters, Homicide Division. Unfortunately no arrests were made.

The robberies continued for the entire summer and fall months. It was getting frustrating. We could not get a handle on these guys. Most of the robberies were taking place between the hours six P.M. to nine P.M. Occasionally a grocery store and a candy store was being hit by the same six robbery suspects. We compiled a good description of the assailants. We knew who to look for if we saw them in the vicinity of Springfield Avenue. In July 1981 they robbed the Exxon Gas Station located at Springfield and Fairmont Avenues. They made off with a good score. The owner was robbed of $2,300. We arrived on the scene five minutes after they hit the gas station. Fortunately no one was injured. The gas attendant was quite shaken up.

In September 1981 we responded to two more robberies. At two-ten P.M. we responded to Herms Liquor Store located at 575 Springfield Avenue. The robbers used the same MO (Modus Operandi). The owner was robbed of $1,100 in cash. Fortunately he was not injured. At four-twenty-five P.M. the radio dispatcher assigned us to the Foodtown Supermarket located at Springfield Avenue and Tenth Street.

He said, "Unit 491, we have a code 510 robbery in progress. Use extreme caution. We have a off duty police officer shot. The robbers are armed and extremely dangerous." Officer D'Angelo acknowledged the dispatcher and advised him that we will check conditions. At the scene I advised him to put a push on the EMS emergency unit. We have a wounded police officer shot in the chest with a shotgun. I told Bobby to call teletype and give them a description of the suspects. The radio dispatcher broadcasted the following description. "All units be advised we are looking for five black male teenagers. Use extreme caution they are armed with guns. The sixth suspect is a black male adult. He is armed with a sawed-off shotgun. Approximate age twenty-seven, Height 5'10", short black hair, clean shaven.

"He is wearing a black leather jacket, light blue denims, brown hat, yellow sweatshirt, white sneakers. He has one broken front tooth. He is armed with a sawed-off shotgun. Suspect is wanted for shooting a police officer at the Foodtown Market. All units from Unit 491, use extreme caution. All six robbers should be considered armed and dangerous. They have committed seventeen previous robberies. They are wanted for killing a store owner. They are wanted for shooting an off duty police officer."

The wounded officer was transported to University Hospital. He was in the intensive care unit and listed in critical condition. The supermarket was robbed of $3,700. These robbers had become vicious assailants. I stated to Officer D'Angelo, "I can see that the inevitable showdown is coming." We realized that sooner or later we were going to catch up with these punks. They had terrorized Springfield Avenue for eight months.

We were disgusted that during an eight month period, seventeen robberies occurred on our post. "Don't let it upset your, Bobby, we are both frustrated that they have embarrassed us on several occasions. Eventually we will catch up with these guys. I promise you that we will one day very soon arrest them."

Lieutenant Sheedy advised us to report to the Captain's office at 1400 hours. Captain Rox advised us that he was assigning another safe streets unit to our post. We continued to work the shift assigned to us. We desperately wanted to catch these thugs. They were terrorizing the merchants of Springfield Avenue.

Captain Rox said to us in a very stern voice, "I want you to be extremely careful, but use an aggressive approach. Good luck on your special assignment. If you have any leads as to their whereabouts, you have my permission to travel off your assigned post." The confidence that Captain Rox had in us was a great morale builder. He told us to wear our bulletproof vests at all times.

During the first two weeks of February 1982, this vicious gang changed their modus operandi. We had five victims robbed at gunpoint. The victims came out of the grocery store and they were robbed. Two victims were violently mugged and pistol-whipped.

Officer D'Angelo and I talked about our confrontation with these robbers. We both could sense that eventually we were going to have a showdown with these criminals. We invisioned ourselves in a gun battle like the *Gunfight at the O.K. Corral*. The inevitable showdown occurred on May 21, 1982.

The radio dispatcher assigned us to 474 Springfield Avenue. In front of Marty's Food Market, we had a code 510 robbery in progress. Six black males were robbing and pistol-whipping a victim. Officer D'Angelo asked the radio dispatcher to keep the air clear. When we got to the scene we advised the dispatcher to put a push on an ambulance. The victim had a severe head wound and was unconscious. We had two witnesses that gave a good description of the robbery suspects. Officer D'Angelo questioned the witnesses and transmitted a description to Central Communications. I stayed with the victim. He was bleeding profusely from the back of his head. His clothes were ripped apart by the thugs.

The witnesses, Mr. Carl Brooks and his brother Mr. Ray Brown, are both Councilman Aides. They are employed by the City of Newark. Carl Brooks said he was driving west on Springfield Avenue. His brother Ray was in the front passenger seat.

Carl Brooks stated: "The robbers dragged the victim into an alleyway on Blum Street. One of the robbers was hitting the victim in the head with the butt of his gun. The other five assailants were kicking and stomping him in the chest, back and legs. They ripped his pants off and stole his wallet. When we got out of our car the suspects fled north of Blum Street." Ray Brooks added, "These bastards are animals; they battered that old man."

Officer D'Angelo gave an excellent description of the robbery suspects. The radio dispatcher broadcasted the description to the units in the field. I said to Bobby, "These guys have once again eluded us."

EMS Emergency Unit 324 arrived on the scene a few minutes later. The robbery victim was a black male in his late sixties. He was viciously beaten up and in critical condition. A few minutes after the ambulance transported the victim to College University Hospital. The two witnesses returned to the scene of the crime.

Mr. Carl Brooks stated: "Officers, we drove our car north on Blum Street hoping to find the robbery suspects. We observed the suspects on Sixteenth Avenue intersecting Fifteenth Avenue. They are walking north on Fifteenth Street and heading towards Fifteenth Avenue. I told Mr. Brooks to get in his car. We wanted them to positively identify the robbers.

"Come on Bobby, let's get these sons of bitches." The curtain was coming down on these vicious assailants. We were going to arrest them if it took us all night.

Officer D'Angelo contacted Central Communications and stated: "Unit 491 clear the air, clear the air." The radio dispatcher advised all units in the field to stand by and keep the air clear. "Come in Unit 491. We need backup units to respond to Fifteenth Street and Fifteenth Avenue. Six robbery suspects are walking in the vicinity of that location."

I drove the police car near the intersection of Fifteen Street and Fifteen Avenue. We observed six black males who fit the description. They were walking gingerly north of Fifteenth Street. Mr. Ray Brooks got out of his brother's car. He shouted out to us, "Officers, that's them, that's them." We immediately got out of the car. We had taken our guns out of our holsters minutes before arriving on the scene. We knew that these were the guys terrorizing victims for the past eight months. We were ready to challenge and arrest them. I told my partner that the robbery spree was going to end that night.

When we approached the suspects, they were approximately twenty feet in front of us. When they saw us, they made a dash to escape. They ran into a dark alleyway near the intersection of Fifteenth Avenue and Fifteenth Street. Officer D'Angelo ran east on Fifteenth Avenue. We wanted to cover both escape routes. Officer D'Angelo was going to prevent them from escaping out of the alleyway on Fifteenth Avenue. All six suspects fled into the alleyway. They were approximately 200 feet from the corner of Fifteenth Avenue and Fifteenth Street. I relentlessly pursued the robbers into the alleyway. It was very dark and ominous. Having no shield to protect myself, conditions were not in my favor. I feared that I was going to be shot and killed. The alleyway stretched out to approximately 300 feet. It extended through an abandoned vacant lot and warehouse. When I was about twenty feet into the alleyway, the robbers were approximately 100 feet in front of me. I could barely see them. Visibility was poor.

Suddenly a volley of shots were fired at me. The shots rang out into the quiet night. I quickly dropped down to the ground. I fired five shots at the robbers. I saw two of the assailants wheel around and fire shots at me. I could only hope that I killed them before they killed me. From the instant that they fired and shot at me, I thought I was shot. Fortunately I was not shot. However, my adrenalin was so high and intense. I would not have felt the shot until I collapsed. I reloaded my gun and cautiously approached the back lot of the alleyway. You don't have time to be scared. Your body and mind are very tense. I cautiously continued searching for the robbery suspects. When I got to the other side of the alleyway the suspects were gone. I called the police dispatcher with my portable police radio.

"Unit 491 the robbery suspects have escaped through a rear back lot on Fifteenth Street. They are running east on Fifteenth Avenue from Fifteenth Street. Unit 491 shots were fired at the robbers and they might be wounded." I also requested to have internals affairs respond.

When I came out of the alleyway onto Fifteenth Avenue, I observed Officer D'Angelo putting handcuffs on one of the robbery suspects. He caught him on the corner of Fifteenth Street and Fifteenth Avenue. Officer D'Angelo asked me if I was injured. He said that he heard shots fired from the alleyway. We took the suspect to our police car. Officer D'Angelo said that when we ran around the corner, he saw five suspects run east on Fifteenth Avenue. Officer D'Angelo said he chose to capture and arrest the robber who fled west on Fifteenth Avenue.

I said to my partner, "Bobby, I cannot believe that I did not wound anyone. I fired five shots at the robbery suspects. Two of the robbers fired several shots at me. I know that I am very fortunate to be alive!" I told my partner that these were the robbers we were looking for the past eight months. "Bob, I know that I must have shot at least one of the robbers." I needed a couple of minutes to catch my breath. I was shaken up; it was my first shootout. When you as a police officer watch a movie involving cops in a shootout, your first reaction is to wonder how you would react to the situation. I can only tell you that it is not as easy as it looks. It is a very intense moment and your life passes right in front of you.

We were transporting our prisoner to the West Precinct. Suddenly Officer Odell Field's working Unit 416 called Central Communications.

"Unit 416 to dispatcher, I have a possible suspect lying wounded in a vacant lot. He has a bullet wound in the groin area. He is bleeding profusely." Officer Fields was located in the rear lot of Ninth Street and Fifteenth Avenue. The radio dispatcher acknowledged Officer Fields' transmission. "Unit 416 we have EMS Emergency Unit 522 responding. Unit 129 Lieutenant Reed from Internal Affairs is responding. Unit 402 Sergeant Tassie and Unit 491 Officer Moravek and D'Angelo are responding." Officer D'Angelo and I were advised that one of our robbery suspects was shot. Officer Fields said he was in critical condition.

We responded to Unit 416's location. I talked with Officer Fields. He told me that he had not shot the guy lying on the ground. I informed Officer Fields that he was the robbery suspect who tried to kill me. I told Officer Fields that I shot him. We searched the suspect. There was no gun found on him. I found $2,147 in the suspect's left rear pocket. The suspect was advised of his rights. Sergeant Tassie arrived at the scene. He told Officer Fields to go down to University Hospital with EMS Unit 522. A police guard was authorized by Sergeant Tassie.

Lieutenant James Reed from Internal Affairs Division arrived at the scene of the shooting. He told me that a .357 Magnum gun was recovered. He found it in the rear yard located at Fifteenth Street and Fifteenth Avenue. Lieutenant Reed asked me if I positively identified the suspect. "Lieutenant Reed, this is the guy that fired shots at me in the alleyway." Lieutenant Reed told Officer D'Angelo and me to take the other suspect to the homicide squad. All police reports were executed at the detective division. Lieutenant Reed advised me to go to the ballistic division. I turned my gun over to the lieutenant in charge. A new gun was issued to me at that time.

At the scene of Ninth Street and Fifteenth Avenue I remember looking at the robbery suspect that tried to kill me. The assailant, who was later identified as Willie Smith, he was in a great deal of excruciating pain. The suspect was grasping the area of his groin. His testicles and penis were blown apart by the two bullets that struck him. The suspect was transported to University Hospital. The prisoner was guarded by Officer Odell Fields. Officer D'Angelo and I took the other prisoner to Police Headquarters Homicide Squad.

The two were slated and charged with two counts of

homicide. They were charged with seventeen counts of armed robbery. Willie Smith was slated on an additional charge of aggravated assault with intent to kill a police officer.

Detective Harry Coleman was the detective from homicide assigned to the investigation. He stated to Officer D'Angelo and me: "I have statements from four witnesses. They live adjacent to the alleyway where you were in the shootout with Willie Smith. The witnesses stated that Willie Smith is well known in the Central Ward of the West District Precinct. He is the ringleader along with five juveniles. They have been robbing and terrorizing the citizens of the Central Ward for the past eight months. The witnesses further stated that they observed Willie Smith fire several shots at Officer Moravek."

"When Officer Moravek dropped to the ground I said to my wife, my God he killed the cop. A few seconds later Officer Moravek fired several shots at the suspect," one of the witnesses said.

Detective Coleman advised us that he has statements from Mr. Carl Brooks, and Mr. Ray Brown. They gave a complete detailed account of the robbery. They positively identified the teenage suspect that was arrested. They also identified Willie Smith as the guy who robbed the victim and battered him. The victim of the robbery and brutal attack, Mr. Isiah Wright, was pronounced dead at University Hospital. The doctors told us that he died from extensive brain damage. Detective Chuck Conte went to the victim's house and notified his wife. Mrs. Wright told the detectives that her husband worked in New York. "My husband always had well over $2,000 dollars on him every Friday," she said.

Mrs. Wright was taken to University Hospital where she identified her deceased husband. She said her husband was in poor health. "He was sixty-four years old."

Sergeant Steven Tassie had the preliminary investigation. His assignment was to make sure that Officer Moravek's shooting was justified. Lieutenant Reed was handling the Internal Affairs routine shooting investigation.

I submitted a property sheet on the .357 Magnum gun recovered by Lieutenant Reed. The juvenile that we arrested was sentenced to ten years in prison. His name cannot be released because he is only fifteen years old. Willie

Smith was sentenced to life in prison. He is currently on death row.

When Officer D'Angelo and I went to work the next day, Lieutenant Sheedy told us to report to the Captain's office. Captain Rox was very pleased with the arrests of the robbery suspects. He congratulated us on a job well done. Captain Rox told us that Sergeant Tassie recommended valor awards for Officer D'Angelo and I.

Police Week May 1983 Chief Zizza presented Officer Moravek with the Class "A" Valor Award. Officer D'Angelo was presented with the Class "C" police excellence award.

We went back to our regular hours of work on Springfield Avenue. During the last ten months that we worked in Springfield Avenue, the streets were relatively quiet.

6 The Wild West (Tragedy of a Princess)

It was a warm night in July 1984. There was a full moon ablaze. You could almost sense an eerie night was going to haunt us with a rude awakening. We were working the midnight graveyard shift. On this night we were in for a horrifying nightmare. The radio dispatcher called us on the air. "Unit 411 respond to 313 West Kinney Street on a code 514 stabbing in progress."

My partner Officer Kurtz said to me, "Jerry, it looks like you are going to be right. This is going to be one of those crazy wild west nights in the city. Jerry I think we are getting too old. I don't like climbing up ten flights of stairs."

The elevators in the high rise apartments rarely operate properly. Climbing up ten flights doesn't make it any easier. Especially when the humidity outside is close to 100 percent. Adding to our misery was a sultry temperature of eight-four degrees.

When Officer James Kurtz and I got to apartment 10D, we knocked on the door several times. We were getting no response. I started to knock again when the door opened. Mrs. Julie Starks let us enter her apartment. She told us that her grandson, Caril Withers, stabbed his niece in the chest across the hallway in another apartment. Several people were screaming hysterically and crying. They were very distraught and upset. Mrs. Starks told us that that the little girl was seven years old. We did not have to ask where the girl was. We went right to the apartment where everyone was screaming hysterically. The victim was across the hallway with her mother holding her in her arms. The cute little princess was bleeding profusely. She had a deep knife wound in the center of her chest. I immediately told the police dispatcher to have an ambulance respond quickly. I put a compress on the girl's chest and held it firmly. The victim's pulse was very weak. She had lost a great deal of blood. We decided to take her to the hospital. There was no time left to wait for an ambulance. I cautiously carried the girl in my arms. Carrying her down the stairs was dangerous. I could not afford to slip and fall on the stairs. The balance of her life was held in my hands. We hoped there was time to save her life. I knew that every minute I could save, would give the victim a better chance to live.

Officer Kurtz called radio communications: "Unit 411 we are taking a victim to University Hospital. She has a stab wound in the chest area. Please notify the emergency room that we are bringing in a seven-year-old black female. She has lost a considerable amount of blood."

Officer Kurtz drove the police car to University Hospital. My police uniform shirt and pants were drenched with blood. The blood from the girl's mouth and chest flowed out like a broken water faucet. It took us approximately six minutes to arrive at University Hospital.

I had the little girl clutched in my arms. I quickly took the girl into the emergency room. The surgeons were on standby and I handed the victim to the doctors. We became emotionally involved in this case. Even though we are trained to stay neutral. We broke the rules, for this was a special little princess. I held that little child in my arms. I treated her as if she were my own daughter. We are professional police officers who are not supposed to show emotion. This case was different from any of the thousands of tragedies I have encountered.

We remained at University Hospital. We watched intently from the surgeons observation window. They were doing open heart surgery on her. The tears from my eyes were flowing down my cheeks. I watched five surgeons try desperately to save the little girl's precious life. She was an innocent victim of a violent crime, committed by her sick, demented uncle. The little girl was a cute little princess. When I saw her lying on the operating table unconscious, I felt a deep hopeless emptiness inside. My subconscious thoughts sensed that the little girl was on her way to heaven. The surgeons opened up her chest cavity. They desperately tried to stop the massive bleeding. It was such a tragic view to see the little girls punctured heart. The size of her heart was no bigger than a plum.

"What kind of a sick son of a bitch could commit such a brutal attack on this little girl?" said one of the surgeons.

The surgeons came out of the operating room two hours later. They were all drained from the operation. The chief surgeon approached us and stated. "I'm sorry, officers, we lost the little girl. We did everything possible to save her life. The surgeon said she was stabbed with a very large knife. The knife penetrated her chest cavity and it punctured her heart." Detective Chuck Conte from the Homicide Division responded to the hospital.

We left the hospital and called Central Communications. We requested a back up unit to respond with us to 313 West Kinney Street, Apartment 10D. We were determined to arrest the guy who killed this little girl. The suspects name was Carl "Batman" Petersen. He was a former mental patient from Marlboro, New Jersey. Residents from the apartment told us why they call this guy "Batman." "We call him 'Batman' because he dressed up in a Batman costume," one resident said. Another resident stated, "He dressed up in that silly outfit. He thinks that he is the savior of the people."

We asked Central Communications to check his record for previous arrests. The radio dispatcher notified all units in the field. "Units 410, 411, 412 use extreme caution. The suspect, Carl Petersen, aka (also known as) 'Batman.' He has been arrested on previous occasions for aggravated assault on police officers."

When we arrived at the scene, Mr. Petersen would not let us in his apartment. We went into the adjacent apartment and retrieved the apartment keys from his grandmother, Mrs. Starks. When we opened the apartment door all of us had our guns drawn. "Batman" was in the deceased little girl's bedroom. There was blood splattered all over the floor. "Batman's" eyes looked like Satan's himself.

"Batman" had a demonic look on his face. His mouth had saliva dripping out. He stood there motionless, armed with a twelve-inch Bowie knife. There was dry blood on the knife. We were expecting him to lunge at us, and we were ready for his attack.

We considered this guy to be an extremely dangerous foe. A guy with his mental capacity only made out task worse. A mentally deranged person can be ten times stronger than an average man. I thought that at any second, we were going to unload a barrage of bullets into his body. He never said a word to us. He just gave us that demonic look. I said to the other cops, "I could shoot this guy with six bullets; frankly I don't think they would kill him. How do you kill someone that looks like a zombie?" I said to the officers. "If this guy does not drop his knife after two warnings, I am going to blow his ass to hell." I had my gun pointed at the suspect at point blank range. In a stern loud voice I said, "Carl, you are under arrest, drop the knife and drop to the floor."

Suddenly, to our amazement, "Batman" dropped the knife and lay his body flat on the floor. Officer Kurtz put the handcuffs on the prisoner. He was advised of his Miranda warning. We transported the suspect to the homicide division. He was slated for murder. He is presently in a mental institution.

My heart went out to the beautiful little princess. I consoled the victim's parents at the funeral. They were very appreciative. They thanked us for the effort we made. The tragedies that we encounter are not easy to cope with.

7 The Wild West (Shootout into the Darkness)

One intangible sequence is unique in the profession of a police officer. Every assignment is handled differently. We never know when a robbery in progress is going to be for real. No one ever said that our job was easy. You always have to be ready for the unexpected. Ninety percent of the time, when a police car is dispatched to respond to a robbery in progress or holdup alarms, the suspects are gone when we arrive at the scene. We also respond to thousands of false alarms and an occasional trip of an alarm system. When officers respond to hold-up alarms, our blood pressure goes up 100 points. The tension and stress level increases your heartbeat by fifty ticks a minute.

On the night of March 20, 1984, we were dispatched on a routine assignment. It involved an altercation between a girl and her boyfriend. Minutes after arriving on the scene, we were rudely interrupted by a young couple that told us that they were robbed at gunpoint. They told us that it had happened three minutes ago. Ironic twists, such as this incident, will occur from time to time in your career as a police officer. On this night we were very lucky that we were not killed. My regular partner booked off sick. I was working with a young police officer. His name was Officer Brian Morris. He was an excellent police officer who had on many occasions displayed courage and dedication.

Officer Brian Morris said that he was pleased with the opportunity to work with me. He said that he heard a lot of stories about the shoot-outs I have encountered in the wild west district.

"Jerry, you have become a legend in the Precinct. I noticed that you have been decorated with three 'A' valor awards. You are an outstanding police officer and have displayed great courage and fortitude."

Brian told me that he would like to someday be the recipient of a class "A" valor award. He asked me what it was like to be in a shootout.

"Brian, it is a nightmare that you don't want to experience."

I thanked Officer Morris for the compliments. I told Brian that I was very fortunate. I always try to be a professional at all times. Officer Morris has been awarded the class "B" Medal of Honor twice. I told Brian that to attain the Class "B" awards is something he can be proud of. A police officer has to display courage and excellent police awareness. You cannot attain police excellence without those qualities. "Brian you can wear your medals proudly."

Heroes to me are soldiers that have sacrificed their lives in a war zone. Police Officers are heroes of the people, and for the people. Obviously I have never backed away from a dangerous situation. However, it is important to know that I never venture to put myself in life threatening situations.

"Please believe me Brian, if you can survive through your twenty-five year career without receiving a class 'A' award, go to church when you retire and light twenty-five candles. Thank the Lord that you never had to risk your life in a shoot-out."

I still get nightmares from the three shoot-outs I was in.

No police officer should ever want to receive a valor award, knowing that he will be in a shoot-out to attain one. When you receive a class "B" award display your medal proudly. You have earned it by displaying courage and dedication. I have confronted death three times in my career. I consider myself very fortunate to be here talking about it. The tension and stress you develop after being involved in a shoot-out is serious. The stress and fear stay with you. It is a nightmare we all can do without. I said it before and it is worth repeating. No police officer wants to receive a class "A" award posthumously. Don't go out on the streets looking to be a hero.

The conversation that Officer Morris and I were having took place while we were on routine patrol. I was hungry, so we drove down to a good restaurant. We ate a couple of hamburgers and fries. We resumed patrol at 0045 hours. Minutes later we were assigned our fourth job.

Central Communication called us on the air. "Unit 416, respond to Alexander Street and South Orange Avenue. The landlord has a complaint of a Code 083 boyfriend, girlfriend dispute in the hallway." We arrived at the scene and adjusted the altercation. We advised them to go their separate ways.

A young couple approached us and stated to us, "Officers, we were just robbed about three minutes ago. Two black males pointed a gun at us. They robbed us of all our money and jewelry."

"All right listen carefully and calm down. I want you to give me a description of the robbery suspects."

"Officer the robber with the gun was 5'10", 165 pounds, he was a light skinned black male. He was wearing blue jeans, a green teashirt, white sneakers, a blue yankee baseball cap. He was approximately twenty-five years old and he had a black mustache. The second suspect was a black male, 6'2", 180 pounds. He was approximately twenty-two years old. He was wearing a short brown jacket, white sneakers and blue jeans. He had short hair and was clean shaven."

I called Central Communications to execute a police action assignment. "Unit 416 hold us at Boylan Street and South Orange Avenue. We have a Code 519 robbery at gunpoint."

We drove our police cruiser west on South Orange Avenue. The suspects had last been seen on West End Avenue and South Orange Avenue. Officer Morris issued a description of the robbery suspects. We asked the police dispatcher to send us two backup units. Central Communications broadcasted the description of the suspects. We drove the car slowly west on South Orange Avenue.

We told the victims to look carefully for the robbery suspects. When I got to the corner of Boylan Street and South Orange Avenue, we observed two black males walking west on South Orange Avenue. I said to Bryan. "That looks like the robbery suspects." The victims saw them and yelled out in a very excited voice.

"Officers, those are the robbery suspects on the corner." She pointed to the guy who has the gun and stated, "That's him." I stopped the police car in the middle of the intersection of South Orange Avenue and Boyland Street. Officer Morris exited from the police car. He immediately drew his weapon when he approached the suspects. They saw us when we stopped the police car. The robbery suspect armed with a gun fled south on Boylan Street. The other suspect ran west on South Orange Avenue. Officer Morris wisely chose to pursue the robbery suspect who was armed with a gun. He pursued the suspect south on Boylan Street. I quickly exited from the car and ran in back of Brian. I didn't care about the other suspect. My partner was pursuing a robber armed with a gun. Officer Morris trailed in back of the suspect by 300 feet. I called Central Communications and stated. "Unit 416 clear the air. We are chasing a robbery suspect on foot. He is armed with a gun. We are running south on Boylan Street." The radio dispatcher alerted to all units in the field.

I followed Officer Morris in the intense pursuit. I was approximately 100 feet in back of Officer Morris. We were running at least three blocks down Boylan Street. Suddenly the assailant wheeled around and fired several shots at Officer Morris and me. We each fired two shots at the suspect. The suspect ran into the rear yard of a vacant lot. The suspect fired several more shots at us. Officer Morris fired three shots at the suspect. I fired four shots at the suspect. The vacant lot was very dark. We saw the suspect climb over a cyclone fence. We reloaded our service revolvers. I said to my partner, "Brian are you all right? We must have wounded him." Officer Morris pursued the suspect by climbing over fences. He bravely stalked the suspect under extremely dangerous conditions. It was very dark in the backyards. I flanked Officer Morris from the street. We were in communication with each other at all times. We both had portable police radios.

Officer Morris contacted me on the police radio. "Jerry I have climbed over several fences pursuing the suspect. He has to be trapped in the alleyway. Jerry, he can't go over any more fences. There are guard dogs impeding his escape."

I told Bryan that I saw the suspect climb on top of a porch roof. "Brian this guy thinks he is a weasel. He is hiding on a small extended porch roof in the alleyway."

I notified Central Communications that we had the robbery suspect trapped on a porch roof located at 212 Boylan Street. We had Units 415 and 417 responding along with Unit 402 Sergeant Paglia.

The alleyway was very dark. I could not see two feet in front of me. I approached the alleyway cautiously. I hugged the house as a shield. I did not want to leave myself vulnerable. I observed the suspect lying flat on the porch roof. I stated to the robbery suspect. "You are surrounded by police officers. Throw your gun off the roof and jump off the roof."

The suspect replied. "Hey man, are you crazy? If I jump off the roof I'm gonna mess myself up." The suspect said that he'd thrown the gun in an abandoned lot. I told the suspect that he has five seconds to jump.

"I can't see you and I don't know if you have a gun pointed at me. I will only warn you one more time, brother. If you choose not to jump at the count of five, I am going to blow your ass away."

Fortunately the suspect had run out of options and chose to jump off the roof. He landed flat on his butt and was not injured. I had my gun drawn and held him at bay. I didn't want to search or handcuff him. I eliminated the chance of the suspect making a slick move on me. I waited for my partner to arrive. I stood about three feet from the suspect.

The suspect stated, "Officer don't shoot me; I don't have the gun anymore."

I replied, "You just keep your hands behind your back and you won't get hurt."

The suspect lay on his stomach and he never blinked an eye. Apparently the suspect was afraid that I would shoot him. Officer Morris arrived at the scene a few minutes later.

The suspect was handcuffed by Officer Morris. He was advised of his Miranda warning. We took the victims to the Robbery Squad Detective Bureau. The suspect was placed in a lineup with five other guys. The victims identified the robbery suspect. We submitted as evidence $600 in cash. We also recovered two gold watches and a diamond ring. Officer Morris searched the suspect at the scene where we arrested him. We advised the victims that their property would be released to them after the trial. The suspect was slated and charged with armed robbery and aggravated assault on police officers with intent to kill. There was no gun found on the suspect. He said that the gun was tossed away in the weeds.

Sergeant Paglia advised the radio dispatcher to have a police emergency unit respond. Unit 84 responded to 202 Boylan Street. Officer Michael Lamotta was at the scene within ten minutes. Sergeant Paglia told Officer LaMotta to set up the floodlights at 202 Boyland Street. Officer Michael LaMotta along with Unit 417 searched the dense area for the gun. The weeds and grass was very high. The conditions were very poor; it was difficult to find the gun. Sergeant Paglia called off the search after a two hour effort. Sergeant Paglia got a statement from a witness who stated that he observed a teenager take the gun from the suspect. The teenager was last seen getting on a bus on South Orange Avenue.

Dangerous ground lightning and thunderstorms was hampering our investigation. We responded to the Detective Bureau and executed our arrest sheets. The robbery suspect was fortunate that he was not killed. A barrage of bullets was fired at him during our gun battle with him. Sergeant Paglia advised all units to return to their sectors. We thanked the police officers who assisted us on the scene.

Sergeant Paglia told us that he was recommending class "A" valor awards.

"Congratulations you have both displayed courage beyond the line of duty. Continue your excellent efforts in the field. I am forwarding my investigation to Captain Rox." Sergeant Paglia advised us that Lieutenant Reed from Internal Affairs had the shooting investigation. Detective Coleman would conduct the robbery investigation.

Detective Coleman told us that he recovered two bullets lodged in a car on Boylan Street. "Based on your reports on where you were located during the line of fire, ballistic analysis will confirm that these bullets were fired by the robbery suspect," Detective Coleman said.

We were very fortunate that the heavy rain, thunder and lightning held off until we were in the Detective Bureau. The heavy downpours and dangerous ground lightning would have hampered our efforts to arrest the suspect.

Officer Morris and I were awarded the class "A" medal of valor. It was presented to us by the Police Director during Police Week, May 1985. Officer Morris had an interesting comment that he related to me after he received his Medal. "Jerry, I have to hand it to you. When you told me that getting involved in a shootout is extremely stressful, you were absolutely right. I remember you telling me how intense and frightening it is when someone is shooting at you. Jerry, when the robbery suspect wheeled around and fired several shots at us, it was a bizarre feeling. I felt one of those bullets buzzing right by my left ear. Jerry, you can't come any closer to death than at that split second. That bullet was marked to blow my head off. I will always remember that my life could have been snuffed out by a one inch projectile path. Jerry I know you were flanked behind me. You had a good angle on the suspect. The position you were in enabled you to fire several shots at the suspect. I will always be indebted to you for saving my life. He continued to run after the shots were fired at him. I thought I shot him in the back Jerry. I hope that I never have to get involved in another shootout, but I will be ready for whatever challenge arises. It was a privilege working with you that night Jerry."

I told Brian that it was his speed, agility and courage that enabled us to arrest the robber. Eight months later the robber was sentenced to fifteen years in prison. In May

1990 Officer Morris was promoted to Sergeant. He presently works as a drill instructor.

In August 1994, Bryan Morris was promoted to Lieutenant. He is currently a Detective Lt. Investigator for Internal Affairs Division.

8 Take Back the Streets

I was assigned to the Safe Streets Program in the spring of 1980. We had a new Police Captain at the West District. Captain Edward Duffy took over the reigns as Commanding Officer of the West District Precinct. During the two years that I was under his command, I was inspired and motivated to take back the streets from the criminals. Captain Duffy wanted to give back the streets to the citizens of Newark. Under the leadership of Captain Duffy's Command, I received two class "A" valor awards and eight command citations. Police officers who displayed exemplary police work were always backed up by Captain Duffy. He always kept the officers under his command well disciplined. He always displayed the kind of dedication and fortitude that gained the respect of all the police officers. Lieutenant Pepek advised me to report to Captain Duffy's office at 0900 hours.

Captain Duffy told me that I was detailed to the Safe

Streets Program. The Captain went on to say, "Officer Moravek, it will be your responsibility to cover Springfield Avenue. You will be covering a two-mile radius from Springfield Avenue intersecting Irving Turner Boulevard to Seventeenth Street intersecting Springfield Avenue. You will have a police car to transport you from the extended area of Springfield Avenue. Use the police car as an asset. Visit as many merchants as you can. Log in your report the business stores that you visit each day. I want you to have a police car as a means to respond to all areas of Springfield Avenue. The police car will be to your advantage. A quick response when a crime is committed will enhance your chances of arresting the suspects. You can also use the police car as a decoy to distract the criminal element. Let's make every effort to take back the streets from the criminals. When I ride along Springfield Avenue, I have observed seven to ten guys hanging out in front of business stores. They are blocking the passageway preventing patrons from entering the stores," Captain Duffy said.

"Officer Moravek I am telling you that this is going to cease. Everyone hanging in front of stores and blocking passageways is to be interrogated. Advise them that the next time they are caught, they will be arrested for blocking a store passageway. Citizens are being robbed and are having their pocketbooks and wallets snatched by these individuals. The citizens of Newark are afraid to go shopping. Be careful and good luck with your assignment."

Captain Duffy told me to report to Lieutenant Barone's office. Lieutenant Barone greeted me.

"Good morning, Officer Moravek. You will be working in the Safe Streets Program. You will report to work at eleven A.M. and your shift will end at seven P.M. You will be assigned to police radio car unit number 491. All interrogation reports will be forwarded to my office. Captain Duffy wants a daily log sheet. Keep a record of all suspicious persons who are interrogated and arrested."

I had a format planned that was going to make this challenging assignment successful. I was assigned the Springfield Avenue Post for fourteen months. Everyday I averaged interrogating eight 170s (suspicious persons). They were continually blocking the passageway of the merchants' stores. Usually half of the violators whose record I checked were wanted on bench warrants for crimes committed. After nine months of taking the violators off of the streets, the message started to sink into their heads. The City of Newark was not going to tolerate their criminal acts of preying on innocent victims. Most of my days on the street were very busy. A typical day on my post went something like this.

I called Central Communications. "Unit 491, I need a back up unit and a squadroll. I am located at Springfield Avenue and Bergen Street. I need transportation for twelve 170s (suspicious persons). They have to be interrogated and record checked at the West District Precinct."

Units 410 and 412 responded to the scene. The violators were transported to the Precinct. After being detained for three hours, the violators that who not wanted on warrants were released.

When I arrived at a business store, I had to keep control of the violators. I had no alternative. My gun was always drawn and pointed at the violators. Most of the time I was confronted with eight to twelve violators. As a police officer you can never take a situation for granted. There are no free meal tickets. There are no situations that you can consider routine. I could not contain ten wise guys. I had my gun drawn on them. I ordered them to obey my instructions. You also have to take into consideration one very important asset. It is not an easy task for one officer to contain eight to twelve wise guys. When you approach them, you have no idea who may be armed with a gun or knife. You have no idea who might be wanted for a homicide, a rape, a robbery warrant. You have to be ready for action at all times. This profession does not afford you the luxury of making a fatal mistake. You cannot assume that everyone of these guys are good upright citizens. As a police officer we have to be focused on reality. Most of the guys hanging on the corners are drug addicts. Some are vagrants, however most of these 170s are waiting to mug someone for their money. This was one of the reasons why the Captain wanted these guys taken off the streets. These guys were ruthless predators waiting for a victim.

My approach to challenging the violators was executed by stating to them, "You will all drop to the ground and lie prone on your stomach. Keep your hands and arms in front of you. Anyone making a move to reach for a gun in their waist will be shot and killed. Obey and listen to my orders and no one will get hurt."

Those words used are only a threat tactic. An officer would not shoot a suspect without a gun pointed at him by the assailant. We are all trained on the proper use of deadly force. Every officer uses his own discretion. We only have a split second to decide the fate of a person's life. My attitude is if a suspect is taking a gun out of his waist, I will not give him the opportunity to draw his gun on me. That split second is my advantage to shoot him.

I have been involved in three shootouts during my career. I know that I am very fortunate to be here. I could have been killed by the assailants who fired shots at me. Every suspect that you encounter is a police officer's enemy. You always have to be prepared to face the reality of life. If a suspect is armed with a gun, he will blow you away if given the opportunity. You have to stay alert.

Working this post alone made the risk very dangerous. I accepted the challenge. I wanted to give the streets back to the citizens. It was always a high risk controlling eight to twelve violators at one location. However it should be noted that I wasn't holding ten robbery suspects. Most of these guys were small time petty thieves who were robbing elderly people. These guys are slick slimy weasels. They hang around the stores and observe the patrons. They wait patiently for the right opportunity to prey on their victims. They choose to prey on elderly men and women. They wait for the patron to leave the store. The patron will have a few dollars in their hand. When they put the money in their wallet or pocketbook, the actor (robber) will ask the victim for the time. He will ask for a match or cigarette. The actor now will knock the victim to the ground. He will quickly snatch their pocketbook or wallet. The poor victims not only lose their hard-earned money, most victims suffer a broken collarbone, broken wrists, broken hands, broken legs, broken ankles, broken ribs. Some elderly victims suffer critical head and back injuries.

I have no sympathy for the male and female violators. They have to go thorough the hassle of being detained. They are secured in a holding cell for three to five hours. During their time that they were detained. I record checked each individual and executed interrogation sheets on all of them. Usually half of them were wanted on traffic or bench warrants. No one is released until I have completed my reports. The violators who record checked negative were released. They were advised as follows. "The Police Captain of the West District and the City of Newark does not want anyone loitering on the corners. We do not want you blocking the passageway of a merchant's store. You are forewarned that their will be no second chances. I am advising all of you to stay off of Springfield Avenue. You have no business loitering and blocking a merchants store. Anyone caught violating the city ordinance will be arrested. If you are a resident of the area, you can patronize the store."

During the fourteen months that I was assigned to the Safe Streets Program, I gave the merchants and the patrons a chance to feel as if they could shop at a store without the fear of being robbed. The dedication involved was well worth the effort. It also increased the awareness of good community relations. The merchants who owned the stores were elated by my presence.

After nine months of relentless hampering of the violators who were arrested at the business stores, the message started to sink into their heads. We were going to take back the streets and give them back to the citizens. The following five months my efforts was beginning to succeed. The 170s who were continuously loitering in front of stores slacked off dramatically. During the first nine months I was averaging fifty interrogations a week. The last five months the interrogations and record checks slacked off to less than twenty a week. Most of the violators were arrested for blocking a passageway. Some of the violators were arrested for loitering. I very rarely arrested the same violator more than twice. They were advised and forewarned, no one was arrested unless they were caught on a previous occasion. There were no second chances.

Fortunately during the fourteen months that I was detailed to this post, I never had any of the violators challenge my authority. I never had to use physical force. I never had to shoot anyone. I found that my method of having my gun pointed at the potential suspects and violators eliminated a potential confrontation and kept the situation under control. Occasionally I did have several violators file complaints against me. They disliked the fact that I had my gun pointed at them.

I was in uniform and if they obeyed my orders, the violators would have no reason to fear me. My life was always on the line not theirs. Those violators who made a beef of my method were advised accordingly. They knew who I was. I never knew who I was confronting. I always was facing the unknown element. When I confronted and challenged ten subjects, I looked at them and said to myself, I better watch these guys carefully. One or more of these guys could be armed with a gun or knife. I always considered every suspect as a threat to me.

Captain Duffy often would call me into his office. He praised me for the outstanding effort I was doing. He told me that he has received hundreds of phone calls and letters from citizens. They were elated that Springfield Avenue was changing for the better. Citizens of the central ward were not in fear to go shopping at the store. The merchants who owned businesses on the avenue were delighted by the presence of a police officer at their store. It was very rewarding to me when I heard that the citizens of the Central Ward commended my police performance. It was rewarding to have the citizens of the community telling the Captain of the Precinct that they were feeling safe to go to a store. Captain Duffy always backed me up. Complaints that were lodged against me by violators were dealt with accordingly.

During my fourteen month campaign of patrolling Springfield Avenue, I am proud and elated to say that Captain Duffy's quest for taking back the streets was successful. Obviously it was not achieved overnight. It was executed by making a commitment to take back the streets.

The crimes that were committed during my fourteen months of Springfield Avenue were three robberies, eight purse snatches and six aggravated assaults. There were no shootings on my post. There were two business stores held up at gunpoint. The backup units that assisted me were the backbone that made my effort successful. During my fourteen months I executed 2,614 interrogations, 574 arrests. The efforts of me and the backup units that assisted me gave the citizens of the central ward the streets that were taken away from them. Unfortunately, the lack of federal funds disbanded the program.

9 Friday Night Bloodbath at Fort Apache (The Wild West)

In the city of Newark, we average approximately 150 homicides a year. That number is well below the number of homicides in other big cities. Detroit, Michigan 300 homicides. Washington, D.C. 425 homicides. New York 440 homicides. On a Friday night in July, my partner, Officer Opie Smith, and I were involved in a bloody night of death. It involved domestic violence, jealousy and deceit. It was a night that seemed as if it would never end. We were dispatched to the scenes of gruesome bizarre homicides.

Officer Opie Smith and I were assigned to Unit 411. This area has always been drug infested within the projects on Prince Street. It is also prevalent in regards to having numerous domestic violence reports occurring. This night I will always remember as the Friday night bloodbath.

The radio dispatcher sent us to 214 Prince Street, Apartment 8C. We were issued a code 514 stabbing. EMS Unit 382 and Emergency Unit 184 were responding. The dispatcher gave us a time of 0115 hours. We arrived at the scene at 0122 hours. We had to run up the stairs as the elevators were not working. It was a very warm night with a temperature hovering at eighty degrees. The high humidity outside made it feel like a wet blanket. When we arrived on the eighth floor, we needed to regroup and catch our second wind. We were out of breath and sweating profusely. We knocked on the apartment door several times. It was very quiet in the apartment. We placed our ears on the door. It became apparent that no one was going to answer the door. We had to wake up the tenants next door. We had to have probable cause to break down the door. We had witnesses tell us that there was a violent confrontation.

We went back downstairs to the first floor. We contacted the superintendent. He went upstairs with us to open the door. When we walked in the apartment. We observed blood splattered everywhere. It covered the gold woolen rug and two blush white couches.

The furniture, consisting of a television, dining table, and three night tables, was busted up. There were busted vases and antique pottery scattered on the living room floor. The apartment looked as if a tornado had hit it. When we walked into the kitchen, we observed two bodies lying motionless on the floor in a pool of blood. The female had a stab wound in her lower abdomen. The blood was oozing down her thighs onto the floor. The male victim had a stab wound deeply cut into his left forearm. He was inflicted with multiple stab wounds to his lower back. His throat was slit across approximately three inches. The male victim's eyes were wide open. He was lying motionless, the blood was flowing profusely from his mouth and throat. He was bleeding internally from the severe stab wounds inflicted on his back. The female victim had a rug cutter gripped tightly in her right hand. The male victim had a steakknife gripped tightly in his right hand. Shortly after death, rigormortis sets in causing a muscular rigidity; this is why the victims had a tight grip on their deadly weapons.

Officer Smith called the radio dispatcher on the air. "Unit 411 we have two victims with critical stab wounds. Please put a push on those emergency medical units. We also need a homicide team for a possible double homicide." The emergency units arrived five minutes after we requested them for a second time. We also needed a photo team from the identification bureau. The EMS technicians transported the victims to University Hospital. Both victims were DOA (dead on arrival) at the hospital.

We talked with three tenants that knew the deceased couple very well. Mrs. Joan Slater stated, "The couple were fighting bitterly the past two nights. They exchanged some violent words and threats. The female victim, Thelma Brown, was a very jealous young lady. She has been living with her boyfriend, Gary Tingus, for three years."

Another witness, Carolyn Jacobs, stated, "The couple were screaming and cursing at each other. Thelma said to Gary that she found out he was having an affair with Diane Thomas. Thelma became enraged and she was slashing Gary with a rug cutter. Gary picked up a kitchen steak knife and stabbed Thelma in her stomach."

We held the witnesses for the homicide detectives. They were transported to Police Headquarters.

Officer Smith and I were shocked by the amount of blood that was splattered across the kitchen floor. The autopsy revealed that both victims died at approximately 0100 hours. We never had a chance of saving them. Time of reasonable response will always determine the fate of victims. Especially when it involves a violent domestic confrontation. The homicide team arrived at the scene. After we completed our preliminary reports, we resumed patrol knowing full well that we still had five hours left to the night. With a full moon blazing in the northern skies, I had a gut feeling that this night was not over. We received another deadly job.

The radio dispatcher called us on the air: "Unit 411 respond to 642 High Street on a code 513 shooting. Use extreme caution. We have received several phone calls alleging that three people are shot. EMS Unit 322 and Emergency Unit 84 are responding. Take a time of 0317 hours."

Officer Smith and I arrived at the scene at 0321 hours. When we opened the front door to the apartment building, we observed three bodies sprawled out on the bottom of the stairs in the vestibule. The victims were two females and one male. All three victims had multiple gun shot wounds. One of the female victims was later identified as Jane Roberts. Jane had a gun clutched in her left hand. Miss Roberts had two bullet wounds in her chest. Another bullet was lodged in her chin. Jane's sister, Diane Roberts, had a bullet wound in her right eye. She had another bullet lodged in her left cheek.

The male victim was later identified as Jeffrey Gibson. He was thirty one years old. He had a .45 automatic gripped in his right hand. Jeffrey was shot twice in the upper chest. He also had a bullet lodged in his left ear. The two female victims were in their mid-twenties. All three victims were DOA at the scene.

We called the dispatcher and had a homicide team notified to respond. We only had two witnesses who saw the tragic shootout. Mrs. Audrey Morris stated, "The two guys were fighting over the young lady Jane Roberts. Neither guy knew that Jane was having an affair with two men. One of the guys, Jeffery Gibson, came over to see Jane. The other guy Ray Crowley showed up at the wrong time. The guys were intangled in a heated argument. Jeffrey fired several shots at Ray Crowley. The stray bullets missed him and fatally shot Jane Roberts' sister, Diane Roberts. Jane went to get a gun when she saw her sister gunned down by Jeffrey. Both of them exchanged gunfire, shooting each other several times."

It was a nightmare that Ray Crowley will never forget. He was very fortunate that he was not gunned down with all those bullets exchanged. Ray Crowley told us that he dove for the bottom of the stairs.

We submitted our preliminary reports to the homicide detectives. Both witnesses were held for questioning by the detectives. We resumed patrol at 0455 hours.

You would have thought that the rest of the night would be tranquil. Not a chance, we had a full moon remember! We had the dubious distinction of handling three assignments that involved seven homicides.

The radio dispatcher called us on the air. "Unit 411 respond to 444 South Orange Avenue on a code 510 robbery in progress. Use extreme caution. We have several phone calls of shots fired and possible victims shot. Units 412 and 414 back up Unit 411. We also have EMS Unit 324 and

Emergency Unit 83 responding to the scene. All units keep
the air clear. First unit on the scene advise us of the situation." Officer Smith advised the dispatcher that we had two
victims shot. They were in critical condition.

We arrived at the scene at 0544 hours. When entering the
bar we observed two males lying on the floor. The bartender and a patron were shot several times. The bartender
was shot three times in the chest. The bartender was DOA
at University Hospital. The patron, a young male in his
twenties, was DOA at the scene. The patron was shot one
time with a bullet lodged in his left temple. All the patrons
in the bar were held there as witnesses. Homicide Detective
Gary Miller was notified to respond.

One of the witnesses, Mr. John Barnes stated: "The bartender attempted to wrestle the gun away from the robbery
suspect. Suddenly the gun fired and the bullet struck a
patron sitting on a bar stool. The robbery suspect gained
control of his gun with the help of another robbery suspect.
The robber than shot the bartender at point blank range.
The robber shot him three times." The autopsy revealed
that the bartender took two bullets that penetrated his chest
cavity. The bullets pierced his heart and spleen.

Two weeks later the suspect was gunned down by Detective James Nance. He was the triggerman who executed
the victims in the bar. The second suspect was caught by
Detective Gary Miller. The suspect who surrendered was
Harold Reynolds. He was convicted of two counts of homicide and armed robbery. He is presently serving twenty-
five years to life. Our tour of duty normally ends at seven-
thirty A.M. This nightmare of a endless night did not end
until 1030 hours in the morning. It was an unforgettable
night. Officer Smith and I were completely stressed out.

I hope that I never again have to endure that many homicides in one night. The frustrating part of our job is that
we would like to be on the scene before the tragedies occur.
Unfortunately, that is a very rare occurrence.

The following night we had another night of intense
trauma. The radio dispatcher sent us to 468 South Eleventh
Street. "Unit 411 we have a code 508 rape in progress. The
victim is a twelve-year-old girl. The suspect is a black male,
5'9", 165 pounds. He is wearing a light green shirt, blue
jeans, white sneakers. Witnesses state the suspect abducted

the teenager at knife point. He allegedly is raping her on the second floor apartment 2-E. Unit 411 take a time of 0354 hours. Unit 413 will back you up."

We arrived at the scene at 0405 hours. The building was very dark and abandoned. Officer Opie Smith and I heard screams coming from the second floor. We immediately dashed up the staircase, jumping two stairs at a time. When we arrived at apartment 2E, the door was bolted locked. We forcefully busted the door open. We observed the victim on the floor in the living room. The suspect was on top of her. They were both nude. The only clothing she had on her was a white pair of bobby-socks. The victim was screaming hysterically. She was bleeding profusely from the vaginal area. The blood was running down her thighs. The suspect later identified as Robert Manning was ordered to get off her. We had our guns pointed directly at him. The rape suspect was a deranged madman. I thought we were going to shoot him. He was armed with a hunting knife. He had it clutched in his right hand. He was approximately fifteen feet from us. He stood there motionless for a minute. He was told to drop the knife. I warned the suspect a second time. "Drop the knife or I will shoot your ass dead." Fortunately he dropped the knife. The suspect was handcuffed, advised of his rights and slated at the precinct. The victim was admitted at Presbyterian Hospital. A rape kit was sent to the SARA detectives. Robert Manning was convicted of aggravated rape, inprisonment and abduction. He is presently serving twenty five years to life. The victim's name will respectfully remain Jane Doe.

10 Wild Car Chase into Hell

When police officers talk about the intensity level that we have to deal with on a daily basis, getting involved in a relentless high speed chase with robbery suspects is a frightening and stressful experience. On one hot sultry summer night in July 1981, Officer Ed Norvilas and I were involved in an intense wild car chase that lasted forty minutes. It was unforgettable pursuit of four robbery suspects.

The radio dispatcher called us for an assignment. "Unit 414 respond to the Red Star Food Market at 516 Springfield Avenue. We have a code 560 hold up in progress. Take a time of 2120 hours."

We arrived at the scene at 2123 hours. We observed four black males leaving the store. Two of the robbery suspects were armed with shotguns. They quickly got into a red Buick Century. They fled east on Springfield Avenue. I was driving the police cruiser. Officer Norvilas notified the dispatcher. The car chase continued for seventeen miles from Newark to Bayonne, New Jersey.

Officer Norvilas requested the radio dispatcher to have the radio airwaves cleared.

"Unit 414 clear the air. We are in pursuit of a 1984 Red Buick Century, New Jersey Plate Number HJK-344. The suspects are armed with two sawed off shotguns. Unit 414, have a police unit check if anyone was injured in the Supermarket. Unit 414 we are chasing the suspects east on Springfield Avenue. We just crossed the intersection of Bergen Street–Springfield Avenue. Unit 414, our location is east on Springfield Avenue intersecting Market Street. Unit 414 we are in pursuit heading east on Market Street intersecting Broad Street. Unit 414 we are located at the intersection of Green Street. We are heading south on Mulberry Street. Unit 414, the suspects are driving at a high erratic speed. We are pursuing the suspects east on South Street intersecting Adams Street.

"Unit 414, we are pursuing the suspect east on 1 and 9 north. The driver is accelerating at speeds in access of ninety miles per hour. Unit 414 please notify Jersey City Police and Bayonne Police to set up road blocks in their city. Unit 414, we are heading east on the Pulaski Highway. Unit 414, we are crossing the borderline of Newark and Jersey City. Unit 414 we are chasing the suspects east on Commonwealth Avenue in Jersey City. We have two Jersey City Police Cruisers following us in pursuit. Unit 414, suspects just went through a red light at the intersection of Commonwealth Avenue and Kennedy Boulevard. Unit 414, the suspects are driving north on Kennedy Boulevard."

Suddenly the driver attempted to negotiate a left turn at speeds of seventy miles per hour. The driver lost control of the vehicle and violently crashed through a cyclone fence. The car catapulted up seven cement stairs; it then crashed through a picture window. The car came to rest in a young couple's living room. I notified the dispatcher that the car crashed into a house at 1260 Kennedy Boulevard.

I was driving the police car at speeds of eighty to ninety miles per hour. I was continuously weaving in and out of traffic to maintain a visible pursuit of the robbery suspects. Driving the car at such a high speed made the pursuit very intense and challenging. Our lives were always at stake. These assailants were playing Russian roulette with our lives. I tried my best to avoid injuring ourselves and other people who were driving on the congested highway. We had five Jersey City Police, three Bayonne Police and two Newark Police cars pursuing the robbers.

Seconds after the suspects crashed into the house, we ran up the stairs to capture the suspects. We also were concerned for the owners of the house. Fortunately the owners of the house were sleeping in the bedroom. Their bedroom was approximately twenty feet from the living room. To say the least, the young couple was rudely awakened.

Two robbery suspects that were sitting in the rear seats were ejected from the car. They were both critically injured with broken legs, cracked ribs and a fractured skull. The driver had a fractured jaw and lacerations deeply cut into his face. The front seat passenger was ejected out of the front window. He had a fractured skull, a fractured pelvis and severe lacerations to the face. They were transported to the Jersey City Medical Center. The Bergen County Sheriffs Department guarded the prisoners. They were released five weeks later from the hospital.

We found in their possession two shotguns, one .38 revolver and one stolen M16 rifle. We also recovered $2,855 of the money they robbed from the supermarket. The suspects were formally charged and arrested. They were all advised of their Miranda warning. They were slated for armed robbery, knowingly fleeing police officers, possession of weapons, possession of stolen cash. The driver was issued traffic summons for speeding, reckless driving, running six red lights, and voice in hand. Five weeks later the suspects were extradited to the Essex County Jail.

The prisoners were convicted eight months later. They were sentenced to nine to twelve jail terms. Fortunately no one was injured at the Red Star Food Market.

I only worked with Officer Ed Norvilas for eight months. During the stretch of time that we teamed up we made some excellent collars. Eddie had an uncanny talent for catching stolen car thieves. We made twenty-four collars on the apprehension and conviction of stolen car thieves. If we were patrolling the streets today, we would be arresting thirty car thieves a week. Lieutenant Edward Norvilas is an outstanding and dedicated professional. He has always performed excellently in the field. I'm proud to say that

Another stolen car. This time, a passenger in the rear was ejected out the window and was DOA at the scene.

Ed was recently promoted to Lieutenant. He currently is assigned to Central Communications.

11 Inferno into Hell on South 12th Street

As police officers we very rarely have the occasion of performing the heroic role of a fireman. It is a dangerous situation that we are reluctant to perform. Firemen are trained in technique as to how you enter and exit a burning building.

I recall the night we were on routine patrol on South Twelfth Street. We suddenly observed a house engulfed in flames. It was a warm summer night in June 1982. The apartment complex was shooting flames fifty feet in the air.

Officer Joe Smith called the radio dispatcher."Unit 410, clear the air. We need a couple of fire trucks, police units, and emergency units. We have a three-bagger ignited at 534 South Twelfth Street. Hold us here, we are going inside the building to save the tenants."

The radio dispatcher acknowledged our transmission: "Unit 410 take a time of 0322 hours, Emergency Units, Fire

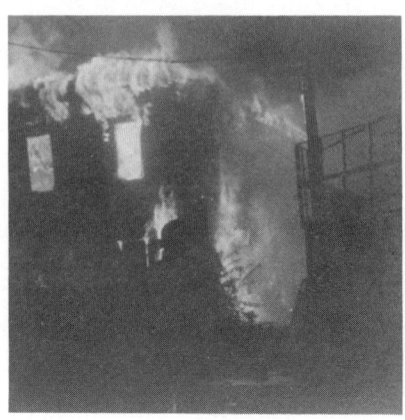

As we approached the house on 12th Street, it was engulfed in flames.

O.J. Moravek

Apparatus, Captain Rox, Command Post, Units 412 and 415 and Sergeant Tassie Unit 402 are responding to the scene."

The term three-bagger means there are three buildings on fire simultaneously and they are out of control.

Officer Smith and I entered each apartment. There were three apartments on each floor. We alerted and woke up all the tenants on all three floors.

The fire wall was extremely intense on the second floor. It was as if we entered the gates of hell. The heat was unbearable and the billowing smoke became blinding and choking.

Officer Smith carried an elderly lady out of her burning apartment. They both got out of the building safely.

I carried a sixteen-year-old female out of her second floor apartment. She was unconscious and was suffering from smoke inhalation.

When I got the fire victim out of the building, she was gasping for air. I applied an emergency portable oxygen tank to her mouth. She regained consciousness a few moments later.

We could hear the sirens of the fire trucks getting closer. Thank God they were only minutes away.

Two adult females came running out of the building. They were hysterical.

"Officer, our babies are trapped on the third floor!" she said.

"Ladies you are going to have to get a grip on yourself. Now tell us exactly where the babies are located. Give us the apartment number and the room you left them in," Officer Moravek said.

"Officer my child is in apartment 3D. My two-year old son is in the room adjacent to the kitchen." Mrs. Walker said. The second woman, Mrs. Levy, said, "Officer my baby is in apartment 3C. My four-year-old daughter is in the bedroom adjacent to the bathroom."

Both women had tears in their eyes and pleaded, "Officers please save our babies and God be with you."

We could hear the fire truck sirens becoming much louder. They were only a few block away from the fire.

We were both reluctant to go into the building. The fire was getting intense, but we had no choice. We had to save the babies.

Precious minutes meant life or death for the kids.

When we got to the second floor, the stairs and the apartments were almost completely engulfed in flames. We did not have time to think of our lives, we wanted to try to save the little toddlers. There really is no time to think of your own life. Neither one of us thought we would get out of the building alive.

When we got to the third floor, the apartments were engulfed in flames. The smoke was choking us.

Officer Smith went into apartment 3D. He snatched the toddler out of his playpen. He grabbed the bedsheets from the bed and soaked them with cold water.

Smith used the sheets as a shield to escape from the burning building. I had a difficult time locating the baby in apartment 3C. The smoke was building up to a thick black choking mist. The flames were very intense. I heard the little baby crying, that was a life-saving blessing. Her cries led me in the right direction. I went into the bathroom with two bedsheets. I soaked the sheets with cold water and wrapped a sheet around the baby's body. I used the toddler's blanket as a shield to get us out of the building.

When I started going down the stairs, I was getting dizzy, I thought I was going to black out. The heat was extremely intense. If the heat wasn't going to kill me, the smoke would surely do me in.

When I got to the second floor, I was suddenly trapped. The stairs between the first and second floors collapsed from the intense fire wall. My best move was to get to the fire escape. The stairs were very hot from the flames shooting out the windows. The baby and I managed to descend from the building.

I quickly gave the baby to a fireman. He administered oxygen to her.

Officer Smith and I were taken to University Hospital for smoke inhalation.

The toddlers were taken to Presbyterian Hospital with their mothers.

The other two buildings were abandoned match boxes. Both of those buildings were burned down to the ground. Fortunately, no one lived in those condemned buildings.

The babies were released a week later, having only minor burns. Officer Smith and I were released a few hours later.

Officer Smith and I booked off sick for three weeks. The fire took quite a bit of energy from both of us. We needed time to clear our lungs.

I will never forget how close we both came to being roasted in that inferno. I felt like a "cooked hotdog."

Anyone who thinks being a fireman is an easy job—forget it. They have to fight fires on a continuous basis. Their job is just as dangerous as a police officer's job. I have a great deal of respect for the courage that firemen display when fighting a fire.

Captain Rox praised Officer Smith and I for our courage.

We woke up thirty-seven people who were sleeping in the building. Most of them would have perished if we hadn't knocked on their doors.

The greatest challenge was saving the babies that were trapped. Saving their lives is a reward I will cherish the rest of my life.

Fortunately Officer Smith and I did not suffer any degree of fire burns.

We both consider ourselves lucky to be alive. It was truly a miracle that we got ourselves and the babies out of the building.

If I had to do it over again, I would still want to sacrifice my life to save the toddlers.

In my twenty-three years in the police department this was the only occasion that I had to play the role of fireman.

Captain Rox awarded Officer Smith and me the Medal of Valor class "A" award for the courage we displayed.

The rest of this chapter will deal with your chances of surviving a fire. More than 400 people died in residential fires in 1992. I want to address some of the mistakes people make when they are in a fire. Reading this could save your life.

Listed below are some of the most important things you should do in a fire. Make an effort to practice fire safety. If you can get rid of bad habits, especially smoking cigarettes in bed, you could avoid the horror of becoming a fire victim. You do not want your children to perish in a fire.

If the fire alarm wakes you, roll out of bed to the floor. Always stay as close to the floor as possible; the air is cleaner and cooler near the ground. In a blaze the temperature at knee level may be as cool as 90 degrees, but a burning 690 degrees at shoulder level! Stay on your hands and knees to avoid the heat and smoke.

Crawl to the door and touch it to see if it's hot.

If the door is cool, open it a crack to check for smoke. If there is none, leave by your escape route. Remember to crawl and keep your head low. On your way out make sure to close all doors behind you. This can delay the fire for hours.

Do not open the door if it feels hot!

Opening the door will only let in the harmful smoke and gas. Keep the door shut and look for an alternate route. Go out the window if possible.

If you are unable to leave your room or apartment, seal the cracks around the door with wet towels or blankets, and try to let some fresh air in through the window. Call the fire department if you can and tell them exactly where you are. Shout for help and signal your position by waving a bright cloth, towel or sheet.

If your clothes catch fire, do not run! Stop where you are, drop to the ground and roll to put out the flames.

Here are some other very important fire safety tips to practice and get into a habit to follow all the time. They may save your life and your family.

Always sleep with your bedroom door closed. The closed door will delay the fire and give you time to escape. Seconds can mean life. It is also a good idea to keep a flashlight near your bed so you can find your way around. Remember, in a real life fire there is no light!

Make sure your family has a fire escape plan. Everyone in your home should know two escape routes from every room. With your family, decide on a place outside where you can meet to be sure everyone has escaped safely. *Practice* a home fire drill often!

Teach your children to memorize the 911 emergency number. Post the number near the phone where it will be easily seen. Have your children memorize your complete address so they can tell the fire department where to go.

One of the biggest tragedies today is that hundreds of people are fire victims because they don't check their smoke detectors. *PLEASE CHANGE THE BATTERY!*

Try to remember that because the smell of smoke will not wake you while you sleep, you must relay on a smoke alarm to save your life. Make sure your home or apartment has a smoke detector near each sleeping area and escape route. Please remember to *change the batteries often.* If you don't have smoke detectors in your house, purchase them. It will be the best investment of your life.

At Christmas time there are more fires than at any other time of the year. Get rid of those wire light sets that are exposed. Check your sockets at least once every five years. Have an electrician check that the inside wires are not worn out and exposed. Do not overload your sockets. Turn the Christmas tree off when you go to sleep or go out. Throw the tree out if it is dry. Feed the tree with water twice a day. Pine trees drink a lot of water. Keep your holiday season a happy one. I have seen too many Christmas tragedies. Keep the book matches out of the reach of your children.

I got most of my material from Dr. Frank Field's book "Get out alive." It is available at all book stores.

12 Three Babies Named Jerry

In January 1994, I completed my twenty-third year as a member of Newark's Finest. During those years I delivered three babies into the world.

I recall the first time that I was called on to play doctor. I still consider that day as the toughest and the most challenging day of my life. Needless to say, the first baby your deliver is obviously going to be the most memorable.

The first baby I delivered was on a Sunday in May 1973.

The radio dispatcher called us on the air. "Unit 312, respond to 212 Market Street on a code 150. See the store manager in his office at Newberry's Department Store. A young lady is in labor. EMS Unit 324 is responding."

My partner, Officer Ken Burchard, asked me, "Jerry have you ever delivered a baby?" I replied. "Hell no, I have only been a cop for two years, give me a break." Burchardt blurted out, "Well Jerry, I guess there's a first time."

When you respond on a woman in labor call, you always hope and pray that the ambulance arrived there before you.

As a police officer, being assigned this type of responsibility is usually a once in a lifetime experience. We have to maintain our composure and be prepared to play the role of obstetrician.

We arrived at Newberry's at 1430 hours. When we got to the manager's office, we were greeted by a very nervous store manager, Mr. Warwick.

We talked with Mrs. Joan Lentz. She said she was well into her ninth months of pregnancy. "Officer my labor pains started over an hour ago," she said, "My water broke a few minutes ago." When Mrs. Lentz said that, we knew the baby was soon to be on its way.

It was time to prepare ourselves to deliver our first baby. I told Mr. Warwick to bring us some white sheets and hot water. We cleared off his office desk table.

We notified the radio dispatcher, to put a push on the EMS ambulance. "We have a woman in labor, and the baby is on the way into the world."

Mrs. Lentz went into full labor and within three minutes I was telling her "push . . . push . . . push. . . ." Within the next eight minutes, the miracle of life happened. We had a little five pound baby boy born.

I used our maternity kit utensils, I carefully cut off the umbilical cord. I used a sterilized surgical knife.

The baby infant was placed on the mother's chest. We began cleaning the afterbirth off of the babies face. Mrs. Lentz held the baby gently in her arms.

Within minutes after we delivered the baby, EMS unit 324 arrived at the scene. Both mother and baby were taken to United Presbyterian Hospital.

A week later I received a letter from the Lentz family. Mr. Lentz said in his letter: "Dear Officer Moravek,

"We graciously appreciate the professionalism you exercised during the delivery of our son. My wife told me that you handled the situation with tender and responsible care. We salute the Newark Police Department for having officers like yourself. We wish only the best in health and happiness to you and your family.

"P.S. we named our son 'Jerry' in your honor."

The second baby that I delivered occurred on September 14, 1976.

The radio dispatcher called us on the air. "Unit 316, respond to 457 Waydell Street on a code 150 woman in labor. EMS Unit 344 is also responding."

When we arrived at the scene, the young lady Mrs. Carol Romano was already in labor. My partner, Officer Carl Sprull, assisted me in delivering a seven-pound baby boy. Carl got the maternity kit out of the police car. Fortunately we didn't have to cut the umbilical cord. EMS Unit 344 arrived at the scene two minutes after we delivered the baby. I was cleaning the afterbirth off the babies face when the EMS technicians arrived. Both mother and baby were transported to St. James Hospital.

We transported the proud father along with his two daughters. We stayed at the hospital for an hour. The doctors told us everyone was doing fine.

Mr. Romano called me at the precinct three days later. He informed me that his wife and him decided to named their baby Jerry. I told him that I had now delivered two babies in the last five years. Both babies were named after me.

The Romanos sent Captain Tenpenny a letter of appreciation. They said Officer Sprull and I were a credit to the Newark Police Department.

The third and last baby that I delivered occurred in the West District in July 1982.

The radio dispatcher called us on the air. "Unit 413 respond to Springfield Avenue and South Tenth Street on a Code 150 woman in labor. See the driver of New Jersey Transit Bus number 423.

When we arrived on the scene, we cleared everyone off the bus. We took out our green blanket and spread it out on the back seat of the bus. Mrs. Teresa Brown said her water had broken ten minutes before. We got out the maternity kit and were ready to help Mrs. Brown. I told Mrs. Brown to relax, this was my third delivery. Five minutes later I delivered a seven-pound baby girl. Mrs. Brown sent me a letter of appreciation. She told me she named her daughter "Gerry."

13 Requiem for a Rape Suspect

I remember the night quite vividly, and every detail leading to the aftermath is very sad and tragic. As police officers we have to try our best to bury our fears and frustrations.

The reason why we have this stress factor is because unfortunately we cannot arrive at the scene of a crime. We would like to occasionally catch the suspect in the act of the crime. The victim too frequently is falling prey to an assailant. It is a very rare occasion that we observe a robbery in progress.

The chances of a police officer witnessing a rape in progress is very slim. The victim of a rape usually is the person calling the police to report the incident. Only on a rare occasion do we get a call from a witness.

The radio dispatcher called us on the air. "Unit 411, respond on a Code 507 rape in progress at 611 High Street, apartment 10B. Take a time of one thirty eight A.M.

We arrived at the scene at one forty four A.M. We ran up

ten flight of stairs, two stairs at a time. We chose not to wait for an elevator. We know that minutes are the precious time in an hourglass that can determine the fate of victim living or dying. The elevators are slow and the seconds you can save are valuable seconds that can cheat death. As police officers who experience tragedies everyday, we know how to cut the corners to cheat death. Unfortunately we don't have that many police officers that would break their butt to run up ten flight of stairs. Most of the officers were top cops that were decorated heroes. The problem was that Father Time had caught up with them.

When I was patrolling the streets in the early seventies, sixty-five percent of the officers in the Patrol Division were in their late forties. We were the new breed of officers filtering into the precincts from 1971–1979. During this period of time 520 officers were sworn into office. Ninety percent of the officers from the seventies and early eighties were an elite group of Newark's finest. Newark was fortunate in the detective division. They had top notch investigators.

When we arrived on the sixth floor, we could hear a female screaming for help. When we finally reached the tenth floor, we were both out of breath.

We cautiously entered apartment 10B. The victim was still screaming hysterically. The door was bolted firmly, we both simultaneously busted the door down. When we entered the bedroom adjacent to the kitchen, we observed a young Hispanic girl lying nude on a mattress. The victim appeared to be in a state of shock and trauma.

The assailant, was a black male in his mid-thirties. He immediately got off the mattress and tried to escape when he saw us approaching. He quickly ran into another room. My partner, Officer Kurtz, blocked off the entrance to the apartment door. I told Jim not to handcuff or search him till I took care of the victim. Kurtz held the suspect at bay with his gun pointed at him.

The young lady was a twelve-year-old Hispanic female. I calmed the victim down. She had suffered an extremely traumatic experience. It took time to reassure her that we had the situation under control. She was terrified from the nightmare experience she encountered.

I notified the radio dispatcher to put a push on the EMS emergency unit.

The victim stated that she was abducted at knife point. She said the assailant forced her to go to the tenth floor. With tears in her eyes she stated, "He forced me to have sex with him. He made me do oral sex with him." The victim said that the assailant threatened her by holding a knife at her throat.

The victim was bleeding profusely from the vaginal area. She was in a great deal of discomfort. We thought the victim might die from either the loss of blood or from shock and trauma.

The EMS technicians arrived several minutes later. They transported the victim to United Presbyterian Hospital.

I went into the abandoned room to assist my partner. When I arrived in the room Officer Kurtz stood fast about fifteen feet from the suspect. I was ready to search the suspect. Suddenly the assailant wheeled around and took a hunting knife out of his right pocket. He had the fourteen-inch knife gripped tightly in his right hand. I'm glad I told Jimmy not to search the suspect without me backing him. This guy would think nothing of slicing my partner to pieces.

The rape suspect stated, "You fuckin' cops are going to have to shoot me. You chicken ass bastards are not going to take me to jail." The suspect said that if we wanted to arrest him we would have to disarm him.

The suspect appeared to be high on drugs. We felt he was a deranged, mentally unstable opponent.

We had our guns pointed at him and warned him several times to drop the knife. The assailant was approximately fifteen feet from us. He never made an aggressive move to stab us with his knife. The suspect stood fast.

I felt that I was going to shoot him at any given second. If the suspect had taken one step toward my partner and me, there would be no alternative. I would have fired several shots into his body, whatever it would take to bring him down. Suspects who are heavily drugged with narcotics are difficult to take down. People have no idea how difficult the decision is to shoot someone.

You only have a split second to decide if you are going to kill an assailant. As a police officer you have the face the reality of life and death. When a suspect threatens to kill you he has to be dealt with accordingly. When a suspect fails to listen to your warning, if he is armed and dangerous you have to defend yourself. This guy was capable of cutting us to pieces.

It is not an easy decision to shoot at anyone. As a police officer you have to face the reality of taking out ("shoot to kill") a suspect as a professional law enforcement officer.

Officer Kurtz and I maintained our composure. We held our ground and were within seconds of shooting this assailant. As a police officer we are trained to be a professional. As much as I would have liked to shoot this scumbag for the heinous crime he had committed, I knew that I couldn't shoot him. We had to let the criminal justice system give this guy his day in court.

We cannot let our emotions take control of our actions.

Suddenly the suspect made a dash to escape. He ran toward the front apartment door. Officer Kurtz was a split second in decision. He was going to shoot the assailant. The suspect approached the front door and I shouted to Jimmy. "Don't shoot the bastard. We will catch him on the roof, he can't go anywhere."

We both could have shot justifiably the rape suspect. I just can't shoot someone in the back, regardless of the fact that he committed a rape. In 1990, the use of deadly force was updated. An officer cannot shoot at a fleeing suspect.

We chased the suspect relentlessly to the roof. When we reached the top floor he opened the wooden roof hatch.

The assailant became enraged when we had him cornered like a rat. The assailant turned into a madman. The assailant stated to us, "If you come any closer I will slash your asses to pieces. If you attempt to handcuff and arrest me, I will kill both of you."

The suspect had a "death wish" evil look on his face. My inner senses told me that I would have to kill him. There was no doubt in my mind. This guy was going to kill us if we didn't kill him. There was little or no options left.

We gave the suspect one last chance to give up and surrender his weapon. The suspect was approximately twelve feet from us. He was two feet from the edge of the roof. He was given a final warning to drop the knife.

We took two steps toward him. He was ten feet in front of us.

Suddenly he took three steps toward us and said. "I'm

going to kill you." I fired five shots at the assailant. The suspect staggered backwards and plunged ten stories to his death.

The autopsy showed that one bullet pierced the suspect's heart. Another bullet was lodged in his left cheek. Two bullets were lodged in his chest. The fifth bullet was lodged in his right knee.

EMS technicians pronounced him dead of arrival at University Hospital.

A grand jury inquest convened several weeks following the police shooting. They sent back a no bill finding. The prosecutor's office declared the investigation a justifiable homicide.

The young rape victim was taken to Prysbyterian Hospital. She was detained there for several days. It would take the victim years of therapy to recover from her nightmare.

A rape kit was executed and sent to our SARA detective unit.

The assailant, Robert Townson, was a repeat offender of several rapes. He served six years in prison from 1974 to 1980. He also had two previous rape cases pending. The suspect died at the ripe age of thirty-four.

14 Death Has No Remorse

It was a hot and sultry day in August 1984. My partner and I were assigned to Unit 411.

The radio dispatcher called us on the air. "Unit 411, respond to 23 Spruce Street on a Code 509 possible DOA. Mrs. Peters is the superintendent of the apartment building. She reported that a foul odor is coming out of apartment L-3. Take a time of ten twenty A.M." We arrived at the scene at ten twenty-six A.M.

We observed Mrs. Peters waiting in front of apartment L-3. When we approached the hallway, we smelled a foul stench.

When Mrs. Peters opened the door, the smell of death was apparent. The living room was not ransacked. We checked the bedrooms and they were not ransacked. We were looking for a body and to find evidence leading to foul play.

When we entered the kitchen, we observed a black female on the kitchen floor lying motionless. She was approximately fifty years old and weighed about 350 pounds. She apparently had suffered a heart attack, there was no sign of foul play.

The Essex County Coroner's detectives arrived. They said she had been dead for three days. They placed her body in a green plastic bag. Her body was taken to the forensic lab at the City Morgue on Bergen Street in Newark.

Officer Green and I searched the entire apartment. There was no indication of a burglary. We double-checked the entire apartment. There was no break-in at the deceased's apartment. The homicide detectives notified the next of kin of the untimely death of Mrs. Roseta Smith.

On a cool crisp morning in the spring of 1985, Officer Dennis Kihlberg and I were assigned to Unit 217. On April 12, 1985 we were dispatched to an eerie assignment that would make a great horror movie for Stephen King.

The radio dispatcher called us on the air. "Unit 217, respond to 193 Roseville Avenue, apartment 7A. We have a signal 509 DOA.

Officer Kihlberg said to me, "King Kong's carcass smells better than the odor in this building. Damn it Jerry I hate these elavators. I don't trust them. One of these days the cables are going to snap. Jerry can you smell that odor? the stench is worse than a dead skunk. This baby is going to be ripe. The stench when we open the apartment door is going to knock us on our butts."

By the time the elavator got us to the seventh floor, I said to Officer Kihlberg, "Dennis, we don't have to worry about the elavator cables snapping. The stench from the corpse coming from the body is going to kill us."

By the time the elavator got us to the seventh floor the stench from the corpse was unbearable. We were reluctant to open the apartment door.

We knocked on the door several times. No one opened the door. We busted the door open. When we entered the apartment we were knocked out by the horrible stench that suffocated the rooms. The apartment appeared to be abandoned. There was little if no furniture in the apartment.

In the living room on the couch. We observed a white hispanic male, thirty years old, 200 pounds. The corpse was sitting in a upright position on an old lounge chair. He was motionless and his eyes were wide open.

The body of the man looked like a corpse mumified and

propped up with added features from a "Creepshow" or "Tales from the Crypt" movie.

It was not only difficult to look at the decaying corpse. The stench was making my skin crawl. Officer Kihlberg's description of the corpse would be a classic horror movie script reading.

Dennis said to me. "Jerry, I am going to stay on the fire escape for a while. I need some fresh air before I die from a lack of oxygen. Jerry let's wait on the roof. I can't go back in that apartment. The detectives and the Coroner take too long to respond. I'm going to sit this one out."

I told Dennis that I wasn't going back into the apartment. I had to stay on the fire escape. I felt like vomitting, fortunately we hadn't eaten lunch yet.

The Coroner's office detectives arrived two hours later. They told us the body was dead approximately five days. The corpse was badly decomposed and bloated.

The autopsy report showed that the deceased man had died of an overdose. The horrible stench spread throughout the entire building. Detective Chuck Conte arrived at the scene. The body was wrapped in a green plastic bag.

Officer Kihlbereg and I will never forget that assignment. The horrifying look on the face of the corpse is unforgettable.

When I got home that afternoon. I stayed in the shower for an hour. I had to get that odor off of my body. I took my uniform to the cleaners.

Eight years later and Officer Kihlberg and I laugh about that unforgettable day. Dennis Kihlberg is a detective in the Police Benevolent Association office. He is first vice president.

15 Death on the Highway (Nightmare on Ice)

Police officers have to deal with death everyday. We find it very difficult to deal with death on the highways. There are many facets that can emotionally hamper a police officer's response to these tragedies.

Ironically, ninety percent of the traffic fatalities that occur could be avoided. I have written an entire chapter on defensive driving. If motorists can change their bad habits and learn to be defensive drivers, we can prevent ourselves from becoming fatalities on the highway.

I remember working the highway car in the East District. Officer Ken Santucci and I were assigned to Unit 317.

It was a bitterly cold and grey day in February 1974. In twenty years no ice storm has ever matched the havoc that menaced the Northeast coast on February 8, 1974.

The radio dispatcher called us on the air. "Unit 317, respond to Route 1 and 9 northbound lanes on Exit 14C. Near the underpass we have a Code 550 accident with casualties. Emergency Units 184 and EMS Unit 283 are responding. Take a time of nine twenty-eight A.M."

The elements for a terrible ice storm were imminent. The temperature was seventeen degrees. A heavy freezing rain and sleet were accumulating rapidly. It created a dangerous blanket of ice on the highways.

Sanitation trucks were out in full force dumping tons of salt that was spread across the four mile stretch of the highway. Unfortunately it was not helping enough because of the adverse conditions.

We had a wind chill factor of five below zero. Winds were blowing at twenty miles an hour. Wind gust were blowing out of the northeast at forty-five miles an hour.

It took us forty-five minutes to get to the scene of the accident. The highway was a skating rink. There were hundreds of fender benders all over the highway. Mother Nature was dealing us a nightmare on ice.

When we arrived at the scene, we observed a tan station wagon overturned. It was located on the center lane on Highway 9 northbound. We saw a young lady pinned to the driver's seat. The driver's daughter was pinned down to the roof of the car. As soon as I got out of the car, I slipped on the ice and fell on my butt.

EMS emergency units arrived minutes after we arrived. Sadly to our dismay, the technicians pronounced both of the car victims dead on arrival.

Unfortunately we had no seat belt laws to enforce in the 1970s. Both victims would be alive today if they had been wearing seat belts.

The twelve-year old girl would have had a better than even chance of survival with a seat belt in use. Her ejection from the vehicle would have been prevented.

I urge every parent reading my book: Buckle up your kids. It's not only the law, seat belts will save your life and your children.

No parent wants to go through the tragedy of losing a child. Double-check that your children are properly fastened when you are ready to drive off. Take an extra minute to double-check that your child is buckled up.

An hour later we received another assignment from the

radio dispatcher. "Unit 317, respond on a Code 550 accident on Pulaski Highway in the northbound lanes. We have a tractor trailer truck driver fatality on the shoulder of the highway. Unit 317, take a time of eleven forty-seven A.M.

When we arrived at the scene, we observed a tractor trailer truck jackknifed on the opposite side of the highway. The driver was lying across the highway near the shoulder of the road.

It took Officer Santucci and I well over an hour to determine how the driver died. We were at odds trying to decide if he had been hit by a car or truck.

The accident victim was apparently run over by his own truck. His head was squashed. A portion of his brains had spurted out next to his head.

We checked his truck very carefully and determined with the assistance of a mechanic, the truck had a mechanical flaw in the brakes.

The truck driver pulled his truck over to the shoulder of the road. He got out of the vehicle and checked under the hood for mechanical problems. Suddenly the brakes failed to keep the truck in park. The right front tire squashed the drivers head. The truck continued to roll and jackknifed across the highway. Fortunately there was no oncoming traffic. That would have caused a major chain reaction accident. Fatalities would have been in abundance.

EMS unit 234 arrived on the scene and pronounced the driver DOA. The entire day became a nightmare on ice. The storm continued to cause havoc. It was an intense nor'-easter. We had a freak occurrence.

We had a temperature inversion occurring: a warm gulf of Mexican air mass at 5,000 feet, feeding a southerly jet stream with warm moist air. Combine that with a bitterly cold pocket of air hovering off the coast. The weathermen call this a temperature inversion. With a temperature of seventeen degrees on the ground, the vaporized water was freezing when it hit the ground. This caused a rare phenonmenon.

At one P.M. we were dispatched to Route 21 (McCarter Highway) and the Route 22 underpass. We had a forty-seven car chain reaction pile-up. Fortunately no one was seriously injured.

All police officer working the morning shift were ordered to work an additional shift.

Routes 1 and 9 were closed along with Route 22 and 21. They were re-opened at five P.M.

During the twenty-seven hour ice storm, we had reports of 1,456 accidents. There were six fatalities reported.

16 Victims of Domestic Violence

The past six years, 1988–1994, I was assigned the responsibility of handling the police incident reports that filter in from the North, East, West and South Precinct Stations. Each night police officers from each Precinct drop off their reports to me at Police Headquarters, Detective Division.

I read hundreds of police reports each night: crimes dealing with narcotics, homicides, assaults, robberies, kidnappings, aggravated assaults, shootings, rapes, burglaries, hit and run accident and domestic violence.

It is my responsibility to assign and distribute the crime committed to the respective detective squad that will eventually complete the assignment. Police officers in the field execute the preliminary report and the detective completes the investigation.

I average working eighty days of overtime each year. My

regular shift starts at eleven thirty P.M. and it ends at seven thirty A.M. However, when I am working an overtime shift the sixteen-hour tour ends at three thirty P.M.

Working here at Police Headquarters I deal with thousands of people each year. Victims come to the Detective Division seeking to have the person who committed a crime against them arrested.

I have calmed down hundreds of victims of crimes committed against them. I give my best effort to make the victim feel that the police department does care about their well-being.

I receive a great deal of satisfaction by helping them. I make sure that I do everything possible to assure the victim that the City of Newark cares about every citizen who had been victimized by a crime.

I had one serious incident that occurred at Police Headquarters in July 1991. I was working the overtime shift (seven thirty A.M.–three thirty P.M.)

A middle-aged female came into Police Headquarters. She was emotionally distressed and feared for her life. She convinced me that her life was in immediate danger.

The victim, Mrs. Jane Darby, was in tears. She told me about the stress that was a part of her life. It started when her estranged husband invaded her house.

I had the victim come into my office. I calmed her down and reassured her. I wanted to give her confidence that we were here to help her. I could not execute a police report until I was able to put her at ease. I assured Mrs. Darby that the detectives would do everything possible to correct the injustice she had suffered.

Mrs Darby stated: "Last night around nine P.M. my estranged husband drove to my house on Tuxedo Parkway. He violently busted my front door down and entered the house. He threatened to kill me if I didn't take him back. He told me that I cannot have a relationship with another man. He had a gun pointed at me and he threatened to kill me if I called the police. He punched me in the face and chest several times. He once again warned me about making a police report."

Mrs. Darby had in her possession three restraining orders that were signed by a judge. One restraining was executed in East Orange. The other two restraining orders were executed in Newark.

Mrs Darby went on to say, "My husband threatened to kill me with a shotgun when we were separated. I had an apartment in East Orange at the time.

"On two other occasions he broke down my door in Newark on Tuxedo Parkway. He threatened to kill me with a gun pointed at my head. Officer, the man has to be put away soon."

Mrs. Darby was in tears and was trembling. She told me how on previous occasions her husband continuously punched her in the face and chest.

Mrs. Darby told me that after two years of being a battered woman victim, she finally built up enough courage to go to the police station. She filed a complaint against her husband for the abusive beatings she suffered at his hands.

Mrs. Darby further stated, "My husband always threatened to kill me if I called the police. When the neighbors called the police, I told the officers that everything was fine."

When Mrs. Darby came into police headquarters she was trembling with fear. It took me ten minutes to calm her down.

Mrs. Darby told me how she managed to escape from her estranged husband. Mrs. Darby said she went through the bathroom window on the first floor. She took refuge at a neighbor's house and called the police.

When the Newark Police Officers arrived, Mrs. Darby told them how her estranged husband broke the door down and threatened to kill her.

"I showed the officers the three restraining orders. The officers searched my house. They searched the area around the house. The officers did not find him. They advised me that their was nothing else they could do. They told me to call back the police operator if he returned," Mrs. Darby said.

Mrs. Darby lost confidence in the court system and in the police department.

The officers should have displayed better judgement and discretion in this dangerous situation.

I did not write this book to criticize police officers. I'm far from perfect. I've made some stupid mistakes along the way. Fortunately I never made a bad discretionary decision that could have cost a domestic violence victim her life. I always called the sergeant if I were unsure what to do. Our job is difficult enough as it is. It is not always that easy to know how to handle situations that are delicate and hard to get a grip on. The public and the press are always watching us. We have to be careful with our decisions.

The officers made an attempt to catch the victim's estranged husband. If they had caught him he would have been arrested.

Mrs. Darby was distraught about the manner in which the officer told her that their was nothing they could do for her.

I told Mrs. Darby that the officers were young and only on the street four months.

The officers were fortunate that a tragedy did not occur at Tuxedo Parkway. The officers should have asked the sergeant for advice. If Mrs. Darby had been killed by her estranged husband, the officers would have faced criminal charges for negligence.

The most important action that could have been done? Mrs. Darby should have been taken to a battered home shelter, at least until her estranged husband was arrested. As an officer your discretion is always going to be the balance between life and death. You have to weigh the situations you face. If you have three restraining orders staring you in the face, I strongly suggest that you make arrangements to put the victim in a safe house. If she refuses, you're covered. Execute a Captain's report on your actions.

I further explained to Mrs. Darby, "You misunderstood what the officers told you. They inadvertently advised you that their was nothing they could do because they didn't find your estranged husband."

To the reader who is a domestic violence victim. If you are in fear of your husband or boyfriend, if you have gone through the hell that Mrs. Darby suffered, New Jersey has a battered women hotline number: (201)(484-4446).

I have an entire forty page chapter on how you can prevent yourself from becoming a victim of domestic violence.

We have safe houses in Newark and Belleville. When a victim goes to a safe house for battered women, the only people who will know she is there are the family members she chooses to tell. It is a clean, well-protected haven. It will safeguard your life from your estranged husband or ex-boyfriend.

Mrs. Darby was very fortunate that her ex-husband did not return that night. He probably would have killed her.

In 1991 there were 1.3 million brutal attacks on women by their spouses. There were over three millions attacks on women unreported. The first week of September 1992, 200 women were killed involved in domestic violence cases.

I talked with Mrs. Darby for twenty minutes. I had the shaken victim calmed down and at ease. After reading the three restraining orders, I listened intently to Mrs. Darby describe how her estranged husband was menacing her at work and at her home for months.

I remember how terrorized Mrs. Darby was. She had tears in her eyes. She was pleading with me and stated, "Officer Moravek, is there anything the Police Department could do for me? My husband is going to kill me."

I told Mrs. Darby that when I was done executing my reports, I would send her to the third floor West Squad Detective Bureau. They will make every effort possible to arrest her estranged husband.

I took Mrs. Darby upstairs. I advised Lieutenant Beard of the situation. I gave him my reports and the three restraining orders.

Mrs. Darby described in detail the terror she encountered with her ex-spouse. Detective Lieutenant Beard assigned the investigation to Detective Underwood.

Detective Underwood was apprised of the situation. He completed the complaints that was going to put this guy away.

Detective Underwood called East Orange Detective Sergeant Cochrea. He was apprised of the complaints executed by the Newark Police Detective Bureau.

Sergeant Cochrea sent two detectives to Mr. John Wright's place of employment. He was arrested and slated at the East Orange Police Precinct.

At 1050 hours Sergeant Cochrea notified Detective Lieutenant Beard that Mr. Wright has been sent to Essex County Jail.

Lt. Beard thanked the East Orange Detectives and especially Detective Sergeant Cochrea. Their quick response to arrest him was appreciated.

Detective Lieutenant Beard advised Mrs. Wright Darby, that her estranged husband had been arrested by the East Orange Detective Bureau.

Mrs. Darby had tears of joy in her eyes. She graciously thanked Lieutenant Beard and Detective Underwood.

Mrs. Darby took the elevator to the first floor. She knocked on the door of my office. She gave me a big hug and a kiss on the cheek.

Mrs. Darby had tears of happiness and relief on her face. The stress, tension, fear, and remorse had vanished from her face.

I will never forget the look on her face when she entered Police Headquarters seeking help. I will never forget the beautiful smile she had when she left. I will always remember the kind words she said to me before she went home.

Mrs. Jean Wright Darby stated. "Officer Moravek, God bless you for everything that you have done for me. It is nice to know that there are officers like you, Who sincerely care about victims of domestic violence. You are a very special police officer. I will always remember the compassion and concern you showed me. Lt. Beard told me that the bail was set at $25,000 cash. I hope he rots in jail for a long time. Again Officer Moravek thank you for your kindness and your professionalism."

Mr. Wright is presently serving an eight-year prison term.

To all the police officers who are reading this book, we can all learn from other officers' mistakes. You can also learn from this situation. The greatest reward that can be attained from this profession, is by being there for the victims of crime. Let the victims know that you care about their safety.

17 Communities Under Siege (Carjackings: A Societal Nightmare)

Cities in Newark and the small communities like Irvington, Piscataway, Elizabeth and East Orange are under siege. Fear is riding Jersey roads in the wake of a rash of carjackings. These carjackings are occurring along the entire East Coast. Los Angeles Police report that they average three carjackings a week. Drivers across the State of New Jersey are locking their doors, arming themselves with tear gas and planning shopping trips as though they were patrols through war zones in the wake of the murder of Gail Shollar and other recent carjackings. In the month of October I wrote reports from victims of three carjackings. Our government has to make carjackings a federal crime.

A victim of a carjacking said to me the other day, ''Fear is killing Americans love affair with the automobile, and

O.J. Moravek
Badge #677

Police surround teenage suspects in the death of Betty Perry during their arrest at Hawthorne Avenue and Bergen Street in Newark.

Police work to remove Betty Perry and Mamie Branch from their overturned car at Hawthorne Avenue and Bergen Street in Newark.

The bodies of car crash victims are covered with sheets in the wreckage of an Acura Legend at South 12th Street and 14th Avenue in Newark.

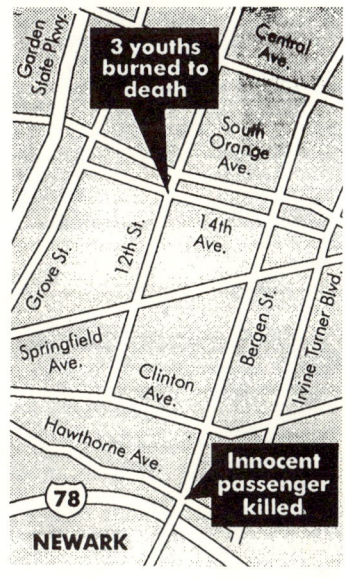

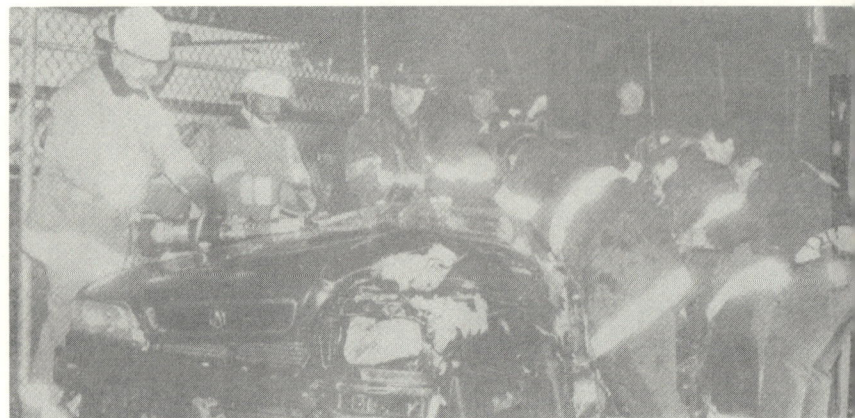

Emergency crews work to remove the teenage victims of an early morni car crash from the wreckage of an Acura Legend that crashed and burst into flames at South 12th Street and 14th Avenue in Newark.

A large hole is visible in the windshield of a van where it was struck by a concrete block thrown from a highway overpass in Somerset County.

changing their cars from relaxing havens of security to places where too often they feel trapped and vulnerable. He further commented, "You sit at a light now, and instead of listening to the radio you are always looking around."

On November 8, 1992, a missing mom was found slain in a drainage ditch. A massive search for a Piscataway kidnap victim ended when the woman's nude body was pulled from a lumber yard drainage ditch, where she had been dumped after being stabbed multiple times.

The body of Gail F. Shollar, the thirty-five-year-old mother of three young children, was discovered in the ditch at the Stelton Lumber Co. on Stelton Road in Piscataway at five after ten A.M. about an hour after 350 police and civilian volunteers began combing nearby woods for the woman, who had been missing since Tuesday night November 3.

Shollar who was abducted in her van as she and her three-year-old daughter sat at a traffic light and died after being stabbed "multiple times with a knife or a sharp instrument," according to Middlesex County Prosecutor Robert Gluck.

The daughter, Andrea, was left unharmed outside a day care center shortly after the kidnapping and was not found until the following morning.

The victim was found nude but covered with her sweater. The ditch from which the body was recovered is about fifty feet from the entrance of the lumber yard, which is less than a mile from a supermarket where the victim had bought groceries shortly before the tragic abduction. Police had searched the lumber yard previously but did not see the body, which probably was submerged by the week's heavy rains, the prosecutor said.

Authorities from Piscataway stated that Shollar and her three-year-old daughter were not kidnapped at a traffic light. They were kidnapped as they headed for their minivan in the parking lot of a South Plainfield supermarket. The daughter was dropped off on the lawn of a daycare center, and Shollar was stabbed to death shortly thereafter, authorities said. A suspect, Scott Johnson, 23, of Plainfield, was arrested and charged with murder. The State of New Jersey is seeking the death penalty for Johnson.

My wife, Aida, said to me yesterday, "It scares me to death. I now lock my doors all the time." She noted that before the recent spate of carjackings, women worried someone might break the car window to grab a purse. "Now, the idea that they are going to pull you out and drive off with the kids. . . . I am terrified. It makes you afraid to go to the malls and other areas. Its really sad that we have to live like that."

Drivers are being injected with a wakeup call. Drivers are now on guard as fear rides Jersey roads in the wake of carjackings. I advise people everyday that because of today's overall crime problem we have to be extremely careful. We have to adjust to the society we live in. That lesson is one being learned by more and more drivers. I advise all my neighbors in Berkeley Heights, if you have to commute from Newark, Irvington, Jersey City, etc., you have to hide your purses under the car seat floor, lock your doors and leave space between their cars and other vehicles so that you can drive away quickly if you are being accosted. A few weeks ago people were telling me that they were only afraid of someone stealing their cars. Thousands of drivers have told me that they never bothered to lock their car doors before now.

Fright has led drivers to purchase mace and other brands of chemical sprays. Chapter eighteen is composed entirely of the many of ways that people can prevent themselves from becoming a victim of a crime.

Try to memorize the twenty-seven precautions I have listed in this chapter. They will diminish the chances of becoming a victim of a carjacking.

Purchase the product pepper defense. I have tried it on myself. It will save your life. Spray the assailant in the face. The chemical spray will knock the assailant down. It causes blindness and convulsions. (*Do not use this spray on people.*) This product is strictly to be used in a life or death situation only.

New Jersey has been under siege for the last six months. Sholar's death was the most recent tragedy in a series of incidents that have struck New Jersey and other states violently.

In October 1992, a fifty-eight-year-old woman was shot and seriously wounded in a South Orange supermarket parking lot by a man who stole her car, and other carjackings have occurred with alarming frequency in recent months in the state's urban areas.

The phenomenon has not been limited to New Jersey. The

New York and Washington, D.C., metropolitan areas have been plagued with carjackings this year.

But carjackings have not been the only assault on drivers' security.

A Pennsylvania man was killed on Route 78 in Bernards Township in September when a chunk of concrete thrown from an overpass slammed through his windshield and into his body as he drove a group of sightseers home from New York.

New Jersey State Police made it one of their "very high priorities" to find out whoever hurled a concrete block from an overpass through the windshield of a van on Route 78 in Somerset County, killing a 44-year-old Pennsylvania man.

After the five-inch chunk of concrete hit the driver, John S. Gensicki Jr. of Reading, crushing his chest, two of his six passengers were able to steer the van and stop it safely.

"We heard this noise like a gunshot. I asked, 'My God, what happened?' My husband said, 'Something got thrown through the window,' and my first thought was, 'Get the car stopped.' Our driver was knocked out," said Susan Thomas, of Laureldale, Pa., a passenger in the van. The quick reaction of the passengers saved lives.

Autopsy results showed Gensicki died of blunt force trauma to the chest. The victim also suffered rib fractures and lacerations of the heart.

Gensicki, a part-time driver for DeSantis Transportation in Reading, was bringing the group home from a theater trip to New York Saturday when he went under the Sommerville Road in Bernards Township at about nine thirty P.M., authorities said. Horrible tragedies like this are occurring too frequently lately.

The concrete block crashed through the windshield, struck the top part of the steering wheel and hit the driver in the chest. Police are treating this horrible senseless tragedy as a homicide.

The overpass is in a heavily wooded area on a street with few houses. On both sides of the bridge are chainlink fences about seven feet high.

Authorities have stated. "It could have been deliberately done; it could have been kids, just (using) poor judgment and making a big mistake.

"The people in Reading are really shocked. A lot of people

knew him. He was very well liked," said Gregory DeSantis. "It is a horrible tragedy."

Thomas said her husband, James, was sitting on a bench seat behind Gensicki, talking to him, and saw the piece of concrete come crashing through the window. He squeezed between the van's front seats to apply the brakes, while Jeffrey Warmkessel, Thomas's brother-in-law, reaching over and grabbed the wheel.

They brought the van to the shoulder and flagged down a volunteer firefighter, who tried to resuscitate Gensicki.

Gensicki was transported by the Liberty Corner First Air Squad to Morristown Memorial Hospital, where he was pronounced dead at ten twenty-five P.M.

"We are all very upset. It's an unbelievable thing. You never thought it could happen to you, but it did," said Susan Thomas. "It's like a bad nightmare."

Use caution when you enter an overpass. If you see juveniles on the overpass, drive to a lane where they are not going to hit your car. Call your local police and notify them. It sounds ludicrous to suggest that motorist have to where helmets on Interstate Highways. We just have to be aware of the tragic occurrences that are happening in our communities.

Four years ago, motorists on Route 78 and Route 287 in Somerset County reported being bombarded with rocks and cinder blocks from overpasses, including the same Somerville Road overpass.

Police arrested two men, a firefighter and a rescue squad member, who were charged with showering cars with debris, then running to the rescue of the motorists when they pulled over.

No one was seriously injured in the incidents, although one person suffered a dislocated shoulder when a cinder block crashed through a car's sun roof.

David Domanski of Passaic Township, and Michael Havekost of Warren Township, who both pleaded guilty, were sentenced to ten years prison terms last year.

If it were not enough that communities are under siege with regard to carjackings, the wave of stolen car violence is on the increase. Teenagers are driving recklessly in stolen cars. They have no fear of losing their life. They will fearlessly drive through a red light at ninety miles per hour. Innocent motorists are going through green lights. They are broadsided and being killed.

In the past year Newark has tragically lost the lives of seven women. They drove their cars through green lights and were killed instantly by teenagers in stolen cars. I have devoted a substantial chapter on defensive driving. In the chapter motorists are warned. There is no free pass when you go through a green light. You have to treat a green light as if it were a red light.

Once again I have to reiterate, you have to adjust to the society we live in. There are teenagers on the streets who are a breed of their own. People who do not focus on themselves will become a victim of a crime. People who do not focus on reality will become a victim of society, if you do not develop the attitude that it can happen to you.

The wave of stolen car violence escalated on November 11, 1992. Four Newark residents were killed in two separate crashes.

One of the victims was a mother of four children who was a passenger in a car rammed by a stolen vehicle and three were joyriding teenagers trapped in a stolen car that exploded in flames after crashing into a utility pole.

Three other people were seriously injured in the accidents, said Newark Police Chief Thomas O'Reilly, who called the night "tragic" for the families of the Newark residents involved in the crashes.

His words were echoed by acting Newark Mayor Glenn Grant, who said, "These are tragic incidents and our condolences go out to the families of all the people who died in these accidents today. We're concerned with the needless loss of life and outraged that the children are not hearing our message.

"They are not hearing the hue and cry by the community, that they shouldn't get involved with stolen cars," Grant said. He promised the city will double its efforts to press its message.

It was too late for Betty Perry, 38, of Seventeenth Avenue, who died at nine fifty A.M. of internal injuries she suffered at two A.M. when the car she was riding in was rammed by a stolen Honda and flipped over, Chief O'Reilly said.

Perry, the mother of four children ages fourteen to nineteen, and grandmother to two, was to have been married next summer. Ironically, she was pronounced dead at University Hospital in Newark, where she worked in the mental health unit.

The driver of the car Perry was in, Mamie Branch, forty-one, of Treacy Avenue, was in stable condition at Newark Beth Israel Medical Center, suffering from cuts and bruises, hospital officials said.

The driver of the Honda had earlier tried to ram two police cars and its five occupants were fleeing from a patrol car when their car ran a red light at Hawthorne Avenue and Bergen Street and collided with Branch's Oldsmobile, Chief O'Reilly said. These tragedies can be avoided if we become defensive drivers.

Colon Sowell, eighteen, of Fairfield Avenue, a passenger in the Honda, was treated at University Hospital for a broken pelvis and shoulder, officials said.

In the second crash at five A.M. three teenagers were killed when the stolen 1992 Acura Legend they were in ran out of control, flew through the air after hitting a bump and crashed into a traffic signal and a utility pole at South Twelfth Street and Fourteenth Avenue. It was one of the worst car crashes I have ever seen. A few years ago four women were badly burned in a car crash. Their car went out of control and hit a brick building. This occurred at the bottom of the ramp on First Street when you come off of the 280 East ramp. This crash will remain in my memory for the rest of my life.

Their car (the Acura Legend) burst into flames, trapping the trio, tentatively identified as Omar Lewter, twelve, of South Sixteenth Street, Lateef Phipps, fourteen, of Springfield Avenue and Qsan Williams, eighteen, of South Seventh Street, officials said. Witnesses told me that they had in the past stolen a lot of cars.

Three other teenagers in the car, including Timothy Johnson, eighteen of Fifteenth Avenue, a fourteen-year old and a seventeen-year old, were pulled from the vehicle by residents before it burst into flames.

Johnson suffered multiple fractures of both legs, back injuries and paralysis and was in stable condition at University Hospital, officials said. He and two other surviving teenagers were charged yesterday with receiving stolen property. There was one witness who is a night owl watching television.

Betty Steele of South Twelfth Street said she was watching television when she heard a "loud bang" about five A.M.

"It sounded as if someone were tearing up the cars on the street."

Steele said she looked out her window and saw the car burst into flames and heard one of the youths call for help. "I didn't realize there were three other kids in the car," she said, explaining she saw someone pull a teenager out and she then called the fire department.

When three men pulled two teenagers from a burning car early in the morning, they were not thinking of joyriding, stolen cars, crime and violence—only of helping people in distress.

One of the heroes, Arthur Jones, sixty, of Orange, N.J. stated, "The first kid slid out easily, compared to the second one we pulled out. The second one came out and his legs were all twisted up. We had to pull on him a long time."

Jones, Gabriel L. Arace and Nathaniel Crawford were opening Arace Brother garbage disposal company at South Twelfth Street and Fourteenth Avenue at five A.M. Wednesday November 11, 1992 when the noise of the accident brought them running to the corner.

"The car was lying there and started burning around the back," Gabriel Arace said, explaining that he told Jones and Crawford to help the people in the car while he ran to call the fire department and the police. The fifty-four year old Livingston resident ran back outside to help pull the teenagers from the burning vehicle. Arace stated. "We pull one guy and laid him on the sidewalk and then we pulled the second one from the car. The rest of them didn't get out. We could hear them screaming for help."

When the men looked back to where they had left the first victim, dazed and banged up, he was gone. "He ran away," said the men. "He never said thank you."

Qsan Williams, eighteen, was the driver of the ill-fated car. An autopsy showed that his heart burst from the force of the crash impact.

The two other youths in the car may have died in the fire, officials said. Police were awaiting toxicological reports to determine the cause of their death.

In all, three youths escaped from the blazing vehicle: fourteen-year old Alim McCollough, of Springfield Avenue, who was treated for minor injuries in University Hospital; Dequan Boyton, seventeen, of S. Seventeenth Street, who was released from the hospital after being treated for back injuries and Timothy Johnson, eighteen, of Fifteenth Avenue, who was in stable condition in the hospital with leg fractures and a broken ankle. All three survivors were charged with receiving stolen property.

"It took a lot of courage to go up to that car, it could have exploded," said Arace as he remembered the events of that tragic morning.

"There was fuel on the sidewalk, I guess that's what caught on fire, and maybe that's why it didn't explode," he mused. "If it had, we could have died as well." Heroes are born every day and these three men deserve a lot of credit.

"We were lucky the car veered toward the right side of the street instead of to the left when it hit that bump, otherwise, it could have crashed into the garage," Arace said.

What the teenagers thought was going to be fun for them —racing around in a sporty car—turned into tragedy.

Witnesses and neighbors that I talked with stated, "The motorists fly through the intersection of South Twelfth Street and Fourteenth Avenue regularly and on one occasion two kids driving a stolen car crashed into a company garbage truck parked on Fourteenth Avenue."

Every teenager who is driving stolen cars should witness this tragedy, hear teenagers hollering for their lives. When I saw their charred bodies trapped in the vehicle, they looked like melted wax figures. The frightening truth is that they really have no value of life and no fear of death. This driver was racing an Acura Legend at close to 100 miles an hour. When he lost control of the car, it flew through the air, slammed into a traffic signal and sheared through a utility pole before skidding to a stop against a chain link fence and catching fire.

"Three young people were burned to death and one innocent woman was killed," Mulvihill said. "This is not a simple theft of an auto—it's a very dangerous pastime—for the public, the police and the kids, themselves."

Police charged the teenagers involved in the first accident, Sowell and Malik Yarrell, eighteen, of West Kinney Street, and three youths, a fifteen-year old Styvescent Avenue resident and two Wainwright Street residents, one sixteen and one seventeen, with four counts of aggravated assault, illegal possession of a dangerous weapon, the car, and its possession for an unlawful purpose and receiving stolen property. Detective Noreen Britt-Headen continued the investigation into the accident and Perry's death.

Mulvihill said the sixteen year old driver will be charged with homicide under the statute that makes a driver eluding police responsible for any death or injury resulting from the chase.

"It appears the captain took proper action in terms of handling the situation," Mulvihill said, referring to Captain Alan Marion's actions in the chase that culminated in the collision of the Honda and the Oldsmobile. Newark was second in the nation per capita, having 15,019 cars stolen in 1993.

While the reports will be presented to a grand jury for review, Mulvihill said the Captain appears to have followed county and city chase guidelines.

"The Captain was keeping a safe distance between the Honda and his patrol car," Chief O'Reilly said. "Both cars stopped at all the traffic signals and signs. This was not a high speed chase.

Captain Marion, a twenty-five year veteran of the department, was returning to the South District precinct at one fifty-three A.M. when he saw two speeding cars approaching the intersection of West Bigelow Street and Johnson Avenue, just as he was preparing to enter the crossing, Chief O'Reilly said.

One car sped through the intersection, followed closely be a second, a 1991 Honda Accord reported stolen in Newark. As Marion waited for the cars to speed through the intersection, the second one veered toward him and would have crashed into the marked patrol car if Marion hadn't reversed to avoid the maneuver, O'Reilly said.

The captain switched on his siren and overhead lights and followed the Honda, notifying the dispatcher of the pursuit and calling for backup units.

Marion was still a few blocks behind the stolen car when the Honda reached Hawthorne Avenue and Bergen Street and sped through an amber light.

Captain Marion took evasive action when the driver of the Honda turned west onto West Bigelow Street, and Marion followed, considering the attempted ramming as an assault on a police officer.

The Honda was speeding when it reached Hawthorne Avenue and Bergen Street. The timing of the light changing red was a bad omen. Apparently the other car, traveling north on Bergen Street, saw the light was changing and did not stop before going through the intersection. When officers John Underwood and Israel Caraballo, Jr. arrived at the scene of the crash, they recognized the Honda as the vehicle that had tried to ram them at Chancellor Avenue and Wainwright Street earlier that morning.

They told Marion they had been dispatched to the neighborhood to investigate a car "doing doughnuts," at twelve thirty A.M. and while there, the carload of teenagers drove straight at the marked patrol car.

The officers avoided the collision and the Honda disappeared down Schley Street. The teenagers spitefully taunt the police officers. They play these cat and mouse games. They dare the officers to challenge them.

The second accident was reported at nine after five A.M. The six teenagers in the Acura had been riding around in the stolen car for several hours, Chief O'Reilly said, explaining the vehicle, reported stolen in Jersey City was equipped with a telephone. They used the phone and called their friends, picking people up around the city, and driving around.

The teenagers were speeding down a long stretch of South Twelfth Street and were traveling at over ninety-five miles an hour when they hit a bump in the road or a pothole and went airborne.

"At those speeds, anything, even a stone, could send them airborne," said Detective Jack Eutsey. Jack Eutsey and Detective Anthony Ambrose had the investigation. Detective Eutsey is one of the top homicide detectives in the state.

In its flight, the Acura hit a traffic light, knocking that over a ten-foot fence and sliced through the middle of a telephone pole, leaving a three-foot stump on the pavement and the top section with the transformer dangling by its wires. The middle section of the pole also flew over the fence, landing on a parked car. The Acura landed and skidded to a stop.

On a highway (Interstate 95) in Jacksonville, Florida, sniper shots were being fired—at motorists. The National

Guard was patrolling the highway for weeks. Fortunately the suspects were arrested on November 11, 1992.

The Washington, D.C. carjack epidemic was eyed wearily in New York and New Jersey. The D.C. area was under siege with a epidemic of carjackings.

New Jersey officials, plagued by car thefts, kept a watchful eye on the nations capital.

The situation in the Washington D.C., area became so bad that the Federal Bureau of Investigation said it might set up undercover decoys to discourage thieves who have been strong-arming motorists out of their autos.

A woman was dragged a mile-and-a-half and killed as thieves sped away in her auto—prompting calls to Congress to make carjacking a federal crime.

Three days later on a Saturday night, an off-duty FBI agent killed a thief as he drove away in the agent's auto in Largo, Maryland.

The FBI agent had interrupted two men as they allegedly tried to steal a car, and one suspect turned a gun on the agent, ordering him to hand over his keys. If our nation's capital was under siege, the small surrounding communities along the East Coast were in deep trouble. Motorists had to extreme caution.

The terror on the streets continued. On November 11, 1992, New York Detectives originally believed that an off-duty New York female officer was shot and killed in a carjacking incident.

An intense round the clock investigation led to the arrest of her assailants. Probers say the N.Y. officer picked up her killer.

Police Officer Milagros Johnson was killed for her gun by one of two men she picked up early Wednesday (11-11-92), apparently strangers who may not have known she was an off-duty cop, the chief of detectives said yesterday.

Both suspects were taken into custody Thursday (11-12-92) on information from a number of callers who said they heard the men boasting of the slaying.

Chief Joseph Borrelli said Johnson was killed by Kwame (Kiki) Jackson, 24, of Jamaica, Queens, an unemployed father of two with a record of drug and assault convictions.

He was charged with murder and robbery.

The second man, Anthony Joseph, 20, of St. Albans,

Queens, was charged with hindering prosecution, tampering with evidence and weapon possession.

Investigators believed the slain officer picked up the two men sometime around one A.M. and drove with them to Joseph's home. "They went inside, where there may have been some sexual activity, probably consensual, between her and Jackson," Borrelli said. "We don't believe there was force," he said.

"Around two thirty A.M., back in Johnson's car, the men saw her gun in the storage compartment between the front seats and admired it," said Borrelli.

"Then, Kiki shot Officer Johnson three times in the head," he said.

The slain officer was dumped, naked and covered with a coat, in a weeded lot in Rosedale. Her car was abandoned in the West New York section of Brooklyn.

Her gun, along with the .25-caliber pistol used to kill her, were found together in a sewer in South Jamaica. The officer's badge was missing and it was not known whether anything else was stolen from her.

Since early October, 1992, Washington-area police reported there were a half-dozen carjackings—stealing a car by force while a driver is in it. Police arrested two gun-wielding teenage girls in one incident.

Recently, a Maryland woman, Pamela Basu, was taking her daughter to preschool when two men commandeered her BMW at an intersection. As the woman was forced out of the car, her arm became entangled in a seat belt and the thieves drove off. Along the way, they pitched the child in her car seat out the window. She was unharmed, but her mother was killed.

"What happened in Maryland should be a wakeup call," said Representative Charles Schumer. "We can't just throw our hands in the air and lament that car thieves have taken over the streets." Our streets in communities are under siege. People are in fear from the terror that is stalking motorists.

Schumer's bill would make carjacking a federal crime and require that more car parts be marked with identification numbers. Congress must act soon on a bill.

A computer study by the Washington Post showed that

at least 245 carjackings occurred between January 1 and August 16, 1992 in the area. Five resulted in death.

The Los Angelas Police Department has seen a rise in carjackings, particularly in affluent neighborhoods along the San Fernando Valley. Detroit suffered a well-publicized wave of carjacking in the summer of 1991.

People are "really frightened to the bone," said Robert Krebs, a spokesman for the American Automobile Association chapter covering Washington and its suburbs. Congress just passed a bill that allows all states to sell three-ounce canisters of teargas. People over the age of eighteen should be permitted to purchase it. That small canister could mean the different between life and death. It is an effective safety measure that will immobilize an assailant.

The FBI's Washington field office has been working with Arlington County, Virginia police since March, 1992 to curb car thefts. Scafidi said 25,000 to 30,000 car thefts occurred in the region in 1991. The team has already spend considerable time working on carjackings, Scafidi added.

The possible FBI decoy operation would be carried out with the District of Columbia Police Department.

Residents living along Interstate 95 in Howard County, Md.—where Basu died—say the highway connecting Baltimore and Washington brings crime into their area. Many were so alarmed that they called on local officials to build a new, higher fence with barbed wire along the top near the highway's rest areas.

According to the FBI, an automobile is stolen in the United States every nineteen seconds, with more than 1.7 million vehicles stolen in 1991. The FBI has said that the number of auto thefts increased thirty-eight percent from 1986 to 1991.

(New Jersey ranks fourth in auto thefts nationally behind California, New York and Texas, according to the National Insurance Crime Bureau. It said 925.9 cars per 100,000 were stolen in New Jersey in 1991. The Bureau also placed Newark, Irvington, Camden, East Orange and Trenton among the worst cities nationwide when ranked by the average number of thefts per 100,000 vehicles. However, when ranked in terms of the number of vehicles stolen, Newark and its 13,961 thefts came in eleventh nationally. New York led the way with an incredible 139,977 car thefts.)

"Decoys are a viable option," FBI special agent Frank Scafidi said of the situation in Washington. "If the FBI can help in any way to turn around what's beginning to be a real escalating problem, we'll spare no expense in equipment and manpower." The operation could involve unmarked cars, plainclothes officers and decoy drivers in luxury cars that have been the targets of the armed auto thefts, Scafidi said.

The communities (towns and cities) are under siege with regards to robberies, rapes, carjackings and stolen cars, which has to come to an abrupt end. Drastic measures have to be undertaken and a statewide cooperation has to be effectively executed. At the time of this writing, State Attorney General Del Tufo is undertaking the burden of putting together a strategy to combat the siege of terror occurring in New Jersey.

Recently State Attorney General Robert Del Tufo announced law enforcement officials are putting together a comprehensive effort to cut down and eliminate carjackings in New Jersey, just as Essex County officials said two area men were arrested for a two-hour armed crime spree on Saturday November 7, 1992.

"I'm here to make a few statements about the problem (of carjacking) in general," Del Tufo said during a press conference called by acting Essex County Prosecutor James Mulvihill to announce the arrests of Frederick White, 20, of East Orange and Frederick Ludiver, eighteen, of Newark.

"Carjacking is a very great concern," Del Tufo said, calling it a "mutant" form of armed robbery that seems to be increasing. "It affects the quality of life of the people."

He called the two suspects "thugs" in his remarks, promising that their type of conduct will not be tolerated in New Jersey. Del Tufo was being kind. These guys are "maggots" they are decaying our society. "They are preying on innocent victims," Moravek said. But the state is turning the tide on the criminals.

"There will be no plea bargaining for carjackers. We're going to press them to the hilt. They will go away—go to jail and will be punished for their acts," Del Tufo promised.

He outlined a combined prevention and enforcement effort being hammered out by state and local enforcement officials, the business community and local residents. Del

Tufo forsaw increased security in the parking lots of shopping centers and malls, increased mobile police patrols and promulgation of a series of safety tips to educate motorists. Motorists must not panic but learn to "lock their doors, take safe, well-lit routes, be aware of their surroundings," Officer Moravek said.

The charges against White and Ludiver include armed robbery, aggravated assault, weapons offenses, receiving stolen property, theft and conspiracy, Mulvihill said.

Officials said there may have been a third person involved in the robberies and have other incidents that could be linked to the spree. The men took turns brandishing a shotgun, first one, then the other threatening the victims with the weapon.

The two men were arraigned in Central Judicial Processing before Judge Clifford J. Minor. They pleaded innocent to all charges and were each ordered held on a $250,000 cash bail, set by Minor, who said theirs were the "most heinous crimes," he had heard in a long time.

Assistant Prosecutor Ted Brown, in charge of the auto theft prosecution unit, had originally requested a $200,000 cash bail but Minor set it higher to the consternation of the attorneys representing the men.

Lon Taylor, representing White, said the prosecutor's office had an on-going investigation and that such a high bail was premature. Attorney Taylor is missing the point. Minor increased the bail because of the criminal element that is gripping the city. Judge minor was setting a new standard.

The two men were accused of a crime spree Saturday night in which one man was shot in the hand and arm with birdshot pellets from a ten-gauge shotgun, nine other people were terrorized and robbed and one woman was beaten up.

These ruthless maggots held Essex County under siege for two hours.

"There were ten incidents in Newark, East Orange, Irvington, Hillside, and South Orange, during a period of one hour and forty-five minutes. Police found the minivan used in some of the incidents Saturday, and found two other cars stolen at gunpoint and used in subsequent robberies on Monday November 9, 1992.

"The assailants had a game plan to off set any police action.

"One of the cars was to be a ram car. If the police showed up, whichever was in the best position to hinder detention would have been used against the police," said South Orange Police Director Steven Palamara.

The rampage started with the theft of a minivan parked on Epprit Street in East Orange at seven P.M., Mulvihill said.

By seven thirty-four P.M., the suspects had driven to Milton Street in South Orange, where they tried to rob a fifty-one year old woman in her driveway, Mulvihill said. When the victim screamed and fell on the ground, the suspects, one brandishing a sawed-off shotgun, fled the scene.

Less than ten minutes later, the suspects approached a thirty-three year old woman in a Stanley Street driveway, dragging her from her 1984 BMW and driving away with her car and purse. One of the men fired a round. Fortunately it missed.

By eight P.M. the suspects were in Irvington, where they approached two women unloading groceries in a Vermont Avenue driveway. One man put the shotgun to the chest of one of the victims and demanded their pocketbooks. The gunmen fled in their gold BMW, police said.

Five minutes later, the suspects allegedly robbed a fifty-seven year old woman of her totebag and surfaced at eight fifteen P.M. on Williamson Avenue in Hillside where they shot a thirty-year old man who was sitting in his car.

The victim put his hands to his head to protect his face and suffered wounds to his hands and arm, Mulvihill said. Doctors removed thirty-six pellets.

At eight twenty P.M., still on Williamson Avenue, the suspects put the shotgun to the face of a woman who was getting out of her 1991 Toyota Camry carrying her two year old daughter. They forced her to remove the steering lock from her car and drove off with the vehicle and the victim's money.

Ten minutes later, the men were on Hansbury Avenue in Newark where they approached a twenty-one year old woman, pointed the shotgun at her and demanded her property. The assailants beat her with the gun when she started screaming, pistol-whipping her three times in the head and fleeing when her family came to her aid.

At eight thirty-five P.M., the assailants approached a woman on Pamona Avenue and stole her pocketbook. At eight forty-five P.M., they attacked a twenty-six year old man as he walked along Lehigh Avenue. The assailants put the shotgun to the man's chest and demanded he empty his pockets. They fled with $40 in cash and his leather coat.

Del Tufo praised the law enforcement officials involved in the investigation, as did Mulvihill, who cited the FBI Violent Crimes Task Force for its help, his own investigators and police in the departments where the crimes occured.

When you have team work and cohesiveness we can get the job done. This was excellent police work by all the departments combined.

These guys caused havoc for nearly two hours. During the string of incidents, one man was shot in the hand and arm with birdshot pellets from a ten-gauge shotgun.

The assailants also terrorized and robbed nine persons and beat one woman.

Robert Davis, of Sunset Street, Newark, turned himself in on November 11, 1992. He is charged with armed robbery, weapons offenses and conspiracy.

Summit meetings convened in mid-November 1992 to mobilize Jersey state drive against carjacking. The big and small cities and towns in New Jersey were under siege. State officials met to counter the growing fears about the spate of auto theft violence.

At the urging of Governor Jim Florio, representatives of the state Attorney General's office huddled with FBI officials, county prosecutors, chiefs of police and members of the business community.

"You have almost a new crime. Now we have carjacking that is taking the form of armed robbery," said Florio.

Immediate fears resulted from the November 3 murder of Gail Shollar, abducted as she headed for her minivan in a shopping center.

Numerous drivers around the state expressed fears about carjacking and reported taking increased precautions lately, including packing tear gas in their travels. We had a breed of assailants out there lurking. They were terrorizing the communities. As a law enforcement officer I could only hope that this wave of terror ended soon.

Both State Police and FBI officials said that to date they do not have specific statistics for carjackings, explaining they are wrapped into overall car theft and armed robbery data. There are plans to keep such statistics in the wake of the increased violence.

Jim Lamb, FBI spokeman, estimated there were some twenty carjackings a month in the northern New Jersey area, with more than 5,000 since January 1990 in the New York metropolitan area and surrounding New York State counties. Carjackings were a small percentage of the nearly 1.7 million cars stolen nationwide last year.

From everything that I'm seeing, the violent nature of car theft is increasing. There is a breed of individuals out there who have no value on life. They will stop at nothing to gain their peers' respect. Police officials will have to get a handle on the extent of the problem.

In Middlesex County, where Gail Shollar was murdered, residents were "really frightened" about carjacking as the holiday shopping season neared. People won't go to shopping malls until they can feel secure.

New Jersey's carjacking woes mirrored similar troubles in other parts of the nation, including New York City, the District of Columbia, and Detroit.

In Nassau County on Long Island, police reported more than forty carjackings since January compared with a negligible number in 1991. But even the forty plus carjackings were a small number of more than 1,500 robberies in the county in '92.

The frightening and realistic aspect of every armed robbery carjacking of this type is a potential homicide. We as police officers cannot underestimate the crime's significance. "The new awareness seems to be the best thing we have going. . . . I'd rather be exaggerating and have people be a little more cautious."

I told Captain Allen Marion he was night command post supervisor. Carjackings are more times than not prompted by the increased use of anti-theft devices (Steering lock, car alarms etc.) in vehicles. The easiest way now for some thieves to take a vehicle is by grabbing the keys from a victimized driver. Others suggest it may be partly be the result of copycat crimes, prompted by increased publicity about the problem.

President Bush signed a new federal carjacking law that highlighted the crime and offered stiff penalties. Those convicted of taking a vehicle by force now faced up to fifteen years imprisonment even is no victim is injured. In cases where a victim sustains serious bodily injury, the assailant was liable for up to twenty-five years in jail, while a homicide carried up to life imprisonment.

New Jersey law said heinous state carjackings could be tried under the new statute if federal authorities desire.

Governor Florio said he would support a similar state law "to send out a message," but stressed there are state laws—including armed robbery charges—to handle carjackers.

Additionally, Senator Richard Codey (D-Essex County) called on the Senate Judiciary Committee to move his bill that would impose harsh penalties for carjacking. He proposed making the crime a first-degree offense, carrying a ten to thirty year jail term and $100,000 fine. I along with all police officers salute and applaud Sen. Codey for his outstanding leadership and his awareness of the epidemic that has terrorized motorists across the state.

Meanwhile, in an unrelated matter involving vehicle safety, Assembly-woman Harriet Derman (R-Middlesex) was particularly concerned about an incident that happened in October 1992 on the New Jersey Turnpike, when a man impersonating a state trooper in an unmarked car pulled over a thirty-two-year old woman and raped her.

Motorists should be made aware that State Police use unmarked cars that have alternating flashing red lights and state troopers are always in uniform.

In the Newark Police Department as well as most police departments, it is against police procedures for police officers to pull cars over when they are off duty and out of uniform. If someone has committed a traffic violation and an officer has his civilian clothes on, you as a police officer would not want to scare the motorist to death. The motorist has no idea who you are. If a police officer is in uniform and off duty, you have a different circumstance. The motorist knows he committed a violation and he can see that you are an officer of the law. Police should avoid getting involved in minor infractions. But at a robbery in progress,

I will be there to make arrests when I am off duty. I will not run away from the protecting the people of this state.

Another new law will help curtail the rash of stolen cars perpetrated by juveniles. Governor Jim Florio signed a curfew law which went into effect Oct. 30. It allowed municipalities to keep those seventeen and under off the streets late at night.

The law, sponsored by state Sen. Ronald Rice (D-Essex), allowed communities to make it unlawful for youths to be in public places between ten P.M. and six A.M., unless accompanied by an adult, or involved in a school, religious or cultural event or a medical emergency.

Sen. Rice did outstanding community work when he was a West District Councilman. He also was a Newark Police Officer for a few years. I worked with Ronald for six months in the West District. We made quite a few good collars together. Ron was always a dedicated cop who was there for the citizens when they needed him.

Police in Essex County Communities began making sure that youngsters under sixteen were not on the streets after ten P.M. during the week and midnight on the weekends, with certain exceptions.

The state's municipal police departments, especially those in urban communities like Newark and Orange, will have to start doing more to help curb the growing acts of crime and violence, many committed by youngsters, that occur during the overnight hours.

Police Director William R. Celester implemented a new unit in Newark. He has eight police officers who ride bicycles. The officers give the people of Newark a new confidence in our Police Department.

Deputy Chief Santiago restructured the entire Patrol Division and the Detective Bureau. He strengthened the Police Department by putting the men where they are needed most.

This chapter was not written with the intent to scare anyone. I wrote it to have people focus in on the reality of what has been occurring in our country.

People have to attain the attitude that "I have to adjust to the society I live in." Read and remember the twenty-seven precautions I have outlined at the end of this chapter.

On November 18, 1992 authorities announced that a

thirty-five-year old Piscataway mother was raped and robbed of $1.90 and a token before she was stabbed and dumped in a drainage ditch. Police said they reached those conclusions on evidence and tests performed on the victim, Gail F. Shollar, whose nude body was pulled from the ditch at Piscataway lumberyard on November 7, 1992.

Police said the testing found evidence of semen, which showed the victim was raped, but they declined to say whether they could link the sample to Scott R. Johnson, twenty-three, of Plainfield, who has been accused of kidnapping and repeatedly stabbing Schollar in the head, neck and chest.

Evidence gathered at the scene of the slaying show Shollar probably was raped in the minivan, and then stabbed outside the van in the lumberyard.

A friend of Johnson's previously claimed the defendant had boasted of stealing $1.90 and a token from the victim.

Johnson was later apprehended at his girlfriend's home, located two doors away from where the van had been discovered, and 100 yards from the lumberyard.

Johnson remains in custody at the Union County Jail in lieu of $1 million.

Carjacking is a violent crime; it's not something to be taken lightly. Please read and memorize the twenty-seven precautions outlined in this chapter. In the wake of the recent rash of carjackings along the entire East Coast, motorists have carried Mace, taken their dogs on trips and purchased cellular phones for their cars, all to prevent from being victimized by the rising tide of carjackings.

People no longer feel invulnerable or independent behind the wheel of their car, especially now that the violence has started a siege in the suburbs and highways.

Since January 1, 1992 there have been 285 car jackings in Essex County.

Purchasing a cellular phone for a loved one at Christmas is a gift of life.

A cellular phone could be your only link between life and death in many situations on the highways. It is a life saving investment.

No one should believe this problem is restricted to Essex County. This way of terror is spreading not only in New Jersey, it's across the nation.

Although President Bush signed a new anti-carjacking law that guaranteed a minimum of fifteen years in jail for offenders, yet stiffer penalties are needed to ensure that crime is curtailed, if not eliminated, altogether.

It might help, of course, if criminals had some sense they might actually get sent away to prison for a long period of time and get refused the right to plea bargain for anything less.

Some criminals used to be satisfied to grab a victim's purse. Now there is a group of assailants that will knock their victims to the ground, kick and viciously punch them and sometimes fatally run them over.

To really counteract violent crimes such as carjackings, we have to administer swift punishment, and get more people to become the eyes and ears of the police by joining neighborhood crime watch groups and tipping off police to any and all suspicious activities.

In closing this chapter I would like to address three departments.

The Piscataway Police Department should have called in detectives from New York and Newark. Obviously they had no relevant ideas on how to handle a heinous crime such as in the Shollar case, when you have a crime scene with possible implementations regarding evidence that will lead to a break in the case.

When Shollars van was found, the detectives should have searched that area with a fine tooth comb. Don't insult my intelligence as a twenty-four year veteran of the police force. Don't tell me an initial search of the area proved negative. Don't tell me a week later that "we searched the area a little better and found the body submerged under the water." That kind of excuse is appalling to have the audacity to make anyone believe that a search party combed a quarter mile area of a crime scene. Piscataway authorities said that they failed to find a body. I find it ludicrous that their can be total incompetence played out by Union County Detectives. They did a terrible job.

I can only hope that Gail Shollar did not lie in that shallow grave severely wounded. Detectives in small towns obviously need better training.

I want to extend my sincere sympathy to the Shollar family. May God rest her soul in peace. I applaud the thousands of people who have extended their hand and contributed donations to the Shollar family. God bless all of you.

In Newark, on November 17, 1992 the body of Miss Simoes was found in a deep ravine off Route 22 East near the entrance to 1 and 9 North.

The Hillside detectives went up and down the road numerous times. They were retracing the routine route she took to work. There was no way possible that they could have possibly spotted her car. It was deeply embedded in the weeds of the swamps. Even if they were at the foot of the railing where she toppled over the rail they would not have seen the car.

The top echelon of the Hillside Police Department and the Union County Detective Bureau should have been held accountable for their poor discretion.

I know if that my wife were lying in a gully for four days, if she were seriously injured from a car accident, I would have nightmares for the rest of my life. Oh sure the Union County Officials got off the hook. The autopsy showed that the victim died instantly. But I don't exactly see it that way. You want to know why? Because the way they conducted the investigation was appalling. I don't want to hear that you could not obtain a helicopter. I don't even want to believe that a Police Chief could be that ignorant. I don't want to hear your excuse that the state police helicopter is in a shop being repaired. Excuses are like assholes—everybody has one.

Four days passed by and the Hillside Police Chief made a brilliant decision. He rented a helicopter from a company in Elizabeth. Well guess what! Forty-five minutes into the search on the same highways the Hillside detectives checked, "Bingo!" They see a car that fit the description deeply entrenched in the weeds. The car was twenty-five feet below in a gully. Newark Detective D'Angelo from the auto task force responded to the scene. He found the body of the missing young lady from Hillside, New Jersey.

Since the rash of carjackings began eleven months ago, you would be led to believe that a police department handling a search for clues would use all the means possible to solve the crime expediently.

Chief D'Esanto and Chief of Detectives, Robert Hack,

Hillside, Police Department: since you don't have the intelligence to use those brilliant police minds that you should have attained over the years, the next time you have a serious homicide that you cannot solve have a talk with our Chief of Detectives. Chief O'Connor will be more than happy to lend you one of our homicide detectives. If I had ever been Chief of Detectives I would have called New's '88 for a chopper. I could have called Donald Trump for a chopper. I could have called the New York Police for a chopper. I will bet you one million dollars to your dollar that they would have gladly assisted you. So while you ponder why you did not use all of those options, think about the mistake you made. You cannot erase your mistakes. But you can get your head and asses wired together. Maybe it's time that you retire. New blood always brings out the best in professionalism. I'm not sorry for being so critical of you. I would love to hear your reasons for waiting four days to obtain a helicopter.

I would also like to know why Governor Florio was not made aware of the situation. I still find it very difficult to believe that all the state police helicopters were out of service. Thank God both victims in Piscataway and Newark were reported killed instantly. I would have been downright nasty.

On November 18, 1992 at approximately eleven ten P.M. Assistant Attorney Mulvihill announced to the press his preliminary findings in regard to the discovery of Miss Simoes. He told the press that the preliminary reports from his prosecutor detectives revealed that the victim possibly was hit by another vehicle. He said that she possibly lost control of the car. He said that he could not rule out a carjacking. He didn't say if she was shot or stabbed.

In light of the wrath of carjackings gripping our communities, it most certainly was out of character for Mulvihill to leave the public hanging on edge. I was at the scene of the accident. The Medical Examiner was at the scene of the accident. The victim died instantly from a broken neck. There was no reason why he could not have released this to the public: The doctor's preliminary report stated she died instantly from a broken neck. He also could have said that there is a strong possibly that she was killed by reason of a side swipe or loss of the control of her car.

Miss Simoes' sister said that she was not a good driver. I know that car had to have been speeding to jump off the highway. She could have lost control or could have been cut off.

You cannot leave the public hanging in fear. There was nothing wrong with telling the press that the victim died of a broken neck.

In the wake of the brutal carjacking murders in Florida on November 29, 1992, we had a rash of carjackings in New York City and in Newark.

On November 25, 1992, a fifty-year old New York woman was thrown out of her car while she still had her seat belt on. The carjackers dragged her eight blocks before she broke loose. Later that night a married couple was forced out of their car. The woman was pregnant and they ran her over.

On December 3, 1992, New York Detectives arrested several gang members who were part of a group carjacking luxurious cars. The cars were shipped to New Mexico.

On the lighter side, a young woman from Piscataway fended off a would be carjacker at the mall site of the Shollar abduction.

In the weekend event, which took place on Sunday November 29, 1992 at five P.M., a female shopper at the Middlesex Mall was approached by a man as she reached her car. He grabbed her shoulder and told her they were going to get into her vehicle. She refused, spun around and grabbed him, then she sprayed him with a pepper like stinging chemical agent similar to mace. The suspect was left standing there. The six percent Pepper Defense gas is the best on the market. It can definitely save your life.

PRECAUTIONS YOU SHOULD TAKE TO PREVENT A CARJACKING

1. Always keep your door locks and windows closed.

2. Park your car in areas that will be well-lighted when you return.

3. Have your keys in your hand minutes before you approach your car.

4. If you are parked in a poorly lighted area, have a pocket

flashlight handy, seconds can be the difference between life and death.

5. Having a can of six percent pepper mace at the ready as a life saving deterrent. Spray the assailant directly in the eyes. He will be out of service for at least a half hour.

6. If you have no one following you within a thousand feet of you, check that your front and rear door locks have not been forced open. Check that all of your windows have not been busted open. If you discover that a door lock has been tampered with or if you find a window busted, go immediately to the store. "Don't panic." Call the police. If you cannot find a phone or the store is closed, go back to your car. Check and make sure no one is hiding in the back seat floor. If you have a minivan make extra sure no one is hiding under the seats. This is another reason why a pocket flashlight can be a lifesaver.

7. When you get into your car, immediately lock the doors. Start the engine and get out of there.

8. A motorist who is being followed should drive to the nearest police or fire station for assistance instead of driving home or attempting to leave the car.

9. Motorists whose vehicles are being bumped from behind should drive to the nearest police station.

10. Lock all the doors and roll up your windows while driving. Be aware of who is in back of you and be aware of where you are.

11. Take well-traveled and well-lit routes, while using facilities for gasolne or telephone stops.

12. Leave space between your car and the one in front while at a traffic light or stopped in traffic. This will give you a quick getaway if necessary.

13. Be cautious of minor rearend accidents in quiet isolated placed. If you do not feel comfortable exiting the vehicle, motion to the driver and proceed to the nearest police station, a twenty-four hour business establishment (Seven Eleven), hospital or fire house.

14. Become familiar with the different routes you can quickly take to your local police stations.

15. Keep your house and driveway well-lit. Be aware of vehicles and pedestrians, and beep your horn to have a family member open doors.

16. Do not keep house keys on the same key chain with your car keys since a carjacker also could gain entry to your home.

17. Always have a small pad and pen handy. You can jot down a description of the assailant. Take the plate number down, even though most cars used are stolen. When you get home, call the police.

18. Make sure you fill your tank with a full tank of gas. Do it during the early morning hours at your local gas station.

19. Make sure you notice any flaws in your car. Maintain your car and change your oil every 5,000 miles and get a tune-up every 20,000 miles. We don't want you breaking down on a unfamiliar street or highway.

20. If you break down on a street or highway, keep your doors locked. Roll your window down one inch. Hang a white cloth or handkerchief on the door.

21. Do not use the same time and pattern when you go to work and when you leave.

22. Do not leave your drivers license, registration and insurance card in the glove compartment. The carjackers will attain your home address. If you have an expensive car, they will visit your house and it won't be for a party.

23. Don't leave any letters or mail with your address on it in the car.

24. When taking a trip to an unfamiliar location looking for a business to shop for a bargain, call the local police of that town or city. Ask for directions. Dial the operator and she will forward the police station you need. We do not want you asking a stranger for directions. If you have no alternative, roll your car to the extreme

shoulder of the road. Keep your four ways on. Roll down your window one inch. Make sure all the windows are up, make sure the doors are locked. Keep the car in drive, keep your left foot on the brakes, and have your right foot ready to zoom out of there if a stranger looks threatening.

25. If an unmarked car pulls you over for speeding, if the officer or state trooper is in plain clothes, use caution. Stay in drive and be ready to leave quickly. If he does not act professional, tell the officer that he can follow you to your police station. Roll your window down one inch when in conversation. Generally most law enforcement officer don't pull motorists over when they are in plain clothes and off duty. If you are violating the law at an excessive speed, a trooper will occasionally pull you over and issue a summons. However, there was a recent rape of a woman by an assailant impersonating a state trooper. You can ask the officer to follow you to a police station. You will not get a summons for fleeing or voice in hand. This does not pertain to uniformed officers in marked or unmarked cars.

26. Motorists returning to their vehicles should walk to a safe place instead, if they spot someone lurking in the shadows near their car.

27. Motorists should carefully and quickly drive away if a suspicious looking person approaches their vehicle.

**MEMORIZE AND REMEMBER
THESE 27 PRECAUTIONS!**

18 How to Prevent Becoming a Victim of Crime

This will deal with the many precautions that people can exercise. Developing good safe habits and awareness will prevent you from becoming a victim of a crime. There are many ways that you can avoid becoming a victim. You will have a better understanding of the realities of life.

We can all learn from other victims' careless mistakes. We can learn from the different patterns of the way criminals think.

I have based my learning on reading about the modus operandi of a criminal, the manner in which a criminal operates and proceeds with his intentions to commit a crime. During the past six years I have assigned and distributed 600,000 police reports to Newark detectives. I read each report and assign the report to the detective division that handles a certain type of crime committed.

It is my responsibility to make sure that the crime committed goes to the Detective that handles that particular crime.

We have ten different detective squads. Our robbery squad handles shootings, robberies, carjackings. Sara squad handles rape, the narcotics squad handle drugs, the youth aid bureau handles all juvenile crimes, the auto squad handles stolen cars, the homicide squad handles all murders and police shootings, internal affairs handles all police complaints, and we also have precinct squad detectives. The west, north, south, and east squads handle several investigations that include domestic violence, aggravated assault, assault, terroristic threats, harassment, forgery, theft by deception, flim flams, found property, lost property, criminal mischief and burglaries. We also have a hit and run detective.

We handle approximately 125,000 reports a year. I have absorbed all of the knowledge involving the techniques that criminals use. We can take advantage of the mistakes made by victims. We can educate ourselves through their actions. Take certain precautions and always remember that everyone is prone to the realization that you can be a victim of a crime. If you have the attitude that it can't happen to you, you are only fooling yourself.

We can survive and make our lives safer. We have to be careful regarding the way we travel on the road. We have to be aware of our everyday habits.

I know that everyone who reads this chapter will diminish the chances of becoming a crime victim. Read the chapter several times and absorb it. You will have a better chance of surviving.

PURSE SNATCHINGS
Purse snatches are generally committed by juvenile offenders. They range in age between the ages of twelve to sixteen years old. Try to avoid carrying a pocketbook. However, if you find it absolutely necessary to use a pocketbook, try to leave the big pocketbooks home. Dump that junk out of your pocketbook. It is recommended that you carry a small pocketbook. Robbers think that a woman with a big pocketbook will be a good score. In their way of thinking, they feel a big pocketbook contains jewelry and money.

Thugs like to focus in on women that walk alone. Criminal thieves will prey particularly on elderly women. They do most of their purse snatches in the first week of each month.

Criminal thieves do most of their purse snatches at check cashing stores, malls, food shopping centers and banks.

If you have a toddler in your arms and are alone, you will make a good victim for him. Assailants always prey on people who are vulnerable.

Be alert, be aware, and always observe a stranger that follows you into a check cashing establishment or a bank. The actor (robbery suspect) will start a friendly conversation with you. He will observe how much money the cashier gives you. If you are receiving a substantial amount of money, chances are very strong that you will become a purse snatch victim.

Robbers are not looking for 100 dollars. They want to feast on the recipient that is going to net them a few hundred dollars.

If you have a strap attached to your pocketbook, make sure you have the strap huddled over your shoulder. Wrap the strap once around your wrist.

Avoid keeping expensive jewelry in your pocketbook. Do not keep identification papers in your pocketbook. When a robber snatches your pocketbook and he scores with $500 in your wallet, the robber envisions a profitable hit at your house. He will be at your house shortly to rob it.

Keep your wallet in your coat pocket. All ID cards and credit cards should be kept in your wallet.

If you have to carry a substantial amount of money to pay a bill, keep the money in your brassiere or your pantyhose. If you have a lot of credit cards, take with you only one credit card that you can use for the day.

A robber can struggle with you when he is trying to take your pocketbook. Learn how to break your fall before you hit the ground. You will avoid a broken wrist or hand. This especially applies to elderly men and women.

I have seen a lot of elderly victims of crime taken to the hospital. They have suffered broken arms, wrists, hands, ankles, legs, collarbones and fractured skulls. Elderly people who frequently shop in stores, try to avoid taking a pocketbook with you. Robbers have no respect for your safety.

These assailants are the lowest scum of the earth. They will take full advantage of your age and they will prey on you.

Robbers generally choose to prey on single individuals. If you are with a group or a friend most of the time they avoid confrontations.

Do not get into conversations with strangers. They will set you up for a purse snatch.

ARMED ROBBERY

A robbery occurs somewhere in the United States every two minutes. Most robberies of a victim are not done randomly in occurrence or frequency. Robbers will generally pick on a victim that is vulnerable.

Robbers will follow a person into a bank or check cashing store. They generally focus in on middle-aged women and men. They will watch how much money you receive from the bank teller. Women who freely showcase their expensive gold necklaces and watches are excellent prey for a robber.

During the first three years of the nineties, robbers were committing robberies in the check cashing industry. The actors (robbery assailants) loiter near these locations. They patiently wait for the right opportunity to prey on their victims (usually elderly females) who cash large checks.

The victims are followed a short distance from the location of the check-cashing establishment or bank. The actor will use a gun or knife to rob the victim. A large percentage of these robberies occur in the metropolitan area.

Eighty percent of the robberies occurring in the cities take place during the first week of each month. The highest rate of robberies occur during the first three weeks of December.

In the early spring and summer months, people have a tendency to leave their windows wide open.

When a motorist is stopped at a traffic light, a robbery suspect will approach your vehicle. He will ask you what time it is. If you are wearing gold jewelry (Watch, necklaces, bracelets), he will snatch it off your neck or wrist faster than you can blink an eye. If you have your passenger side window open and you are waiting for a red light to turn green, if your pocketbook is lying on the passenger side front seat, a thief will snatch it right through your window.

If you have an air-conditioned car, keep the windows and doors closed. If you don't have one, roll down your window two inches for ventilation. Double check that your doors are locked at all times.

In 1992, Essex County had reports of well over 300 carjackings. Assailants were taking motorists cars at gunpoint. Carjacking is nothing more than a slang word for a robbery at gunpoint involving the taking of a car. The past five years we had investigations involving hundreds of robberies at gunpoint that involved the car taken by the robber.

The carjacker will put a gun or knife to your head or throat. He will take your wallet and throw you out of the car. He will use your car for additional robberies. A robber will not hesitate to blow your head off if you try to resist their demands.

You can always recover lost money and material things, but a bullet hitting one of your vital organs can be fatal. Most of your organs cannot be replaced.

RED PEPPER DEFENSE

I have added this effective chemical element to this chapter. Chapter seventeen deals directly with carjackings. However millions of people are purchasing different types of mace. Store owners don't advise people on the procedures that you have to undertake. The Newark Police Department uses a pepper chemical mace with five percent pepper. I have tried the product pepper defense that has six percent pepper. It is extremely effective. It will deter an assailant for forty minutes. This mace will save your life. Keep the mace in your strong hand coat pocket. When you are with 100 feet of your car, take the car keys out of your weak hand coat pocket. The key that opens your door should be in your weak hand (left hand). The mace should be in your strong hand (right hand). Open your door with the mace at the ready. Make sure the mace is pointed in the direction of the assailant. To depress the mace push the button strongly with your index finger. Remember that there is five pounds of pressure in the bottle. It takes a bit of pressure from your finger to release the spray. Take a piece of paper and a thumb tack and nail the paper to a tree. Step back ten feet and spray the paper. The reason for doing this is to become familiar with the amount of pressure it takes for you to release the mace. You will also have confidence on how well it effectively covers the paper. Remember that this spray was strictly made to save your life. Don't use this on a person when you are involved in an ordinary dispute. This product was made strictly for a person who is being carjacked, raped, or murdered.

When an assailant is sprayed, he is blinded for forty minutes.

People coming into Newark on business should not be asking strangers for help regarding directions. You are prone to a robbery at gunpoint. Before entering a city that you are not familiar with, call your local police department for directions. In Newark you can call (203) 733-6018, 733-6245 or 733-6000. When you have the unfortunate experience of being lost in Newark and other cities, robbers will take advantage of the situation.

Do not panic when you are lost. Drive to an open gas station. Dial an operator and ask her to connect you with the local police department.

There is just one of the tricks that an actor will try on you when you ask him for direction: You, the driver, will stop a person and say, "Sir, I am lost could you please give me directions to Broad Street near City Hall in Newark?"

The actor (robber) will say to you. "Yea man, you drive east on Clinton Avenue, than you make a left turn and drive north on Broad Street. Mister, could you do me a favor? I work a couple of blocks from City Hall. Would you give me a lift to Broad Street and Lafayette Street? I can show you how to reach City Hall and you won't get lost in the city." Being a nice guy, you make the fatal mistake of letting the guy get in.

Suddenly, the actor is brandishing a gun or knife. The actor demands that you give up your wallet, jewelry, and car.

For the skeptics that think it can't happen to you, I'm sorry that you have that attitude because it can, and it will, happen to you. Follow the precautions that are stressed in this chapter. Understand the reasoning and remember them.

This chapter too was not written to scare anyone. People have to face up to the reality of the society we live in and adjust to the changing times.

Robberies involving prostitutes and men looking for illicit sex is a dangerous mix. Today it is not only unhealthy it's just a bad habit to engage in.

Prostitutes who are males in female drag and females will rob you for every penny on you. A male victim can lose on both ends of the stick. Males come from outside of the City of Newark. They are looking for a little action.

Victims of robberies who are engaging in sex with a prostitute will get robbed. The actor (prostitute) wants the john (victim) to pay the money up front before they render their services. When the victim is paying the actor, he or she will observe how much money you have in your wallet. If you have a fat wallet, a pimp will be signaled. Now you are prone to lose your money, your jewelry and on many occasions, your car.

The other end of the stick is that Newark has seven female police officers who pose as decoy prostitutes. You will be arrested as a john for soliciting a decoy officers. It is embarrassing to a businessman who is married.

You can lose a third way because most of these prostitutes are infected with the AIDS virus. Most of the prostitutes are drug addicts. If you choose to play Russian roulette with your life, engage in sexual activities with these prostitutes. You will be injecting yourself with the AIDS virus.

You better think twice before deciding to pay $20 for five minutes of satisfaction. Keep in mind that you could be tested positive with the HIV virus. Ask yourself it is worth $20 to die from AIDS. Is it worth getting robbed and possibly shot and killed for a five minute sex act? Life is too precious; be careful and use good common sense.

BURGLARIES

A house or business burglary occurs in the Unites States at a rate of eight per minute. Unfortunately we can't all afford to have an alarm system installed in our house. However, there are other habits that we can adapt to. It will make our homes less vulnerable to a break in.

Hundreds of burglaries are reported in cities and towns.

However, just because you live in the suburbs. You are not eliminated from the potential of your house being burglarized.

The actor (burglar) relies on his instincts to survive in the big cities. When a burglar attempts to break into a house in a rural or suburban area, he is placing himself at a high risk of being caught by the police. A burglar is out of place in the suburbs. He sticks out like jailbird in a jail uniform.

If you observe a pickup truck or a van in your neighbor's driveway, write the plate number on a pad. Call the police and advise the authorites that there is a suspicious auto in your neighbor's driveway. If the same vehicle appears the next day and it has no company logo on the side panel, call the police. They more then likely are breaking into your neighbor's house.

Neighbors should have a good communication with each other. Let your neighbor know if you are expecting a plumber, painter, or electrician.

Tell your neighbor that you are going to be on vacation for two weeks. If you observe a suspicious vehicle in their driveway, take the plate number down and call your local police immediately. It is recommended that you have all emergency telephone numbers above your wall phone. In extreme emergency situations dial "O" for operator. They will connect you directly to the police.

If you have never seen a particular car, van or pick-up truck in your neighbor's driveway, it is likely that these actors are casing the area for a burglary. Band together and develop into a cohesive neighborhood. Work and cooperate with with each other and you will have a safer neighborhood.

Installing flood lights to brighten the front of your house is an excellent investment. Installing double locks on all your outside doors is another good investment. Unfortunately too many homeowners have cheap locks on their doors. A plastic credit card can actually open your door.

When no one is home at your house or apartment, leave a radio and light on.

When you plan a one or two week vacation, develop some good habits that will lessen the chance of your house being burglarized. Notify your local police department that you will be on vacation from June 10–June 24 1995. Notify the post office to hold your mail for two weeks. Cancel your newspaper delivery for two weeks. If you have a neighbor that is trustworthy, ask your neighbor to keep a close watch on your house. You can return the favor when they go on vacation. If you have a second car, leave it in the garage. If you do not have a driveway, leave your car at a relative's house.

Leave a set of house keys for your closest relative to use. They can periodically check your house. Invest $20 and buy an electric timer to flick your radio and night lamp on at sunset and off at eleven P.M.

Make sure all your windows are closed tight on the first floor. On the second floor leave the window open about two inches for ventilation. If you have any twenty foot ladders in the backyard, secure it in your garage.

Before leaving your house, make sure you have unplugged all your electrical appliances. If you own a gun, the gun should be registered. Don't leave it in the house. Take the gun to a bank. Empty the bullets in an envelope and put the gun in a safe deposit box.

As a homeowner or an occupant of an apartment, it is important to have knowledge regarding the use of deadly force. There are intangible elements to remember when you are protecting your home, your family and yourself. If a burglar enters your dwelling and you have a weapon (gun) pointed at the suspect, if he is not armed with a knife or gun, order the burglar to lie down. Make sure you can see him and order the burglar to keep his hands in back of his head. If the suspect should make a sudden move, if he reaches into his pocket or inside his waist, be ready to defend yourself. If the burglar draws a gun you have the right to defend yourself. If he attacks you with a knife and is threatening to kill you, defend yourself if your life is in danger.

If your wife and children are with you, your wife should call the police immediately. Don't lose sight of the burglar and watch his hands. If he is armed he will produce a weapon.

If no one is in the house with you, order the burglar to stand up. Keep his hands constantly in back of his head. Order the suspect to walk into the room where the phone is. Call the Operator and request that a police car respond immediately.

If you don't have a phone and no one is home with you, order the burglar out of the house and take him to your closest neighbor's house. Have your neighbor call the police. Stay a safe distance of at least ten feet in back of the burglar.

The most important thing for you to remember is that you have captured a burglary suspect. However it is essential that you remember when you can use deadly force. If a burglar is not a threat to your life you cannot use deadly force. Do not shoot the burglar if he is not a threat to your family. If the actor does not try to take the gun away from you, don't shoot him.

If the actor (burglar) has a knife in his hand and he makes an aggressive move to stab you, the actor is a threat to your life. If all else fails, shoot him. If the actor has a gun in his hand and it is pointed at you try your best to take cover. Exchanging gunfire could cost you your life. If you have no means of taking cover, a shootout may be your only alternative. Order the suspect to drop the gun. If he has the gun pointed at you and he fails to drop the weapon, you have exhausted all means to have him drop the gun. If you shoot and kill him you are justified to protect yourself.

If a burglar is in your house and he tries to escape when he sees you, let the burglary suspect go. Don't even attempt to catch him. You cannot shoot at a burglar when he is fleeing from your home. The burglar is no longer a threat to you or your family, so let him go.

Call the police and have a burglary report executed. The detectives will eventually arrest him.

Unfortunately apartment burglaries are not as easy to prevent as home burglaries. Burglars have easy access to apartments. They enter from rear fire escapes.

One of the best ways to prevent your apartment from a break in is to install steel bars in the windows. Make sure you purchase the bars that can be unlocked from the inside in case of a fire. Install double locks on your door. You will diminish your chances of a burglary occurring.

Apartment burglaries usually occur during the day when people are at work. If you have a close friend who is your next door neighbor or who resides across the hallway from you and if he or she is at home during the day, ask if they could keep an eye and ear open for a possible burglary.

Be very cautious of who your friends are. Numerous apartment burglaries are committed by tenants that live in the same building you live in. Do not get too friendly with all your tenants. Screen out your friends from your enemies. If a tenant knows that you have a good job, if they observe that you wear expensive clothes and jewelry, her boyfriend may break into your apartment shortly. Don't invite your tenants into your apartment, especially during the first two years. Get to know your neighbors and you will judge whom you can trust.

If you have purchased expensive furniture such as a new color TV, a new bedroom set, a stereo component, and a new kitchen set, you will not have this furniture very long if your neighbors know that you have it. The less people who know about your wealth, the better off you will be. Use good judgment and discretion with the friends you choose. You will diminish the odds of becoming a victim.

HOMICIDE

In 1991 there were 47,354 homicides committed in the United States. Statistics show that many of the big cities showed a drop in homicides. New York City 1990 2,006 homicides, 1991 1,966 homicides, Newark 1990 125 homicides, 1991 94 homicides.

The top three cities with the highest homicide per capital are San Diego, California; Dallas, Texas; and Phoenix, Arizona. In 1990 there were 150 police officers killed in the line of duty. In 1991 there were 131 police officers killed.

Some of the other cities that have a very high homicide rate are Washington, D.C.; Detroit, Michigan; Miami, Florida; and Los Angeles, California.

A great majority of the homicides that are committed today are drug related. They consist in a drug war dispute between rival street gangs who own the turf. Most of the homicides related to narcotics stem from drug overdoses.

The tragic aftermath of the drug epidemic is that innocent people from children to adults are becoming victims of gunfire related to drug fights.

Drug dealers get involved in gun fights with rival gangs. They have deadly confrontations over who owns the turf (an area or location in the city where drug kingpins deal their drugs).

We are faced with a serious epidemic in this country. Drugs have swarmed over our society and have taken control of our cities. Drug dealers are making millions of dollars. They supply the sellers who are pocketing huge profits by becoming the drug dealers' pawns.

A drug dealer's pawn has a three-way ticket to death hanging on his shoulders every night. He risks death in exchange for the untaxed money he reaps.

The drug seller risks three ways of being killed. 1. When a drug seller approaches a buyer. Sooner or later he is going to be set up by the drug buyer. He will be executed by the buyer. 2. The drug seller soon or later is going to be selling his drugs to undercover narcotic officers. Eventually he will be killed without a chance of growing up. He will be involved in a shootout with narcotics detectives. The average age of a drug seller is under twenty-five years old. 3. When a drug seller is caught by a narcotics detective. He will make a deal with the prosecutor's office. He will turn state evidence and will have his drug supplier set up for an arrest. When the drug seller is released and out on the streets, the drug dealer (his supplier) will have the drug seller killed by a hit man. He will be well paid and hired by the drug kingpin. The young drug sellers never get a chance to reap the money they take in from selling drugs.

Three ways to lose your life is not a good percentage. They better think and consider a better way of life.

If you have a serious drug problem in your community, if your apartment building has an influx of drug traffic, the police will combat the situation.

If you live in Newark, contact Lieutenant Esposito or Detective Mario Genzone. Call the narcotics division at (201) 733-6115 nine A.M.–five P.M. At night you can call Lieutenant Gagliano or Sergeant Demaio from seven P.M.to one A.M. Residents outside of Newark should call their local police department. Ask to speak to the lieutenant in charge of Narcotics.

In Newark we have an extremely dangerous drug problem. We have a Narcotics Detective Division that is rated as one of the top ten in the United States. They average seven arrests a night. Occasionally they execute narcotic raids that net twenty-five arrests in a night. Unfortunately in spite of narcotic detectives collaring thousands of arrests a year, we still haven't even touched the surface. Eventually we will defeat this terrible epidemic. We have a county task force that is eliminating the drug traffic.

A citizen has the right to know where the most dangerous drug areas are. Call the desk lieutenant in the precinct that you reside in. The lieutenant will tell you the areas that are under surveillance. Obviously we cannot reveal to the general public when a raid is being conducted. Areas in the city that have produced hundreds of narcotic arrests can't be revealed to a concerned resident. The lieutenant will advise you accordingly that a certain area is dangerous. Although our narcotic detectives collar hundreds of arrest in drug infested areas, the narcotic dealer will consistently return. Get involved with your community leaders and church minister. They are informed of the areas that are look-outs for drug activities and robberies. Use extreme caution and make every effort to avoid these areas in your community.

Tell your children to avoid walking in areas where drug activities are prevalent. We want to avoid a tragedy before it occurs. Your child could be killed in a cross fire incident involving a shootout between drug dealers. Hundreds of children and adults are killed each year by stray bullets that are meant for someone else.

In the summer of 1991 thirty-three children and adults were killed by stray bullets in the boroughs of New York City.

At the time of this writing, Newark Police director Celester with the backing of Mayor James is making every effort possible to take back the streets.

In June 1991 William R. Celester took over the reigns as Police Director. With the combined efforts of Deputy Chief Joe Santiago the entire police department has been restructured. Within the next two years Newark will overcome its shortfalls. We will bring back the days long overdue for safer streets.

When the city of Newark can get back on its feet, the Police Director will have the funds available for additional police officers and street sergeants. They are the backbone that will bring back and strengthen the police force where our capability will flourish.

In 1974 we had 1,353 police officers, we also had 234 superior officers. Attrition has seriously cut the strength of the Newark Police Department.

We are not alone. Mayors and the town and cities they govern are facing familiar shortfalls caused by the recession.

When you are a victim of a crime, especially when an actor has a gun or knife, avoid getting into a struggle with him. A robber will shoot a victim if they do not listen to their commands.

If you are a stranger to the city or town you are in, this applies especially at night. Avoid parking your car at a phone booth on a dark corner. We have quite a few victims of robberies who are shot and killed by assailants.

Ninety percent of the time a victim is robbed like this. The person enters the city or town, They are lost so they subsequently look for a phone booth to call the police for directions. Suddenly a robber points a gun at the victim's head. The victim will be robbed of his money. The robber will take his car and occasionally they do shoot and kill the victim.

You can avoid this confrontation by driving to a gas station that is open. Your other options are a fire station, hospital, food market. If you are running out of gas, go directly to a well-lighted street that has a phone booth.

Avoid going on a trip on half a tank of gas. Keep a county and state map handy in your glove compartment.

Most of the homicides that occur in the city are drug related. Some occur involving a robbery or theft.

Sixty percent of the homicides that occur involve family members. Violent confrontations between girlfriend-boyfriend, husband-wife. Jealousy attributes greatly to the thousands of reports of domestic violence homicides in the U.S.

Women have to use caution and good discretion when they have an estranged husband who continuously threatens to kill them.

It is strongly recommended that women do not take their estranged husbands' threats lightly. Thousands of women are injured and killed by estranged husbands who cannot accept their divorce papers.

When your husband is threatening your life execute a police report. The detective assigned to the investigation will arrest him for terroristic threats.

In Essex County you can have a restraining order executed at the County Court House located at 470 Martin Luther King Boulevard, Room B-10. Keep the restraining order with you at all times. If your estranged husband is caught within a block of your presence, call the police and he will be arrested by police officers for violating the restraining order. Every county has an office.

If you are having a serious problem with your estranged husband, if your life is endangered by his threats, it is strongly recommended that you take your children out of the house. If you need temporary shelter call a state safe house. Please listen to what I'm telling you. Don't wait until it is too late.

I have seen in twenty-three years, hundreds of women brutally slain by their estranged husbands. In September 1992, 250 women were killed by their estranged husbands in the U.S. Last year over one million women were brutally assaulted by their spouses. What we found even more alarming is that 1.3 million brutal assaults on women went unreported.

If you fear for your life and children, move to an address as far away as is possible. Don't leave a forwarding address that he can obtain from the post office. Avoid having any contact with him.

It is very important to realize the reality of life. Every case and every situation is different. Only you know how capable of violence your husband is. However, if he has abused you violently, if he has threatened to kill you if you divorce him, do not take his threats lightly. The possibility of a tragedy is imminent.

If your husband has been arrested for aggravated assault and terroristic threats, take the opportunity to move out of town. It is recommended that you move to the state where your family lives. Move a safe distance from their residence.

When your husband is freed on bail, there is a good

chance that he will stalk you. Don't give him the opportunity to find out where you live. I have seen too many tragedies involving domestic violence. Women make the fatal mistake of taking their estranged husbands' threats lightly. They assume that the restraining order is a safety net. Although it is an effective document to have, it will not prevent your husband from killing you and the children.

There are hundreds of homicides each year that occur after a husband receives his divorce papers. Men have this mental block with reality. They keep a glimmer of hope that their wife will eventually take them back. They feel that as long as their wife has not filed for a divorce, a chance for reconciliation is possible.

There are thousands of unstable men who cannot accept life when they receive their divorce papers. Their minds are weak and they snap. They will stalk you and will kill you and the children, then kill themselves. This is a tragic loss that has to be avoided. You prevent this tragedy by realizing that your husband is a threat to your family's life. The police cannot prevent it from happening. The court system cannot throw the keys away. Your estranged husband cannot be sentenced to life imprisonment when he threatens to kill you.

Women often live close to their family's house. They don't want to move away from them. Women often have excellent jobs that pay good salaries. They don't want to leave their job because of domestic trouble.

The tragedy of life is the reality that your husband will stalk you. If he is a basket case, use extreme caution. Eighty percent of the time, the location where you will be killed is at work. Ninety percent of the time he will kill you after he receives the divorce papers. That good job you have is not going to do you or your children any good. Your estranged husband will kill you in the parking lot where you work.

When you have filed divorce papers with your lawyer, if your husband fits the personality of an estranged husband who has abused you, if your husband has threatened to kill you if you divorce him, make arrangements well in advance of the final divorce papers. Move to an area miles away from where he can find you.

Take this advice seriously, it will save your life. I wrote

the chapter on domestic violence with the hope that it will save thousands of lives.

Another death that is a terrible tragedy for police officers to handle is the tragic death of a toddler who falls out the window of a high rise apartment building. Toddlers fall out of high rise buildings in Newark several times a year. Hundreds of toddlers are killed accidentally each year in the U.S. The tragic fact is that these tragedies could be prevented.

Residents who have little toddlers should make sure they have steel wired safety basket nets installed in their windows. If your landlord refuses to install the safety nets in your windows, go to the city hall annex in the town you live in. Notify the Housing Authority Clerk and file a complaint. The Housing Authority officials will enforce the law. The landlord will be summoned to appear before a Municipal Judge. The landlord will be ordered to install safety nets immediately. City ordinances require that all high rise buildings must have safety nets below the window. If he fails to install the window safety nets, the landlord will be arrested for negligence and contempt of court.

Court procedures in these cases take months to adhere to. You can take upon yourself to hire a carpenter to install the safety nets. Deduct the money spent from your rent check. Don't wait until it is too late. Avoid the horrible tragedy of watching your toddlers fall helplessly to their death.

Another terrible tragedy that police officers witness occurs at the scene of an accident involving cars—the death of a little toddler killed in a traffic fatality. As responsible parents you can prevent these tragedies from occurring by obeying state traffic regulations.

Make sure you double check that your children are properly fastened to their seat belts before starting your car. If you have toddlers, double check that their car seats are fastened securely. It is important to realize the inevitable aftermath if your children do not have seat belts fastened securely. If you are in a serious car accident your child may be ejected out of the vehicle. Unfortunately hundreds of traffic fatalities occur in the United States.

Children and toddlers are needlessly killed because parents negligently fail to make sure their children are securely fastened in their car seats. I have seen several toddlers killed in traffic accidents. It is an extremely traumatic tragedy for the parents to live with. No parent wants to experience the tragedy of their child killed because they failed to execute a simple safety measure. You should also be well aware that it is a state law to fasten your seat belts, for your benefit and your children's safety. Motorists will be fined and charged with negligent homicide if their child is killed due to their failure to fasten their seat belts.

A parent's ordeal from a car accident that causes the death of their child is a tragic burden to bear and live with. Please don't add to the nightmare of the knowing that you could have prevented your child's death.

KIDNAPPING

One of the worst nightmares a parent can face is the kidnapping of their child. How does it happen? Why does it happen? How can it be prevented?

I will cover all the intangibles that are involved in a kidnapping. There are safety habits that you should learn to execute.

Most kidnappings are committed by sick demented people. Serial killers kidnap more children than any other suspect arrested by the police.

There are hundreds of children kidnapped each year in the United States. New York and California lead the nation in children that are reported missing.

Divorced parents often kidnap their children after a bitter custody battle ensues regarding who will have permanent custody of their child.

Most of the cases involved between divorced parents are focused on the father of the child. He will have a one-day visitation right to take the child with him. The father will plan in advance to take the child to another state. The mother of the child is left heartbroken. Her estranged husband used spite and vengeance to hurt her. She is left in a state of shock. It will take years before the police will find out where her estranged husband has moved to.

Only you know the personality of your husband. You have to know your husband's inclinations. Make sure you inform your lawyer accordingly.

If you feel that your estranged husband is a threat to

your child's welfare, if you have concrete evidence that your estranged husband will move your child to another state, when your lawyer arranges court proceedings, request your lawyer to ask the judge to execute an order that will prohibit your husband from taking the child out of your home.

You as a responsible parent can prevent your child from becoming a kidnap victim. You cannot prevent it all the time. However, ninety-five percent of the time a parent who stays alert will prevent the tragedy from occurring.

Unfortunately there are parents who are nonchalant. They develop an attitude that it will not ever happen to them. That kind of frame of mind could someday turn into a nightmare. Anyone can have their child kidnapped if they do not listen to the steps it takes to avoid the mistakes parents make.

It only takes a couple of minutes' carelessness. Kidnappings have no set patterns like a homicide, robbery or a burglary. Kidnappings take place in every city and towns, suburban and rural areas.

The possibility of a kidnapping is more likely in a small community than anywhere else in the state. The reason for a small community to fall victim to a kidnapping is that parents develop a safety blanket attitude. They feel that their children could never be kidnapped in a beautiful quiet community.

Parents become lax and they let their guard down. They are not worried about their child ever becoming a kidnap victim.

The bottom line is that you cannot assume anything. There are no guaranteed safety nets. No town or city is immune to a kidnapping. It can happen anywhere. If you don't want your child to fall prey to a kidnapping, you have to watch your child twenty-four hours a day 365 days a year. If you fail to pay attention to your children's whereabouts, this negligence may bring you the worst nightmare of your life. You may be confronted with the acknowledgment by police officials that your child was kidnapped.

When you have realized that your child is lost or missing, report the incident to the police immediately. The sooner we have a description of your child, the better the chance of finding your child.

In some cases but rarely, kidnapping reports sometimes turn out to be missing person reports. If your child was with you and he suddenly disappears from your sight, he could be missing or lost. The detectives and police officers will consider and determine if your child was abducted, kidnapped, lost or missing. The intangible sequence of events will give the detectives a clue to reach a decision. The location and time element will also come into focus.

If your child is missing in Newark, call 733-6000. If you cannot reach an operator call our emergency line at Police Headquarters (main desk). The phone numbers are 733-6018 and 733-6245. Advise the officer that your child is missing.

Every minute is valuable time wasted. The officer at the desk will assist you. If your son or daughter is under the age of ten, a police sergeant will have two police cars search a one mile radius for two hours. If your child is six years old and under, the search will be extensive with a police Captain and at least twenty officers searching the area extensively.

It is extremely important for you to realize that every minutes lost will lessen the chances of the police finding your child.

Do not panic and foolishly waste hours searching for your child. If you fail to find your child after a five minute search. Don't waste time calling your relatives, call the police.

It is important to remember to report your child missing in the town or city you are in. If you are at a park or a carnival in Kenilworth and you reside in Newark or another town or city, don't drive home to where you live to report your child missing. People assume that you report the crime to the local police department where you reside. You report the crime in the town or city that you are in.

Unfortunately when parents lose their child they panic. You have to try your best to keep your head on straight. You cannot afford to make the mistake of letting an hour dwindle away. Your child is missing and it has to be reported as soon as possible.

The mother who lost her child in Kenilworth made the fatal mistake of driving her car to her residence in Newark. She called the Newark Police Department and reported her child missing. I advised the distraught mother that she would have to go to the Kenilworth Police Department. She has to file a police report with their detectives. I advised her to bring a recent picture of her child.

I called the Kenilworth Police Department and gave their detectives a complete description of the missing eight-year-old boy. This incident occurred in May 1988. Unfortunately five years have passed. They have not found the missing boy.

We will never know if the little boy would have been found in time if the Kenilworth Police had been notified sooner. What we do know is that two hours and twenty minutes of precious time was tragically wasted because the mother did not know that she should have reported her child missing in Kenilworth. The chance of finding her child was greatly diminished.

Victims who have lost their children often ask us, Where is my child? In the past ten years thousands of children have vanished without being found. Children that are kidnapped are sold on the black market. They are filtered into prostitution rings. They are killed by serial killers and deranged sadists.

The mother who lived in Newark and lost her child in Kenilworth: her initial reaction should have been to call the operator and ask her to connect her with the Kenilworth police.

It is always a good policy to keep your local police phone number in your wallet. Most parents both have to work to maintain their home bills. The mother usually takes her child to school. Unfortunately parents do not get out of work at three P.M. so they can't pick up their children. A child who walks alone is more at risk to be kidnapped than children who walk home in a group.

Even though we all teach our children not to talk to strangers, it is frightening and alarming to report to all parents that it continuously occurs. When a child is walking home alone an actor (kidnapper) will pull his car over to the side of the road. He will try to have a friendly conversation with your child. If the actor cannot convince your child to take a ride with him, he will use a knife or gun and will force the child into his car.

The best way for your children to avoid this confrontation is to stay away from strangers. Avoid approaching their cars and walk home with a group.

A better safeguard is to make arrangements with your child's school class mother. She can have a classmate's mother drive your children home.

In New Jersey in 1991–1992 we have been very fortunate. There were very few kidnappings reported. However, we had quite a few missing person reports taken. Hundreds of children are reported missing each year.

The most recent kidnapping occurred in Sayreville, New Jersey in the summer of 1991. Timothy Wilsey a five-year-old boy was reported missing. The mother told police officials that she was at a carnival in Sayreville, New Jersey. She told the police that she went to a stand to get her son a sandwich and soda. When she returned a few minutes later her son was whisked away. The mother said that she was no more than 1,000 feet from her son who was left sitting on a bench.

The Sayreville Police Department conducted a massive search for the little boy. Search parties were organized but mysteriously they never found Timothy Wilsey. The mother changed her story months later. She told the police a woman kidnapped her son. She fabricated her story and in early 1994 detectives still have not solved the mystery.

In May 1992, the body of Timonthy Wikey was found in a shallow pond. It was located in an industrial area near Perth Amboy, New Jersey. No arrests have been made.

Kidnappings at carnivals and amusement parks are rare. There are thousands of people at theme parks. A child struggling with a stranger attempting to kidnap and take him away would be obvious. Another concerned parent would abort the kidnapping. It is very difficult to kidnap a child where hundreds of people would witness the attempt. Someone in the crowd we would hope would aid the child.

We as parents have the responsibility of safeguarding our children. Supervise and always hold the hand of children seven years old and under. As a parent you have to pay close attention to your children at amusement parks.

How many times in a day do you hear on the public address system. "Mrs. Doe please come to the courtesy desk. We have your child Robert here." You hear this all the time at amusement parks.

Fortunately some parents get a second chance to pick up their lost child. They learn a valuable lesson in life that could have turned into a nightmare and a terrible tragedy.

As I mentioned before, it is not a set pattern for a kidnapper to abduct a child from a carnival or amusement park. Lost children are constantly found by other parents who take them to the courtesy desk. But don't assume that your child will be found if he is lost at a theme park. The odds are against you—hold on to your child.

New York City and the surrounding boroughs have recently had a lot of tragedies occurring to young female teenagers who were abducted. Their bodies have been discovered in shallow graves in wooded areas. They were raped and murdered.

Children walking home from school should be in groups or at least pairs. The biggest mistake that parents make regarding their children, is they take it for granted that they live in a safe neighborhood. They feel that this can never happen to their children. That kind of attitude may someday haunt them. Parents have to wake up and realize that we live in a society that we have to adjust to. Take the necessary precautions.

Missing Children

In the United States we have thousands of unsolved mysteries involving missing children. In Newark we have hundreds of investigations involving reports of missing teenagers. Fortunately eighty percent of the children reported missing are found within a week.

The tragic fact remain that in the United States thousands of children have been reported missing for years. Unfortunately there are very few methods that a parent can do to prevent their children from becoming a missing person.

Most children that are reported missing are incorrigible teenagers. Children ten years of age and under are usually found the same day. Although the child is reported missing, when the mothers cancels the teletype it is closed out as a lost child.

In Newark, we have a Youth Aid Detective Bureau that investigates missing children and adults. Our procedure in

Newark requires a report be taken immediately if your child is ten years old or younger. A police car will respond and execute a missing person report.

Give the police officers a good description of your child. Try to remember the color of clothing and give the officers a recent photo of your child.

If your child is eleven years old you are required to wait twenty-four hours before a missing person report can be executed. The procedure of a twenty-four hour waiting period does have its loopholes. Missing person reports are taken sooner when a child is at school and three hours later he is not home from school.

If your child is eleven years old and especially if he or she is a teenager between the age of fourteen and nineteen years of age and if they have been reported missing in the past, you are required to wait twenty-four hours before reporting your teenage child missing.

However, if your child has never been missing and he or she is not an incorrigible youth, if your child is always home at a certain time, a missing person report will be executed immediately. For example, say your child comes home between five P.M. and seven P.M. Five hours later your child has not returned. It is now one A.M. and you are very concerned. Call the police. A missing person report will be executed.

The only difference involving a missing person report is that if it's a teenager the Youth Bureau will do an investigation the following day.

When a child ten years of age and under is missing, a police car accompanied by a sergeant will search a mile radius within the residency for two hours.

If the missing person is a toddler six years old and younger, the sergeant will conduct a search with two police units. They will search the area block by block, house to house. Every effort is made to find the toddler. A thirteen state alarm is also issued to all counties.

The big question is how do we as parents prevent our children from becoming statistics? We raise our children and try our best to teach them the proper way to grow up and to do well in school. What happens is that unfortunately when our children are teenagers between the ages of thirteen and sixteen, they go through sudden changes along with their peers. They have a change of personality that clashes with the way we want them to grow up. They become defiant to the way we want to have them grow up. They dislike our ground rules. Fortunately this does not happen to everyone. However, this is the reason why eventually we have a teenager reported missing.

It is essential and very important to remember that as a parent, you are responsible for your child's welfare and well-being. When he reaches the age of eighteen he is considered under the state law to be an adult. As an adult your child is responsible for his own well-being and his actions. Whether they are bad or good, he is on his own.

A great number of missing children of our society are victims of broken homes. Divorced parents place a heavy burden on a teenager. Single parents have the most difficulty handling their children when they become teenagers.

If you cannot handle your child or children, every state has a family services and counseling department. They can assist and advise you with your crisis.

The unfortunate problem is that most parents try to handle their problem child on their own. It cannot be done and it is almost impossible to accomplish.

You as a parent who has raised good children and do not have problems—you read in the newspaper every day about missing children. You raise the question why does it happen? You want to know what a parent can do to prevent this terrible tragedy of life.

A single parent without a father to discipline the children has a problem. The weight becomes a heavier burden when she has to work every day. The burden gets worse when the child is incorrigible and defiant of the rules of the house. This is a very serious problem that has to be addressed.

What is an incorrigible child? An incorrigible child is a teenager who cannot be controlled by the mother. He or she is defiant to the manner in which you set the house rules. They will do as they please, when they please. They will become defiant, they will taunt you and will disobey what you tell them to do. They will even go as far as assaulting you and stealing from you. They will make your life miserable. They will break your heart and soul. They show complete disrespect for you.

As a parent we love our children dearly. We would sacrifice our lives for them. They are our flesh and blood and we only want the best for them.

If your teenage child is incorrigible, you will eventually have no alternative. You will have to seek outside help from the state.

Don't wait until it is too late. If your child is incorrigible and you can no longer control him, in New Jersey call Dyfus at (800) 792-8610, family intake (201) 482-5510. There is also a National Runaway Hotline (800) 621-4000. Call your local Youth Aid Detective Bureau for help. The detectives will advise you accordingly. Arrangements can be made with the juvenile court system. Your teenage son or daughter can be put in a special school. If they are a threat to themselves and society, make the phone call.

This is the biggest reason why young teenagers are missing. Parents who have incorrigible children wait until it is too late.

The tragic aftermath is that it can get even worse. An incorrigible child will go out at night and come home during the early morning hours. He is more likely hanging with the wrong crowd. He is on the streets risking death. He is either robbing someone or is selling drugs. Why does it happen? Parents unintentionally let it happen by failing to use the programs available that can help their children.

One of the biggest problems is that we all think that this kind of situation could never involve our children. Contact your local Juvenile Detective Bureau for advice and assistance.

Teenagers feel that they do not get enough freedom. They may feel restricted by their parents. Teenagers like to go out with their friends. Some parents are very strict and they limit their curfew time to ten P.M. When their teenager arrives home late there may be a punishment. When parents restrict their children for a long period of time, the problem will escalate. Your loving child may rebel against your ground rules. When you least expect it, he or she will pack up some clothes and leave.

Our problem as a parent is that we have not learned to adjust to the changing times and understanding and communicating with our children.

Teenagers today are very mature. If they have any indications that you don't trust them, they will retaliate and do what they please. It is a two-fold problem that will have to be asserted by the parents. The failure to communicate is one of the biggest problem that families have to deal with.

Only you know if your child is well-behaved and is doing well in school. Or if they are responsible and do chores at home.

You will have to bend with the tide, so to speak. Go with the following flow. Don't try to go against the grain. Young teenagers today who are in their late-teen years are very grown up and mature. You as a parent are only going to make your relationship rocky. Let your child know that you trust his or her demeanor. If your teenager went out on a date at one P.M. and returned home at eight P.M., do you really suspect that during those seven hours your son or daughter was in a motel? Give your teenager some room to breathe. Try to have a better understanding of each other. This attitude will gain more respect and a better communication between a parent and child.

One of our most important problems is the failure to communicate with our teenage son and daughters. The darker side is an incorrigible teenager, when they reach an age from twelve to fifteen and you cannot control their well-being. If your son or daughter stays out late at night against your wishes or if your child has been reported as a runaway missing person on several occasions, seek help immediately before it is too late.

Your child could be hanging with bad influences and could become a victim of a crime. Teenagers that stay out very late at night with their peers are going to eventually get into trouble.

As parents who love and cherish their children, you must take the time to know your child. Periodically go to the school your child attends. Make sure she is regularly attending classes and that she is doing well academically.

If your child is having problems, there are programs available that will benefit him or her. If you are a single parent and you have to work to support your children, the burden can prove to be overwhelming. If you have a serious problem of communicating with your child, or if he or she is defiant to the ground rules that you have laid out to abide by, your alternatives are few—don't wait until it is too late. Teenagers that are incorrigible and defiant to their parents rules will eventually be caught up in the criminal element. They will become a victim of the harsh society we live in. Make it your top priority to talk with a state worker.

Your child can still be saved from the negative attitude she has developed. The state will provide facilities that can help your child.

There are many young teenagers that are habitual runaway children. The tragic news a few weeks later is the notification of your child found in a wooded area raped and brutally murdered.

No parent wants to turn in their child to the state. However, it may be an option when every other effort has been exhausted or when you fear for the safety of your child. The only alternative is to seek the proper advice. The decision obviously is not an easy one to make. There are no drawbacks when you consider the aftermath of a tragedy.

It is better to have your son or daughter rehabilitated. You do not want to be notified by the police that they found your child murdered or arrested for pushing drugs or robbing a store.

Give your children a lot of love. Be understanding and communicate with them. Give them some space. Learn to respect each other. Develop these intangible ingredients and you will increase the chances of having a close knitted family.

THEFT BY DECEPTION

Theft by deception is orchestrated by con artists. Their technique and talent in the field of deception is excellent. This crime occurs to the average person twice and sometimes three times in a lifetime.

Learning from other victim's mistakes is the only way we can prevent you from becoming a victim. Fortunately this is one of the few crimes that has no physical injury.

There are three types of deception consisting of flim flams, counterfeit funny money and forgery.

Forgery crimes do not occur as often as in the past. Banks and check-cashing stores require at least two identification cards. The biggest victims today are the credit card companies (Citibank, Mastercard and Visa Card).

Forgery crimes do not occur as often in big office buildings. People lose their credit cards and they don't realize they lost it until a few days and sometimes a week has passed by. The cashier at the department store is not asking for proper identification. They are negligently allowing actors to use a lost or stolen credit card. The actor (forgery artist) signs the slip and forges the signature. When this occurs the credit card company charges the bill to the department store for failing to follow proper procedures. Occasionally the credit card company gets stuck with the bill. These companies lose millions of dollars. Why do you think they charge nineteen percent on interest?

Remember when you leave the store and are seated in your car. Double check and make sure you have your credit card. Avoid carrying all of your credit cards. Take with you only the card that you are going to use.

Customers have a very bad habit of leaving their credit cards in the cashier's process machine. When you lose your credit card, call the company and cancel your card immediately. Another credit card will be issued within a week.

Another type of theft by deception occurs when the owners of companies have a bad habit of leaving old company blank checks in their office cabinets and desk drawers. When an actor steals the checks he will forge the company boss name. The company is stuck paying the bank thousands of dollars.

If you have a large amount of money deposited in your bank account, the actor will have a field day cashing in your checks when he forges your name. Avoid the lost and stolen checks. Throw away and destroy all of your old checks. Ex-employees and new employees can be a suspect in the forgery caper rip offs.

FLIM FLAMS

Flim flams are done by both amateur and professional con artists. A flim flam is a scam that an actor will present to you. He will convince you that the investment will make your very rich. A flim flam can be a trick, a swindled deal or a hoax. It can be petty trickery or deception.

Who are the victims of a flim flam? It can happen to anyone who is trying to cut the corners to make more money.

Or take young ladies who are trying to become models. They read an advertisement in the newspaper or a magazine promising a modeling career. The price of the contract is affordable. They are lured into the web with a lucrative offer. The hopeful model will go to the studio and will pay a $500 fee up front. They are promised a great future and big bucks. Most of these lucrative arrangements look good but unfortunately the studio is a ripoff scam. The hopeful models wait months for a commercial contract. The young ladies only get heartbroken when they are told that they have been flim flamed.

The same type of flim flam occurs with male and females who are trying to find an agent. They need an agent to become an actor or actress in the movies.

Before you invest money, inquire and ask the agency for its license. Check with the better business bureau. Make sure they have a legitimate business.

Parents of little toddlers have dreams of their kids making thousands of dollars a month. They are lured in by advertisements that promise their child will have the opportunity to make big bucks.

The parent, usually the mother, will take her toddler to the agency. She will invest $700 to $1,000 in photo sessions. They are given the option of acting training for the little toddler. By the time the agency is done injecting his brains with pipe dreams, the victim is hit with a $2,000 dollar ripoff scam.

The studio manager tells the parent that the child will be evaluated. They inform you that they will be in touch with you soon. Unfortunately they give the same promises to hundreds of hopeful parents.

Before you go to an advertised establishment or movie or TV studio, check with the local better business bureau or consumer affairs before you sign any commitments. The agency you are going to may not be licensed with the state or it might have possibly lost its license from previous complaints.

We have flim flams that are more involved in trickery than in deception. In Newark, Elizabeth, Jersey City, and Paterson we receive hundreds of investigations on flim flams that occur at check-cashing establishments and occasionally at banks.

A con artist will approach you after you cash your check. The modus operandi is showing the victim a big roll of counterfeit money. The con artist will cut up newspapers to the exact size of a twenty dollar bill. They will cut up three hundred exact size newspaper sheets. They will cut up the paper on the corners of one dollar bills and carefully paste the corners of a $20 dollar bills onto the one dollar bills. They will than put two twenty-dollar bills on top of the fake roll of money and one twenty dollar bill on the bottom. They complete their trick by laying bills on top using ten single one dollar bills and ten on the bottom. They will put ten counterfeit twenty dollar bills near the top. They complete their roll of money by putting twenty-five one dollar bills in between the cut up newspaper. The roll of money looks very real. With 50 real bills blended in with the three hundred fake bills, the flim flam artist has a roll of money that is alluring to the next victim. They are ready to make a deal.

The con artists now have a thick wad of counterfeit money that looks authentic. When the potential victim sees the money his eyes light up. The roll of money is enticing. When a potential victim is approached by the con artist, the victim sees the money and may think, "Hey, this is a fair exchange and I am going to be in possession of a lot of money."

The con artists are usually a male and a female. They pose as foreigners that have recently come to the United States a short time.

The con artists are very smooth operators. They may try to convince you that they are in fear of losing their money. They may ask you to help them find an apartment. They may tell you that they are not familiar with the area. They may tell you that they are in fear of being robbed of their life savings. They may tell you that they have a large amount of money and that they need a trustworthy person that will safeguard their money.

When the con artists show you the roll of money, they may try to make a lucrative deal with you. They might say to a potential victim, "Miss, excuse me, you seem to look like a person I can trust. I want you to personally hold my money. I have a roll of money containing $4,000. I want you to put it in your pocketbook for safe keeping. However in return and as a security blanket considering that I am entrusting you with all of my money, I would like you in good faith to give me the money in your pocketbook."

The exchange of money is completed. The con artists will go to their car and they will tell you that they will be at your apartment tomorrow to pick up their money after they find an apartment. The victims of these flim flams are usually women in their middle fifties.

Most of the flim flams that occur in Newark usually happen the first week of each month. Their main target area is check-cashing stores and banks.

The question that readers are asking is—How can this happen? One of the reasons that it occurs is because of greed and dishonesty of the victims. What happens is that the victim sees the money and thinks that this will be an easy score. The victims hand over $420 for a bank roll of $4,000. Unfortunately the victim finds out later that they have been swindled by their own game. We call it in the police department "poetic justice."

Other victims that this type of flim flam happens to are respectable citizens that are just trying to be helpful to a person who is a stranger to the area. A word to the wise: hang onto your money and don't get involved with strangers. In 1992, I took reports of flim flams at check-cashing stores on twelve occassions. I assigned well over one hundred flim flams. We also on occasion have flim flams that are done professionally. These con artists have the ability to mesmerize a victim. He does this by taking the victim to their bank and having the victim withdraw all of their life savings.

Last year I remember a fifty-eight-year-old woman that came into Police Headquarters. She reported a flim flam crime in which she was hypnotized by a Haitian female. The victim was taken to her bank and she withdrew $10,000 from her bank account. She gave the money to the flim flam artist.

We can avoid this crime by going with our elderly parents to banks and check-cashing establishments. Stay in a group of two or three people when you cash your check or you are making a deposit at a bank.

Con artists generally do not prey on people that are in pairs or groups. They do not make good prospects so they will focus on single woman in their late forties and middle fifties. On occasion they will prey on a young lady. Avoid getting into conversations with strangers.

It is important to remember that actors often disguise themselves. They do it very well, so use caution.

FUNNY MONEY

Counterfeit bills are handled by the United States Treasury Department. Police officers execute the preliminary report on a counterfeit bill and the Treasury Department follows up the investigation. Store owners of business establishments are the general victims. In 1991 we had a large circulation of excellent counterfeit twenty dollar bills were circulating along the entire East Coast. Recently the Treasury Department stopped the scam.

The secret of detecting a counterfeit bill is by looking closely at the fiber. The multicolored fiber is very fine and it is very difficult to duplicate. You can also detect a good bill by rubbing it on a clean sheet of white paper. If no print comes off it is more than likely a counterfeit bill. If you are not sure of a twenty dollar or fifty dollar or a one hundred dollar bill, ask the patron for his driver's license and social security ID card. Record the persons name, address, and the serial number in a book along with the denomination that you accepted.

Most small business establishments will not cash a bill larger than twenty dollars. This is a good procedure to follow. Those owners who do accept cash of fifty dollars or one hundred dollars ask the customer for at least three credentials. Another alternative is to refuse bills over twenty dollars.

You can also purchase a black fluorescent lamp, which reveals a counterfeit bill.

Another technique that a con artist will cut off the corners of a $1 and $20. The twenty dollar bill corners are pasted onto the one dollar corners. You are now the proud owner of a one dollar bill that you think is a twenty dollar bill. Take a careful look at the next twenty dollar bill you accept. There are thousands of these bills in circulation.

FALSE CONTRACTS

This is the last in the series on prevention of thefts by deception, false contracts that show up in ads that you see in newspapers and magazines. Some examples are ads that state masons for hire, carpenters for hire, painters for hire and general contracting for hire. Use caution and good judgment when you sign an agreement with a contractor. Most of the victims of thefts by deception are homeowners. The unfortunate problem is that in the past several years we have had a serious recession. Middle and low income people are forced to cut back. This has caused people to look for deals that will meet their budget. What is happening is that people are getting deeper in debt and are being swindled out of their hard earned money.

Homeowners are calling up these sleazy contractors who are bigger crooks than Bonnie and Clyde.

Here are some of the recent police reports involving victims that were taken in by deceptive contracts:

A homeowner will call a carpenter to have his porch renovated. The carpenter will give the victim an estimate of how much it will cost to renovate his front porch. The carpenter will ask for a deposit of $2,500. The carpenter immediately starts working on his front porch. A week later he will tell the homeowner that he needs an additional thousand dollars to cover the material. Now the carpenter has $3,500 and he has completed the foundation of the front porch. A month passes by and the homeowner has not seen the carpenter. The victim tries to call the carpenter, but he fails to reach him. The victim waits patiently a few more weeks and than he decides to go to the carpenter's business location. The victim finds out from the landlord of the building that the carpenters have abandoned the building. The homeowner shows up here at Police Headquarters and files a police report charging the carpenter with theft by deception. How do they manage to pull off this slick move? These carpenters had their business located at the address indicated in the report, but when we investigate, they had gone. When we look through our records and reports, we find that this contracting company had several other victims who have filed complaints against these sleazy carpenters. We have to check with other police departments. We make a coordinated effort to pin down where these carpenters are setting up their shops.

These weasels move from town to town over a very short

period of time. They stay a few months, make a few thousand dollars and they move on. They are smart enough to move out of the state after they have pocketed $100,000.

Some contractors set up shop as masons. For homeowners who are looking for a brick type facelift on their house, the mason will give you a reasonable estimate of the cost. They will ask for a twenty-five percent down payment up front. They will not start work on your house without the cash. Once they start working on your house they will ask for additional money. Unfortunately they will never complete the work and the victim is ripped off for thousands of dollars.

These slick rip-off artists don't always get away from the police. Eventually they are caught by the detectives. The problems is too many of these crooks are robbing us of our hard earned money.

Before you agree to a contract with a mason or carpenter after he gives you an estimate on your house, demand that the contractors show you a legitimate license. Call the better business bureau and find out if they have any past complaints against the contracting company you have hired. Don't be so quick and anxious to sign a contract. Before you make a decision on a contract, call several contracting companies and get the best price. It is important for you take make sure you have a reliable company that has gained an excellent reputation. As a homeowner you can go for your best deal but make sure the company is legit.

STOLEN AUTOS

Car thieves love New Jersey. At least that's what the theft figures compiled by the National Automobile Theft Bureau indicate. Of the ten most stolen cars in United States cities, five are in New Jersey. The value of vehicles stolen in New Jersey in 1989 was $452 million. That is up a dramatic 249 percent from 1979.

In Newark, N.J. population 313,839, 15,674 cars were stolen.

In Irvington, N.J. population 61,659, 3,893 cars were stolen.

In Elizabeth, N.J. population 105,324, 2,750 cars were stolen.

In Camden, N.J. population 82,262, 2,614 cars were stolen.

In Trenton, N.J. population 90,975, 2,567 cars were stolen. In 1989 a total of 70,979 cars were stolen. In the United States a car is stolen every 17.3 seconds. Motorists have to purchase good theft prevention devices to eliminate the stolen car epidemic.

1991 statistics reported that the Camaro is the number one car stolen and is stripped for its valuable auto parts. The 1984 Cutless Supreme is the easiest car to steal. In 1991, 71,868 cars were reported stolen. 3,499 suspects were arrested for possession of a stolen car. Sixty percent of the arrests involved juveniles.

In Newark we received more reports of stolen cars than any of the seven major crimes that occur here. New York City, Jersey City, Philadelphia, and Miami are just a few other cities that handle thousands of stolen cars every year.

Your car is stolen by a car thief for many reasons. They use your car for transportation, armed robberies, or car parts, and they sell them to used dealers and "chop shops."

Most of the new and popular cars that are stolen are taken to chop shops. Chop shops are abandoned garages that are set up and used by car thieves. When your car is taken to the chop shop, the boss who runs the shop pays the thieves a substantial amount of money. The chop shop strips the car down and sells the parts to car dealers. Some well organized chop shops will change the appearance of your car.

They can adjust and change your car mileage. They can destroy your vehicle identification number (car serial number). Your car can be sold somewhere in New York. However, most of the cars that are sold are transported to the southern states. Some of the cars are sold overseas. Your car might be stolen just for a joy ride by teenagers. Juveniles and young adults steal cars to go with their friends to New York.

If you have a stereo radio and tape player and excellent tires that you recently installed, the car thieves will drive your car to an isolated area. They will strip your car dashboard to steal the radio and then steal the tires. Some cars are stolen and used for armed robberies.

Juveniles steal cars and are paid good money by the guys who are running these chop shops. The juvenile delinquents also know that the police will not chase them when they are observed in a stolen car. They also know that even when they are caught they are released to their parents.

In 1991, we have been involved in some terrible tragedies that involved juveniles driving stolen cars. In October 1991 on Seventh Street and Fifteenth Avenue, three teenagers were driving a stolen car. They were performing "donut turns" on the four corners of Fifteenth Avenue and South Seventh Street. Donut turns are a showoff craze that teenage juveniles have been doing recently. It is a very dangerous and deadly maneuver. The driver of the car is doing these donut turns at speeds exceeding eighty miles an hour. The rear wheels spin at a high rate revolving hundreds of times per minute. The car is difficult to maintain and control. The driver is showing off his skills to his friends.

On an afternoon in November 1991, the donut show turned into a very sad tragedy. A mother and father and their children were walking on the sidewalk near the intersection of Fifteenth Avenue and Seventh Street. They observed a car spinning recklessly in a circle. The tires were screeching loudly. The family reacted and was ready to take a safer path to their home. Suddenly the car lost control and it hit the father and his three children. The father and two of his children were taken to the hospital. They were treated for injuries sustained when the car struck them, and detained at the hospital for observation. Unfortunately the third child, their two year old daughter, sustained critical injuries and then died.

The juveniles who fled the scene were caught a short time later. They were arrested and slated with a charge of second degree manslaughter. The Essex County Prosecutor's Office recommended that the juveniles stand trial as adults. They will serve the maximum sentence as an adult offender would.

Please advise and teach your children to stay clear of an area where car thieves are showing off these wild donut acts on the streets.

In the summer of 1991 we had another terrible tragedy involving a stolen car. Two juveniles were driving a stolen car at a high speed. They recklessly drove through a red light at an intersecting street an broadsided a car passing through a green light. All three passengers were killed instantly. The three women were sisters in their early twenties. The suspects were arrested and charged with three counts of vehicular manslaughter.

In May 1992 a Belleville police car was chasing a stolen car south on Broad Street. When they passed through the intersection of Broad Street and Market Street, they broadsided a vehicle passing through a green light. The driver was a twenty-five year old female. Her car was demolished when the police car struck her vehicle. The driver died a short time after impact. She was a young mother of three children. The officers crashed into a store and were taken to a hospital.

Car thieves steal cars that are easy to drive away. They also steal cars that will get the best price for car parts.

Based on a national survey, what are the easiest cars to steal? The Buick Century, Oldsmobile Cutless Supreme, and Chevrolet Impala.

Honda Accord and Nissan autos have an excellent steering column lock. These cars are not stolen as frequently because it takes the car thief too long to steal. Unfortunately there is no car on the street today that is spared from car thieves.

If a car thief needs the parts of your car, he will steal your car. Cadillacs, Camaros, Honda Preludes, and other foreign cars are professional car thieves' top choice. They get top dollar for the body parts. Starting in 1994, all car parts have a serial number.

Invest some money and install a car alarm. The best protection today is an instrument called "The Club." Don't buy an imitation brand. The Club is the most popular and the most effective steering column lock on the market. The Club is a steel bar that locks the steering column tightly and securely. When a car thief observes this mechanism fastened securely to the steering wheel, he will not steal your car. It takes too much time to break the mechanism. The car thief is not stupid. Knowing that he is risking a strong possibility of being caught by the police, he will move on to a car that is not guarded.

It is important that you learn from other victims' mistakes. Do not leave your car running when you are only going to the store to buy a pack of cigarettes. If you have a habit of leaving your keys in the car, a thief may jump in your car and steal it before you can blink an eye.

Drivers go into gas stations and leave their cars unattended. The gas attendant will fill your tank with gas. He is also pumping gas in several other cars. The driver goes to the restroom, three minutes later he returns to his car and it is gone with the wind. This crime happens to thousands of drivers every year. It occurs because we fail to take the car keys out of the ignition.

Another bad habit that drivers have is that they leave their expensive coats, suits, and other gear in the front and back seat of their car. This is a lure for a thief. He will bust out your vent window. When you return your clothes will be stolen. Some thieves get greedy and they decide to hot wire your car and steal it.

Thousands of cars are stolen at shopping malls, especially at Christmastime. Avoid leaving Christmas packages in the car.

There is always the possibility that the car thief will steal your car as well as the packages. The thief knows someone might observe his presence. He knows that he is taking a high risk of being caught by transferring packages from your car to his. The professional thief will avoid the risk by stealing your car.

You avoid the possibility of a car theft by leaving your coat, dresses, suits, and valuable gifts in your trunk. Leave an adult or teenager in the car if you have packages in the back seat. Do not leave the keys in the car. Make sure the doors and windows are locked.

I am not trying to scare anyone who is reading this book. This is the reality of life. Learn from other victims' mistakes. Play it safe, play it cautious. Avoid the attitude that you could never be a victim of a crime. The more aware you are of the many ways that you can fall victim to a crime, the chances of you becoming a victim will diminish.

Another bad habit that car drivers continuously exhibit is they keep their car registration and insurance cards in the glove compartment. Although keeping your registration in your wallet will not prevent a thief from stealing your car, it still has intangibles that you could not even venture to comprehend. First of all, when your car is stolen and you left the registration in the car, your very first commitment is to report you car stolen at your local police station. There are a lot of drivers who do not know their plate number, especially on new cars. The problem now is that without a correct license plate, police officers cannot release a statewide teletype and a broadcast of your car over the police radio airwaves. We cannot bring it to the attention of police officers in the street. Obviously without a plate number the police cannot send out a thirteen state teletype notifying other police authorities that your car is stolen.

You have unintentionally delayed a statewide broadcast of your stolen car. In the meantime the car thieves have the advantage. They are driving your car looking for another car to steal or for other victims to rob with your car. Your car can also be heading out of state. The car thieves are getting away with it because your car is not entered into a statewide teletype system as a stolen car.

The most important advantage that the car thief has is your registration. When a car thief steals your car, the first place he looks is in your glove compartment.

Victims ask the detectives in the auto squad, "Why would a car thief want my registration? What can he do with it?" The detective will reply that when the car thief is pulled over for a traffic violation, the police officer asks the driver for his license, registration, and insurance card. The car thief nonchalantly takes out his wallet and gives the officer his credentials. The officer will ask the driver whose car is this? The driver may reply, "Officer this is my girl-friend Cathy Smith's car. We are getting married next year. My car is being repaired. I borrowed the car until my car is repaired. I faithfully drive my girlfriend to work every morning." If the car is registered to a man, the driver may say that it belongs to his brother-in-law. The thief has a slight advantage when he has the credentials.

Now I know we have people reading this book and they're saying. "Wait a minute, don't tell me that officers are not trained on how to be observant." To the readers who have been victimized by a car thief, stand at ease. When a police officer approaches a car the first thing he looks for is the ignition. Officers know that if the ignition is busted and stripped the probable cause exists that the car is stolen. But as a police officer you cannot rule out that the car was recently recovered from a previous stolen car incident. Police officers don't rule out that a car is stolen just because it has keys in the ignition. We know that thousands of drivers carelessly leave their keys in the ignition. A police officer will not rule out any given situation. As a police officer you cannot overreact to a situation. The car thief also might have gone to a locksmith and had a new ignition installed. A car thief always has a ace in his pocket. They are professionals, they know every trick of the trade.

Car owners who keep their car credentials in their wallet may ask, Why do drivers leave important credentials in their glove compartment?

Most car drivers leave the car registration and insurance card in their glove compartment, because other family members use the car. Fortunately, not every victim has to wait until the next day to report their car stolen. If you are fortunate enough to remember your exact license plate number, the police officer executing the report can run your plate into a computer. The high tech state motor vehicle computer will feed back your name, address, and vehicle identification number (VIN). If your plate number is correct the state computer will verify it. With a positive verification the police officer can have a thirteen state alarm transmitted via teletype systems located at each police station. Stolen cars are usually recovered within three to five days.

If you have family members that use your car, have a duplicate copy of your car registration and insurance card made. Make an effort to change your bad habits. Keep your car credentials in your wallet. If you still leave the registration in the car, find a place to conceal it. Place it under the dashboard, under the rug, under the car seat, or under the rug in the trunk. Car thieves don't make a habit of stripping your car frantically searching for your registration. If they don't find your registration in your car, they will assume that you have it in your wallet.

It is important to remember that it is very risky to look for your stolen car. Police officials do not recommend civilians to do this. You are taking a risk of being seriously injured, robbed, or killed. Let your local police find your car, don't go out on the street playing cop. The car thieves will seriously harm you; avoid any confrontation with them.

If you do find your stolen car abandoned on a desolate street, do not enter the car and drive it home. Call your local police department for assistance. A radio car will respond to the scene. Officers will release your car and cancel the teletype. However, if your car was involved in a homicide or armed robbery, it will be towed to your local detective bureau. Fingerprints are dusted by the identification bureau. This is why we do not want civilians entering their stolen car. The suspects fingerprints would be destroyed if you enter the car. Arrests are imminent when we have good fingerprints dusted from the steering wheel and dashboard.

I have taken reports on occasion where victims of stolen cars have made blundering mistakes. Some owners of their car negligently leave their title papers in the glove compartment. The victim is already upset about his car being stolen. It is unfortunate when you have to advise the victim that he has given his car away. The car thief can sign your title and sell your car. The worst news is that your insurance company will not reimburse you after the thirty day period that your car is stolen. Your insurance company will ask you for your ownership title. They will not pay you book value for your car. If you do not have the car title you will not receive payment on your car.

If you leave the car title in your car, a car thief can sell your car without any problem. You just gave your car away for nothing. The car thief will sign the back of your title. He will sell your car for a minimal price. Leave your car title in a safe secure place in your home. Keep the title in a folder with your other important papers.

When your car is stolen and it is not recovered after thirty days, your insurance company will pay you book value of the price of your car. You will have to be covered with comprehensive insurance and most important you have to turn over your car title to them.

You can avoid having your car stolen if you develop good habits. When you park your car at home or at a friend's house, make sure it's on a well-lighted street. If your friend has a driveway, park it there.

When you park your car at a shopping mall, park it as close to the doors as possible. The farther back your car is to the rear of the car lot, the more at risk your car will be stolen.

Thousands of drivers commute to and from New Jersey to New York City. They leave their car in the parking lots (Edison Lanes) located near Penn Station in Newark. Chances are when you return, you may find your car is stolen. The car thief knows that your car is going to be in the car lot for twelve to twenty-four hours. Hundreds of commuters leave their cars in the lot for the entire weekend. This enables the car thief a golden opportunity to drive your car without the risk of being caught. When the car thief finds your credentials in the glove compartment, he has a better than even chance of avoiding an arrest by the police. Your car could be involved in multiple robberies over the weekend. The worst part of it is that the police have no knowledge that your car is stolen. You should not leave your car in a parking lot for three days. If you're planning to stay in New York for the weekend, arrange to have someone give you a ride to the train station. Another excellent suggestion is for you to take a cab to Penn Station.

During the past eighteen months a rash of cars being stolen at gunpoint were reported across the United States. The victim was robbed not only of his car, but also of his jewelry and money. Most of the car robberies occur late at night. Motorists exiting the ramps into Newark asked strangers for directions to a street location. The robber took the victims' car at gun point. They called this phenemenon "carjackings." (Chapter 17 goes into a detailed account of carjackings.)

If you need directions to a street, use a phone on a well-lighted street. Your best bet is to go to a twenty-four hour gas station. When you are going to an out-of-town location, make sure you have a full tank of gas. Keep a county map in your glove compartment. If a you don't have a map, call your local police for directions. Call the police in advance when you are driving to an unfamiliar location. All of these little habits can help you avoid becoming a victim of a crime. Remember and follow the precautions suggested. You will reduce the possibility of becoming a person whose car is stolen every twenty seconds in the U.S.

CHILD ABUSE

From 1992 to 1993 parents saw on television and read in the newspaper the sad and tragic causes that focus on child abuse.

I recall the tragic child abuse case in New York City in January 1990.

A ten-year-old girl died from continous battering from her father. Lisa Steinberg died because school officials negligently failed to report to the police. Lisa came to school several times with scars over her face and body. The case worker failed to take action to save the child. It is also the responsibility of the schoolteacher to report any severe injury that is unusual. Lisa's death has opened up all our eyes. People are not reporting parents who abuse their children.

In early November 1991, TV actor Roseanne told a reporter that her parents abused her when she was a child. Shortly after TV talk show hostess Oprah Winfrey told a Senate committee that she was raped by her nineteen-year old cousin when she was nine years old.

Thousands of children are abused every year. People are asking the Senate committee to help the innocent children in our country to survive.

In Denver, Colorado there is a national hotline number (800) 421-0353 that will assist you in reference to child abuse cases.

As a police officer I have seen relatives perform some of the most diabolical acts. They have made victims of their sons, daughters, nieces, nephews, and cousins.

I have arrested grandfathers that have sexually abused their own grandchildren. I have arrested uncles and fathers for sexually abusing their own children.

Unfortunately we have a small population of people who are mentally sick and unstable. They have to be arrested and committed to a prison facility.

We, as parents, have to accept a greater responsibility regarding the safety of our children.

As a parent, use discretion and make every effort to cross check references when you have a baby sitter watching your children. Be careful of the relatives and friends with whom you entrust your children.

Fortunately, the criminal laws have become stricter. Negligent parents and relatives are being prosecuted to the full extent of the law. Stiff jail sentences and fines are being mandated.

Recently we have been receiving hundreds of reports regarding children being sexually abused and battered by their own parents and relatives. We have been arresting schoolteachers, day care workers, and doctors.

When your child reaches the age of six, if he is being supervised at a facility, it is imperative that you teach them in a light manner about sexual contact. Tell your children that no one is permitted to touch their genital area. Comfort them and tell them not to be afraid to converse with you. They have to be drilled in a smooth matter concerning unusual occurences. They have to feel free to tell you if their schoolteacher or a case worker is touching their private parts.

If your child's personality takes a drastic change, take your child to your family doctor for a complete examination. Don't wait until it is too late. Check your child's body periodically.

Children are generally afraid to tell you if their teacher or a relative has been touching them. Your child thinks that they are doing something wrong. In their mind they are afraid that you will punish them. This is why I stress that having an understanding with your child is important. If you have reassured your child in advance of what is right and wrong, you will not have to experience the horror and pain other parents have been undergoing.

Parents are being arrested at an alarming rate. If a relative is physically abusing your children, call the police and have that person arrested.

As a police officer serving the public for twenty-four years, I have been dispatched to the scene of a child badly beaten by parents and relatives. It is a tragic experience when you see a little toddler's head battered. I have seen hundreds of children rushed to University Hospital by EMS technicians. I have arrested parents for committing horrible injuries to their children. As I am writing this book it brings tears to my eyes to recall the brutal attacks I have seen. EMS technicians transport children to University Hospital with critical injuries inflicted on them. They are treated for broken ribs, busted eye sockets, busted ear drums, perforated ear injuries, broken arms, broken legs, severe burns, fractured skulls, and burns on their penises. Unfortunately there are thousands of parents who lose control. They don't have the patience that is needed to handle little toddlers. If your self-control is at the point of no return, SEEK HELP IMMEDIATELY! Don't wait until the problem escalates into an event that will result in your arrest.

It is very important that you digest and understand full knowledge of the law regarding children that are physically abused by their parents. If you are a schoolteacher or a family physician, you are required by the laws of the state to report to the police any critical bruises that you observe on a child. Police officials urge neighbors that continuously observe and hear children being battered by their parents to become community orientated in regards to safety and welfare of the innocent young victims.

Call your local police department and request that they investigate. In Newark you can call our Youth Aid Bureau at (201) 733-6090. If you observe your child's best friend with deep bruises on his face and body, call Dyfus at (800) 792-8610.

The Police Department cannot prevent these terrible and sad tragedies from occurring. We desperately need the community to assist us and become the eyes and ears of the city.

SEXUAL ASSAULT

Rapes occur in the U.S. once every sixteen minutes. They are committed on children ranging in age from two to ten years of age. It is unfortunate that there are a lot of sick demented individuals lurking in your neighborhood.

FBI national crime statistics report that thousands of rapes are inflicted on teenagers and adults. Sexual assaults on toddlers are committed by friends and relatives. Some teenage rapes occur when students walk home from school, or after school hours and late in the evening. Students can help avoid the trauma of becoming a rape victim by walking home with a friend.

When you're out late in the evening hours, call your parents and make arrangements for them to take you home. If they are not home, have a friend or relative take you home.

Because of the society that we have to deal with on an everyday basis, you have to make adjustments to conform with and become a survivor. You can avoid the agony and nightmare of becoming a rape victim. Use precautions and get rid of the attitude that it could never happen to you. Walking home in a group is another safe precaution to utilize. This habit will greatly diminish the chance of becoming a victim.

Teenagers that have part-time jobs should have a friend, relative, or parent pick them up from work. Take a cab home when you do not have a ride. If you work late evening hours you should definitely call for a cab.

Women have to use extreme caution and discretion when they are walking the dark streets of the city.

It is essential to remember that if you are raped, report the incident to the police immediately. Make the necessary arrangements to have a relative transport you to your local Hospital. Newark residents would go to United Hospital. Doctors, nurses and counselors will comfort you and put you at ease.

In Newark, rape victims are treated at United Hospital on Ninth Avenue and Seventh Street. It is imperative that those who are raped be taken to a hospital the same day that the rape occurred.

A rape kit will be administered as evidence. The detectives from the rape squad will talk with you.

We can only hope and pray that no one close to you is raped. Unfortunately it is inflicted on thousands of women. However, knowing what to do if it does occur is essential.

Rapes can be prevented if you remember to use caution and follow the recommendations given in this chapter.

In Newark, we have a Sara Unit that investigates sexual assaults, (201)733-8728. Victims in other cities and states, dial the operator and ask him to connect you with the detective bureau in the city where the crime occurred.

Hundreds of women are raped at street corners as they wait for a bus late in the evening hours. Make sure that you have enough money with you to take a cab, if necessary, especially if leave work or a night club late in the evening.

Play it on the safe side. Call a friend, relative, or a cab to take you home. If you have learned and digested anything from other's mistakes, you can avoid the agony of becoming a rape victim. Carrying a canister of six percent red pepper mace is an excellent defensive mechanism. Spray the assailant in the face. It causes blindness and nausea for thirty minutes. You can purchase mace in sporting goods stores. It is legal to carry in most states. New York does not allow citizens to carry mace. It is the only state that prohibits the sale of mace.

HARASSMENT

This is a nuisance complaint that is reported by thousands of women. Women are harassed at home and work usually by the phone, and frequently in person.

If someone is harassing you and putting your job in jeopardy, go to your local county court and file a complaint and restraining order. In Newark, on your lunch break or day off, go to the police station and have a police report executed. Bring a copy of the report to the second floor at 31 Green Street. If the harassment persists, go to 470 Martin Luther King Boulevard and execute a restraining order. If he disregards the court order, he will be arrested for violating a retraining order.

STALKING

In February 1993 a new law was passed by the New Jersey State Assembly. Anyone who intently follows someone on a unusual basis will be arrested and charged with stalking. For years men have stalked women by following them to various locations. They have caused women a great deal of stress and fear. Men have gotten away with stalking women for years. They would follow their girlfriends to work. They would follow them to shopping centers.

A perpetrator can be charged with a first, second, third, and fourth degree. The stiffness of the charge depends on the seriousness of the crime committed.

When your spouse says the relationship is over, don't pursue an avenue that is lost. Stalking is a serious crime.

HOME ALONE

Police officials are asking parents to deter themselves from becoming a victim of their own negligence. The hit movies *Home Alone I* and *Home Alone II* were great comedies. Unfortunately 1993 has been a very sad year with terrible tragedies. In Detroit, Michigan a mother of six children went with her husband to the grocery store. They were only gone a short time. One of the kids was playing with matches. When the parents returned their house was an inferno. Six children perished in the fire. The parents were devastated with the horrible death of their loved ones. The parents are not only the tragic victims of losing their children. They are also victims of their own negligence. The police charged them and arrested them for endangering the life of children. In the tri-state area, a mother left two of her toddlers home alone. She left a pot of stew boiling when she went to the store. When she returned both of her children had perished in a terrible house fire. She was charged for endangering the welfare of a child. These parents are suffering dearly with the loss of their children. They face a deeper wound with the ten-year jail sentence.

A mother in Seattle, Washington, left her four children home alone for a month. She went on a vacation trip to Hawaii. She was arrested for endangering the welfare of children.

Hundreds of thousands of parents leave their children home for a short time. Police officials are not looking for you. If your children are eight to ten years of age, it isn't a question of going to the store for an hour. The key element is how much can you trust your children and how you've trained and disciplined them. If your children are well-behaved and know that playing with electrical appliances is dangerous, then your chances of a tragedy occuring is minimal.

Unfortunately there are parents out there who are grossly negligent. You cannot leave toddlers aged two to five home alone. If you are having difficulty finding a sitter, seek state help.

19 How to Prevent Becoming a Victim of Domestic Violence

Aggravated sexual assaults and aggravated assaults—these criminal acts lead to serious injuries, more times then we would like to read about. Violent acts of domestic violence are reported on hundreds of thousands of women every year. A woman is assaulted by her husband every eighteen seconds.

Over the past three years, the criminal laws have been revised to such an extent that the number of battered women is decreasing. Statistics show that more women are alive today because the laws are providing a safety net.

Unfortunately it is not a safety net that will ensure you will not become a casualty of domestic violence. However, it does provide women with more protection than they ever had before. The laws are provided to protect women from their estranged husband. An arrest is mandatory if a man assaults his wife. Officers at the scene will be the complainant if the victim refuses.

In October 1991, the State of New Jersey revised its domestic violence laws. The good news for women was that the State of New Jersey was putting a clamp on tough guys who continually battered their wives and girlfriends. The toughest violence laws in the nation got even tougher. New provisions were implemented advising all law enforcement agencies throughout the state to take strict action against violators of women.

The revised prevention of domestic violence acts of 1991 was a long overdue correction. There were too many loopholes in the state's ten year old· law protecting battered women. The revised domestic violence act not only was expanded to protect all household members, which also included homosexual victims. The new law indicated situations in which police officers had to make arrests. The courts had to act on behalf of the victims.

I can remember quite vividly in the past, judges and the court system used poor discretion, particuarly in custody and visitation cases. Unfortunately, the courts are generally sympathetic to white-collar workers. This policy is a terrible mistake that has in the past couple of years cost the lives of women who were continually victims of the court system. This could be seen in how we have handled, or more accurately, mishandled domestic violence cases.

The tragedy of the laws that provided protection for battered women is that in the past the laws were to thin and vague. Police officers had to hold the line and use good discretion. Officers could only hope that the criminal justice system would conform to stronger restrictions regarding the safety of battered women.

The revised domestic violence law extended equal rights protection to homosexual partners. There were a lot of people out there endangered by domestic violence who couldn't do anything about it. Although many victims may be afraid to expose themselves to the bias in the justice system, at least now they had some legal recourse to take action on. The whole purpose of the domestic violence law was to provide and protect people who were most afraid to call the police or seek help elsewhere. In 1990, there were more than 50,000 cases of domestic violence reported statewide to local police municipalities. Women were the victims in eight-five percent of the cases reported, children were directly involved in ten percent and three percent involved people over sixty. The frightening statistics indicated that, despite declines in some categories, homicides resulting from domestic violence were up sixteen percent, sexual assaults rose seventeen percent, and kidnapping more than doubled.

What makes domestic violence even more of an important issue is the fact that experts in the field of police work believe that only half of all domestic violence incidents are reported. The need for more clarification of the domestic violence law was brought to the attention of the courts in two highly publicized cases.

In November 1991 people in the town of West Milford, New Jersey, protested the death of thirty-one year old Valerie Van Dunk, who was shot to death in front of her two children by an abusive former boyfriend who then turned his gun on himself.

Another recent tragedy that I recall happened in Bergen County. A judge in family court (Judge Roger Kahn), made a fatal mistake; Judge Kahn violated a court policy and allowed an abusive husband back into the home of a Rutherford woman. Tragically, shortly after the restraining order was lifted, Kathleen Quagliani, forty-three years old, a blind school teacher and the mother of two children, was beaten to death with a baseball bat by her estranged husband.

The law, as it was originally written, was fine. The major problem was the parochial and archaic attitudes of the justice community, particularly of the judges. Despite implied protections, police and the court system were reluctant to act, and unfortunately, the burden was on the battered woman.

In May 1992, a Montclair schoolteacher was killed in the school parking lot by her ex-boyfriend. A week later an Elizabeth women was killed by her estranged husband. In March 1993, a New York parole officer was in family court to settle a custody suit over his visitation rights with his daughter. The estranged husband got into a bitter dispute with his ex-wife. The officer shot his wife in the head. She died a short time after.

Police officers are sworn to protect life and property. We have been able to make huge strides in understanding the dynamics of domestic violence and abuse. Unfortunately, the court system with a few exceptions, has been horrendous. Advocates agree that the key changes in the law involve identifying all victims of domestic violence abuse and more important, taking preventive steps to break the pattern of domestic violence abuse.

Fortunately, police officers in the field now have the statutory power to seize all weapons if there is probable cause to believe violence may occur. The key that police officers needed was the authority that has been signed into law by the Attorney General's office.

Now officers have the necessary tools needed in the prevention of domestic violence tragedies. In the past it has always been too late for the police to save a life. This has been the case in so many tragic events that I have seen, I have read about, and I have executed. Tragic domestic violence reports have been reported to me during the past ten years.

Fortunately the Attorney General's office has revised changes in the criminal justice system. The major changes include the expansion of the definition of victims, clearer definition of circumstances under which police officers must make an arrest.

One of the most important new laws implemented is the limiting of a judge's discretion in returning the abuser to the household. If this new law had been implemented years ago, there would be a lot more women alive today.

Another new law revised is establishing new rules for child custody and visitation rights. There is also an expansion of the crimes covered under the statute.

One of the most important sections of the recent law and the most difficult law to get passed was the new definition of who is protected. Under the old law, victim and abuser had to be related by law that pertained to blood or marriage or be of the opposite sex. The new law covered any "person who is present or former household member." In addition to same sex partners, it covered the elderly and the disable who might be abused by a caretaker. The legislation widened the scope of domestic violence offenses, adding homicide, terroristic threats and criminal trespass to assault, kidnapping, criminal restraint, false imprisonment, sexual assault, criminal sexual contact, lewdness, criminal mischief, burglary and harassment.

The most important and essential decision was permitted by the new law and it protected you the innocent victims of the crimes committed by the abusers. But police officers always had the discretion to make an arrest if there was evidence of physical injury or "probable cause" to show that a domestic violence situation has occurred or that a weapon is involved.

Fortunately, for the domestic violence victim, the law requires a thirty-day jail sentence for repeat offenders. In cases involving children, the court must award temporary custody to the nonabusive parent. The court must also consider a request by the plaintiff to limit or suspend visitation by the abusing parent. One of the key gains in the revised laws was the elimination of "in-house" restraining orders under which the abuser was allowed back in the house but ordered to stay away from the victim.

As a police officer who was dispatched to thousands of domestic violence situations, I, like my colleagues, have particular horror stories of vicious and insidious abuses of children and housewives, of women who were victimized by their abusers. Most of these cases involved in-house restraining orders. They resulted in homicides and critical injuries resulting from gunshot or stab wounds.

Just look at the Quagliani case, a woman who moved from New Jersey to Pennsylvania. The judge released the abuser by reducing his $10,000 bail down to $500. Shortly after being released the abuser found out his wife's new address. The abuser drove his car to her house in Pennsylvania and subsequently shot and killed her. I can go on and on with the tragedies. We all read the newspaper and at least once a week you read about an estranged husband or ex-boyfriend killing his spouse.

At the time of this writing, there is an important revised law that will save a lot of women. The new law states a judge is barred from issuing an in house restaint unless it is requested by the victim. Even then, the judge must first determine that the plaintiff understands the risk of an in-house restraint and that he or she was not coerced into the request. Perhaps the most important and essential section of the law is a requirement that all court and law enforcement personnel undergo training before encountering domestic violence cases. The training must be reviewed every two years. Now the victims have the laws to provide protection for them and they, the victims, have police officers on their side. The police officers have the laws to provide the victim, and now the judges must provide the safety net protection.

Unless we hit the abusers where it hurts with sanctions, we will never stop the tragic pattern of domestic violence. We need the neighbors of the community to be the eyes of the law. If you see or hear of unusual occurences next door to your house, don't hesitate to call your local police department. Talk to the desk lieutenant and request that a police unit should respond to your neighbor's house. A police unit will investigate the situation.

The life you save may turn out to be your child's best friend or your neighbor who was battered by her husband. Don't wait to read about a tragedy the next morning. If you have reason to believe that your neighbor needs the police, reach out and lend a hand and show some concern. The police need your help to prevent some of the terrible tragedies. They involve estranged husbands and parents abusing their children and ex-husbands battering their wives.

To the women who have in the past become self-assured to change, remember that when you call the police and you have been assaulted by your husband or boyfriend, it is mandatory by law that the police officers arrest the assailant. If you refuse to make a assault complaint, the officers under the new state guidelines are required to arrest him.

If you have a serious problem and you or your children have been abused by your husband or boyfriend, contact Sandy Clark. She is a spokewoman for the New Jersey Coalition for battered victims. In New Jersey we have a battered women shelter call (201) 484-4446.

In spite of the revised domestic violence laws, battered women who are planning to divorce their husbands are not fully shielded from abuse.

What is the fatal mistake that women are making? Women strongly believe that when they have a restraining order executed, they feel that they have a safety net that will will protect them from their estranged husband.

A restraining order today is a strong document to obtain, and it should be noted that if your husband breaks the restraining order, he will be arrested. However, it will not prevent the inevitable tragedy that is occurring to women.

In May 1992, New Jersey had nine women killed by their estranged husband and boyfriends. The frightening scenario is that all of them had restraining orders. Why isn't the safety net working? It is not working because women have to go a step beyond a restraining order. You cannot assume that a restraining order is going to be your safety net. Only you the victim of domestic violence know the personality of your spouse. If you have the slightest inclination that your spouse is capable of killing you, you will have to go beyond a safety net.

If your husband has threatened to kill you if you divorce him, do not challenge his threats. Your next step is to move out of the state and start a new life. If you have children, explain to them why you have no alternative. You have to move to a place where your family will be safe.

Hundreds of women each year are killed by their estranged husbands. If you assume that it cannot happen to you, I'm sorry to tell you that you may become a tragic victim.

Thousands of women are stalked by their estranged husbands and boyfriends. On January 5, 1993 a new stalking statute was enacted by the Senate and General assembly of the State of New Jersey.

A person is guilty of stalking, a crime of the fourth degree, if he or she purposely and repeatedly follows another person and engages in a course of conduct or makes a credible threat with the intent of annoying or placing that person in reasonable fear of death or bodily harm.

A person is guilty of a crime of the third degree if he commits the crime of stalking in violation of an existing court order probibiting the behavior.

A person who commits a second or subsequent offense of stalking, which involves an act of violence or a credible threat of violence against the same victim, is guilty of a crime of the third degree.

Six months of 1993 have passed, and the stalking law has minimized the crimes that have occurred on women for years. Unfortunately it is not a foolproof safety net. It is sad for me to tell you that on several occasions I have advised women accordingly. They reported that their husband was stalking them and had viciously abused them. They reported that their husband threatened to kill them if they ever divorced them. They were advised to move to a town at least 100 miles from where they currently lived if at all possible. The most important element of surprise is to do it before your husband is served with divorce papers.

These women feared that they would be killed when their husbands were served with divorce papers. Although I advised these women to apply for new jobs months in advance of their inpending divorces, they all stated that they had excellent jobs that they could never replace. I told these women in a stern voice, "No matter how good your job is, no matter how much money and prestige you have attained, the job means absolutely nothing when you are dead."

All of these women that I forewarned were shot and killed in the car lots where they worked.

Estranged husbands, especially those who are still living with their wives, still think that they have a slim chance of mending the marriage. Frightening as it may seem, when husbands are served with divorce papers, reality sets in and their minds snap and an inner explosion erupts. They only want to end your life and their own.

I strongly suggest that you arrange to get a new job, a new life, and a safe place to live miles from your present location. The farther you move the better chance you have of not crossing paths with your estranged husband. The key element is moving out before your husband is served with his divorce papers. If your estranged husband is arrested for violating a restraining order, move to a new location while he is in jail. Police officers cannot prevent your homicide.

20 Defensive Driving May Save Your Life

Most of us who drive cars have been involved in numerous traffic accidents. In 1992 over 50,000 people died in traffic fatalities in the United States. As a motorist you have to develop good driving habits. We all want to avoid a serious car accident. You have to be responsible for your bad driving habits.

I have taken two defensive driving courses. I have assigned over 25,000 accidents in twenty-four years. I have responded to the scene of accident fatalities. Seventy-eight motorists and passengers were pronounced dead in auto accidents.

New Jersey is rated as one of the top ten states in regard to safe roads. Despite this excellent rating based on road mileage and fatalities, hundreds of motorists and passengers are killed every year. In 1992, 870 motorists died on the road.

Most drivers are involved in car accidents when they are within one mile of their homes. It occurs because drivers tend to lose concentration. As a driver if you want to avoid being involved in a car accident, obey all traffic regulations and develop a good attitude. The rules of the road in this chapter will make you a better driver.

If every driver will follow the rules of the road that are showcased in this chapter, your chance of being fatally injured in a car accident will diminish greatly. You will also diminish the risk of a critical car crash by reading and understanding the mistakes that other drivers have made. You will avoid the tragedy of becoming a statistic. Stay alert, stay alive, and focus on the important rules of the road. You will benefit by becoming a good driver, a defensive driver and most important, you will discover that the life you save will be your own. Comprehend and use these important rules of the road.

RULES OF THE ROAD

1. The very first habit you want to develop is to always make sure that you fasten your seat belt. Make sure if you have front seat or rear seat passengers that their seat belts are fastened properly. This applies with strict enforcement especially when children are in your car. It is important for you, the driver, to have knowledge of the dangers involved when seat belts are not fastened properly. Passengers will be ejected from the vehicle if you are involved in a collision.

2. At least once a month check your car. Check the directional signals, headlights, taillights, windshield wipers, wiper water container, erosion building on the battery, oil change at every 7,000 miles, tune-up at every 20,000 miles, brakes at every 25,000 miles. Check that your door locks work properly.

3. When you purchase a new car, request to have an air bag system installed. The investment may someday save your life.

4. Do not drive your vehicle if your brakes are low. The average driver that does not have a heavy foot will install new brake shoes every 30,000 miles. If your car is squeaking loudly, you are grinding the brakes into the drums.

5. Rock throwing missiles—Do not lose control or concentration on the road if you are suddenly bombarded by

a loud thud on your car roof. People lurk on footbridge overpasses. They maliciously throw large rocks at passing cars. Try your best to be alert to this frightening sudden attack. When your car is struck you can very easily lose control of your car. A fatal accident can occur.

6. Stop Sign—Many drivers are seriously injured or killed at stop signs. Here are some of the mistakes that motorists are involved in: a) Drivers do not pay attention to the road. They fail to see that the intersection they are crossing had a stop sign on the corner. b) Drivers who do observe the stop sign fail to come to a complete stop. c) Drivers misjudge the distance that the oncoming car is speeding at. It is important to know that the law states that you cannot pass an intersection unless the crossing lane is clear by five-hundred feet. Drivers fail to realize that the other driver is speeding. As a defensive driver, you will make the adjustment. d) If a car is speeding, you have to make sure that the oncoming car is at least two thousand feet in front of the crossing lane of the intersection so that you can make a safe clearance from the crossing lane. e) Remember as a defensive driver you should never assume that an intersecting street is safe to pass across when the stop sign is situated on the oncoming vehicle's street. There is no guarantee that the other driver will stop. There is also the possibility that the other driver did not see the stop sign. f) Every year there are fatal accidents at stop sign intersections. Nine out of ten times the innocent driver legally crossing the intersection is kill. The other driver is often eluding the police in a stolen car. He is driving a lethal weapon at speeds of eighty miles per hour. He will disregard the stop sign. The other driver is tragically killed by the driver of the stolen car.

7. Amber Traffic Light. How many times have you approached an intersection and the traffic light turned amber? What does the average driver do? Most carelessly accelerate and try to beat the traffic light before it turns red. Well guess what? The only thing you are beating is the grim reaper. The odds are not in your favor. Sooner or later the grim reaper is going to be there to take your life at that fatal traffic light you have beaten a thousand times. This poor driving habit may kill you, or possibly family members and the passengers in the other car. The traffic laws

are enforced for a good reason. When a driver approaches an amber light, he is required by law to stop at the light. If you are at the intersection and a green light turns amber use caution. Look at the intersecting street and cautiously pass through the intersection.

The amber light is a caution warning signal that is telling you to slow down and prepare to stop at a red light. However, most drivers fail to obey this law.

8. Red Light. The average driver accelerates and picks up the speed of his car to beat the red light. As a defensive driver you will develop good driving habits. When a defensive driver observes an amber light, he will automatically slow down at the intersection. If the crossing lanes are clear to pass, he will proceed to drive through the traffic light without incident. However, nine out of ten times a defensive driver will stop when a traffic light turns amber.

9. Green Light. There are thousands of traffic accidents at intersecting streets that are operated by traffic lights. Defensive drivers know that a green light is not a free pass to pass through an intersection. He will cautiously approach the intersection. He will slow down and look to his left and to his right. He will make sure that there is not an oncoming car beating a red light. A defensive driver is programmed to believe that there is no guarantee that a green light will safely get him through the intersection without a critical collision occurring. Hundreds of motorists are killed every year at intersections.

You have to be aware of the simple fact that there are careless drivers who violate the law. Some drivers even read a book or a newspaper while they are driving. There are thousands of intoxicated motorists who pass through red lights. How many people eat while they are driving?

When you are going to attempt to safely pass through a green light, slow down and take a quick look to your left and right before passing the intersecting streets. You can never assume that a green light is a free pass that will safely get you through the intersection.

A driver of a stolen car will shoot through a red light with no regard for the oncoming traffic. It is also important to remember that traffic lights are not without flaws. On various occasions, traffic lights do not function properly.

Use caution when you approach busy intersections especially in the city.

In May 1992 a twenty-six year old driver was killed at the intersection of Broad and Market Street in Newark. She passed through a green light. A stolen car went through the red light. *Use caution.*

10. Left Lane Fatalities. The average driver on the road maintains the left lane of the highway ninety percent of the time. A driver will often question why a police officer issued a traffic summons for failing to get out of the left lane. The state traffic law clearly states that the left lane is to be used as a passing lane exclusively. By law you cannot maintain the left lane for more than three to five miles. There is an essential reason why the left lane should be used as a passing lane only. Defensive drivers do not abusively use the left lane.

There are thousands of people killed in traffic accidents on the highways. Drivers stayed in the left lane for a fifteen to twenty mile stretch on a divided highway with four lanes (two lanes going southbound and two lanes going northbound). If there are no divided retainer walls, the percentage of you becoming a head-on collision fatality increases if you continually use the left lane. If the driver in the southbound lane has a tire blow out, and suddenly loses control of the car and is now in the northbound lanes, a head-on collision is inevitable. The same fatal head-on collision can occur in the east and westbound lanes.

11A. Another type of fatal head-on collisions occurs on divided highways with barrier walls separating the highways. Most highways today have barrier walls made of wooden four by eights, steel girders, and cement retainer walls. Unfortunately these retainer walls will not prevent a car from flipping over and colliding with your car on the other side of the highway.

Truck drivers staying in the center and right lanes are not allowed to use the left lanes. However, they are permitted to use the left lane to pass slow moving vehicles. Remember that a twelve wheeler truck has a tremendous amount of weight. They have to drive at a safe speed to survive. Their air brakes cannot prevent them from a major accident if they exceed the speed limit. Fortunately a good percentage of truck drivers obey the law and maintain a safe speed. They are excellent drivers and are courteous to the other motorists.

11B. It is important to always remember the dangers that exist when you are within 100 feet of a tractor trailer. Trucks that are driving in the center and right lanes are prone to fatal accidents because of other drivers' poor driving manners. They are prone to losing control by being forced to make a drastic sharp lane change because of a stupid mistake by the driver in front of them. Now the truck driver can very easily lose control of his rig. A sharp and sudden lane change can cause an overshift of his freight. This will cause his trailer to overturn across the divided highway retainer wall. The twelve-ton trailer is now in a deadly position. He is in the opposite lanes, which will cause a major disaster on the highway.

If you don't want to become a defensive driver and are going to continously disobey the law, try to develop a habit of continuously looking in your rear mirror. Make sure you always have clearance to quickly manuever into the center lane.

11C. Runaway tires are one of the freak fatalities that occur to drivers who continuously stay in the left lanes. Runaway tires can cause an untimely death. Occasionally somewhere in the United States a driver is killed by a tire that broke lose off a truck loaded with used tires. The tire will plunge over the dividing barrier and will strike the victim's windshield with tremendous force. The driver may lose control and be killed instantly. Some drivers are killed by the impact of the tire crashing through the windshield breaking the victim's neck.

Motorists lose their tires right off the drum itself. This freak accident occurs much more frequently to twelve wheelers. Tires become loose after hitting a huge pothole. The tire breaks loose off the axle and becomes a deadly runaway tire.

11D. There are so many intangible factors involved that can cause your death when you continuously drive in the left lane. Drunk drivers lose control of their cars and flip over the retainer wall. This may cause a fatal head-on collision. Drivers who fall asleep at the wheel can cause head-on collisions. Intoxicated drivers frequently go on the wrong exit and drive right into a head-on collision.

Emergency vehicles need to use the left lane to reach the scene of an accident quickly. Keeping the left lane clear may save the life of a car victim who is critically injured. Seconds are essential to a quick and safe response by emergency vehicles. These are the main reasons why officers enforce the law on left-lane violators.

Avoid the left lane habit that you have become so familiar with. Try to develop better driving habits. If you drive in the left lane, and a driver in your rear continuously flashes his high beam lights on your car, have the courtesy to move to the center lane. It is important to remember that when an irritant driver is tailgating you, it can cause a dangerous situation to you and other drivers. If the car in front of you makes a sudden stop, you will also make a sudden stop. The tailgater may plow right into you. This can cause a major chain reaction causing a multivehicle accident.

If a twelve-wheeler wants to pass you in the left lane, don't even think about playing games with him. Your car will be flattened if he plowed into you. When a truck does pass you, hold on to the steering wheel. The centrifugal force from his wheels can suck your car right into his trailer. At night when you are passing a trailer truck, flick your high beams on for a brief second. This will enable to truck driver to know you are passing him. Showing courtesy and respect for the truck driver may someday save your life. How dangerous would it be if he decided to slide into the left lane when you were passing him? You would be sideswiped and fatally run off the road.

Develop good defensive driving habits. You will diminish your chances of being involved in a fatal car accident. Remember that officers focus their sights on motorists who abuse the privilege of the left lane for obvious reasons.

12. Deer crossings. Use extreme caution when you see deer crossing signs. The warning should focus your attention at night when deer come out of the woods for feeding. In New Jersey and Pennslyvania, hundreds of deer are killed every year. Motorists suffer extensive damage to their cars. Police reports indicate that twenty-five to thirty motorists are killed each year. In 1993 in Pennslyvania, there have been police reports of a few black bears being hit by passing cars. Recently in New England, cars have

been hitting giant moose. Obviously these animals cause extensive damage to your car. They have caused hundreds of critical accidents.

The best way to avoid a deadly collision with animals is to stay in the center lane when you are driving at night. Always be aware of the cars in your rear. When there are no cars in front of you, use your high beams as often as possible for better sight. Don't use your high beams during dense fog conditions. Staying in the center and right lanes will allow you to observe the deer feeding on the grassy hilltops. If you are going to stay in the right lane, make sure you have a clear center lane when making a quick lane change to avoid colliding with a deer.

Driving at a safe speed, especially at night, is imperative. Drivers are killed without hitting a deer or bear. If you are driving at a high speed of seventy or more and suddenly a deer darts out on the road and blocks your path, to make a sudden and quick lane change can be extremely dangerous and difficult. Nine out of ten times you will lose control of your car. Your car will smack into a pole or tree. You have to maintain a safe speed to keep control of your car.

Other drivers fail to watch who are in the rear lanes when a deer suddenly darts out on the road. The driver quickly changes lanes and in turn he will collide with the car in the other lane. When you see a black and yellow deer crossing sign, use caution and slow down. It is important to remember that if a sign is not posted, do not rule out the chances of a deer crossing your path. Northern New Jersey is bear and deer country across the state lines. Pennslyvania has a wide area of deer and bear country.

13. Being blindsided. When you are driving in the center lane, and attempt to negotiate into the right lane, use extreme caution when you change lanes to get off the highway exit. Thousands of accidents occur every year because drivers only look into their rearview mirror. The lane looks clear and subsequently the driver changes lanes. Drivers fail to realize that there is a blindside on the passenger side of the mirror. When a car is within ten feet of your extreme right side, as you maneuver your lane change, it is too late to correct your mistake. Your car is going to sideswipe the car in the right lane. You can avoid this type of an accident two ways: a) Purchase a sideview mirror and continuously

be aware who is in your rear. Use your rearview mirrors. This will avoid the blindside accident that occurs thousands of times each year.

The second type of blindside occurs at six thirty A.M. in the East. The east-bound lanes on a clear day cause an abundance of brilliantly bright sunshine. Always keep a pair of sunglasses handy and use those sun visors. Avoid looking directly into the sunlight glare and slow your vehicle down.

14. Intersections. Drivers enter an intersecting street. The driver looks to his right, then he looks to his left. The crossing lane looks apparently clear. The driver proceeds to accelerate his car through the street or highway. Suddenly the driver spots this car or truck barrelling at a high speed toward his vehicle. The driver is frozen and cannot prevent his car from being creamed. What happened? How and where did that vehicle come from? When you are crossing an intersection, you must look out for impending obstacles.

15. If you are driving south on a street, the east lane usually has a commercial truck double parked. This truck blocks your view from seeing oncoming traffic. You can avoid the accident by cautiously moving out toward the intersection. This tactic will allow you to see the east-bound lanes if a car is traveling in the west-bound lanes. By using this reliable procedure you can easily back your car up and avoid a head-on collision.

16. Stay sober. Hundreds of people are killed every year on the highways by drivers that are intoxicated. It is difficult enough to survive on the highways when you're sober. Your chances are diminished greatly when you are intoxicated. You are driving a lethal weapon when you are intoxicated.

Driving a car requires concentration and quick reflexes. Any driver of a vehicle that has consumed three alcoholic drinks should have a sober friend drive his car home. If everyone's intoxicated at the party or night club, call a friend or relative to take you home. If those options are not open to you, drive slow and cautiously to the nearest restaurant. Drink a couple of cups of coffee. Order a hearty breakfast and take your time eating the food. In three hours you should be able to safely make your way home. If you have consumed four to six drinks, don't even think about driving your car. Park your car on the side of the road and sober up. How would you like to wake up the following morning in jail? You don't want to be advised by the police that you were involved in a head-on collision and four people were killed. I have seen this tragedy one time too many. Drinking and driving is a deadly mixed cocktail. The life you save will not only be your own, it may also be a mother and father of a family.

The police are out there patrolling the roads. They can easily observe your poor driving if you are intoxicated. First offense for drunk driving is $1,000 and a one-year suspension of your license. A second offense is severe. A $5,000 fine will be imposed and a five-year suspension of your license. In addition a six-month jail term and your insurance rates will skyrocket.

If you kill someone in a car accident, you will be charged with second degree vehicular manslaughter. You will be sentenced to a jail term and will lose your driving privileges permanently. Stay safe and sober, avoid the deadly mix of drinking and driving. The risk is too great a burden to handle.

17. Speeding. Millions of drivers across the United States violate our speed zones. You have to realize that there is a good reason why police officers enforce the law when it comes down to motorists violating the speed limit.

Twenty-five mile speed zones were designed for school zones. If you have been driving in excess of thirty to forty miles an hour in a school zone, you may kill a child who darts in front of your car. Hundreds of children are killed every year. It is unlikely that you will be able to brake in time when a child jaywalks in front of your car. If you drive at a speed of twenty-five miles per hour, a child may have a chance of you braking in time. No driver wants to live the nightmare of killing a child. The nightmare will endure in your memory for a lifetime. The tragedy is more than a nightmare for the parents to endure.

18. Cruise control. If you don't have cruise control installed in your car, it would be a good investment of $300 to install the mechanism. What is cruise control? This mechanism is used to keep your speed limit at a controlled pace. When you accelerate your gas pedal to fifty-five miles per hour, press the cruise control button on and it will maintain

your speed at fifty-five. It will remain at that speed for as long as you want it. When you have to slow down or decrease the speed, simply hit your brake lightly and the cruise control automatically decreases the speed.

If you do extensive road travel on the highway, the cruise control is a great investment. The cruise control will discipline you to maintain a safe speed. It will take the stress off of your foot continuously pressing on the gas pedal. It will safe you thousands of dollars in wasted gas. It will save you money and points on speeding tickets you got in the past.

The most important reason for having a cruise control mechanism is it will change your bad driving habits. If you can maintain a speed of sixty miles an hour you will limit your maximum speed on cruise control to sixty-five miles per hour. This will diminish your chances of becoming a traffic fatality. It will reduce your chances of being pulled over by a police cruiser. You will have less tension.

You will have excellent control of your car. Drive your car in the center and right lanes. Maintain a speed control of sixty miles per hour. You will become a safer driver with less stress on your shoulders.

19. Right turn on red. Hundreds of drivers are killed each year making this turn. Stop at the light, look to your left before making that right turn. Make sure that there is no oncoming cars within 500 feet of your vehicle.

20. Black ice. A motorist's worst nightmare on the highway is black ice, water frozen on black asphalt. During the late night and early morning hours moisture freezes on the highway. This creates a thin sheet of ice on the black asphalt surface. Hundreds of motorists are killed each year by this extremely dangerous condition that occurs in the winter months.

When the temperature is thirty-two degrees and below use extreme caution. Maintain a speed of twenty miles per hour or less. Keep a safe distance of seven to ten car lengths, behind the car in front of you. Motorists driving at speeds of thirty to forty miles per hour are risking their lives. Driving at those speeds will cause your car to go out of control. Your car may swerve and hit a tree. Your car may overturn if it hits a divider. Black ice is a dangerous condition that will leave the grim reaper hovering over your vehicle. Slow down and use extreme caution.

21. Fatal moon craters (street potholes). In the early spring highway roads become extremely deadly. The thaw of the cold weather changing to warm weather creates large potholes in the streets. Some of these potholes look like miniature moon craters. Motorists have to become aware of the danger when you hit a pothole.

You have to keep a strong grip on the steering wheel. The impact from the pothole could cause your car to go out of control.

In the early morning hours in March 1993, a young motorist was driving north on the Garden State Parkway. The road was wet and icy at four A.M. in the morning. The motorist was driving at a speed of fifty-five miles per hour when suddenly his car hit a large pothole in the right lane. The fatal accident occurred near Exit 148 in Bloomfield, New Jersey.

When the driver's tire hit the pothole, his vehicle lost control and swerved it to the right side of the retainer wall along the ramp. The vehicle skidded into a snow embankment along the retainer wall. The vehicle catapulted over the wall and plunged seventy feet off the ramp. The motorist died instantly from the impact of the fatal plunge.

Stay alert and aware of the large potholes. Keep a tight grip on the wheel. Report dangerous potholes to your local police department.

22. Fog. Motorists should be given better training and testing on how to drive in fog. On September 29, 1992 a ninety-nine vehicle pileup in Tennessee killed twelve people and injured forty-two. A frightening statistic shows that 6,804 people were killed in accidents on foggy highways from 1982 to 1991.

All of us at some time or another have experienced the scary nightmare when we encountered dense fog at night. The only way to survive on the highway is to use extreme caution. Reduce the speed limit to half of the posted speed limit. Use the center and preferably the right lane. Stay at least two car lengths in back of the car in front of you for every ten miles of speed. Driving at a speed of thirty miles per hour should position your car at six car lengths behind the car in front of you. Do not use your high beams, they will only hinder your vision. Put your four way signals on. When the fog becomes extremely dense, visibility is reduced to less than 500 feet. Your best bet is to pull over to the side of the road or get off of the nearest exit. Wait until the fog lifts.

23. Intangible Dangers. All of us who get behind the wheel feel that they are excellent drivers. Some people think they are better drivers than others. The fact of the matter is basic. The most important and essential fact for good drivers to focus on is that you can be the best driver in the world, but that does not leave you infallible to the high risk of driving on the road.

A good driver has to always remember that he has to be aware of the bad drivers on the road. This is why this chapter was written. When you are aware of the intangible dangers you can avoid the fatal mistakes made by drivers who carelessly drive with reckless abandonment. This chapter contains the techniques that will assist you and help you become a defensive driver.

As a defensive driver who logs thousands of miles on the highway, you have to always be ware of the dangers that can cause a critical accident.

Just when you thought you heard everything: On July 26, 1993, I was working in the south district. I responded to a two-car minor accident. Mr. Paul Phillips told me that the other driver was intoxicated and he plowed into his auto.

As we were talking I observed Mr. Stanley Holden of Vallejo, California vomiting a green liquid from his mouth. "I saw him drinking Flag Anti-Freeze from that gray bottle," Mr. Phillips said. I immediately took Mr. Holden to Beth Israel Hospital. Dr. Dynos treated the patient and pumped his stomach. Mr. Holden was listed in critical condition. A few days later he was downgraded to stable condition.

Police officials are uncertain why Holden drank the coolant. An ethylene glycol product, a typical bottle of antifreeze carries a warning on both the front and rear labels against drinking it and urges consumers to avoid fumes from the product.

Mr. Holden either drank the liquid to commit suicide or

he drank it to alleviate the blood content of the amount of alcohol he had in his bloodstream.

Mr. Holden was very lucky that he received treatment immediately. He was lucky that a hospital was close by. Most people would not have that luxury.

21 Police Officers' Fatal Mistakes

This chapter by no means was intended to criticize police officers. I sincerely dedicate this book and especially this chapter to all the officers who have died valiantly in the line of duty. It may save the lives of hundreds of officers. The officers who are mentioned in this chapter died because of a fatal mistake they made. We can learn from their mistakes. I'm sure they would want all their brother officers to focus on that.

Officers have to face the reality of death everyday. We are the "Blue Warriors" who are sworn to shine above the line of duty.

This book is dedicated to the 13,267 police officers who have died courageously in the line of duty. This chapter is dedicated to Newark's finest and all law enforcement officers in the United States.

Professionalism

Police officers should always remember that they are a part of a semimilitary organization. Officers have to maintain a professional personality and awareness.

We have to set standards that are above reproach by the public. As police officers, we will always be in the public eye. As a police officer we know that if we commit a crime, we will be prosecuted to the fullest extent of the law. We will be treated with no mercy by the judicial system. We are not above the law and we have no excuses for breaking the laws. We are sworn into office to enforce the laws.

As a police officer you will cope with the petty abuse experienced a thousand times in a career. If you cannot handle it, turn in your gun and badge. Only the strong survive the vigorous challenge of the men and women in blue.

Police officers are professional law enforcement servants of the people. Officers have to maintain a clear head at all times. Verbal abuse from people on the street is a common occurrence. Keep in mind that the public is always watching you. Develop a courteous demeanor and always set a good example. Always try to show compassion for victims of a crime. Maintain a good personality. Develop a good standard of community relations. Citizens will respect you and they will turn in a suspect you are looking for.

When a suspect has been arrested for a crime, handcuff the suspect and advise him or her of their rights. Do not pay attention to their taunting remarks. Do not take the handcuffs off the prisoner until he has been transferred to the precinct. Don't let a prisoner get the better of you. Search the prisoner before he is placed in the police car.

Maintain a level head when a citizen is upset about a certain situation. Calm the person down and don't pay attention to the profane words uttered in anger. Adjust the situation to the best of your ability.

ROUTINE ASSIGNMENTS

The most dangerous job that a police officer can respond to is a routine assignment. As a police officer you have to eliminate any thoughts of routine assignments. There is no such a thing as an assignment routine in nature. Police officers cannot take an assignment for granted.

Especially a police officer in a big city, Newark, Philadelphia, Detroit, Washington, Miami Beach, New York City, cannot ever assume that an assignment is routine.

Every assignment you are dispatched to is going to have

a different aftermath. All assignments will be handled in a different manner. Although many assignments are nonviolent in nature, they are all unique and challenging.

When a police officer goes out on the street, he has to be prepared mentally and physically. He has to be on guard always. He must always be aware of the reality that at any given time or place he can be shot, assaulted, stabbed, and critically injured. He must be ready to combat the forces of an environment that is drug infested. Officers know that the criminals are armed and dangerous. Becoming familiar with your post is essential to survival.

This chapter was written to educate the young officers that have not seen enough action on the streets. They might not realize what kind of task is ahead of them. The tragic mistakes of officers fatally wounded are a wakeup call to all of us. Officers in small towns and cities have to realize that they are more prone to a fatal encounter. This is a fact because they are lax in their approach to a routine situation that can be more than it appears on the surface. All police officers are prone to making a fatal mistake. We are all human beings, capable of making mistakes. Unfortunately police officers are not usually allocated second chances. If you make a fatal mistake and don't react to it in time, it will cost you your life. You should learn and remember the fatal mistakes that officers who were killed in the line of duty faced, remember the fallen officers who died valiantly and are mentioned in this chapter. I'm sure they would want all officers to remember and correct the mistakes they made.

Police officers employed in small towns and cities of rural communities are less prone to critical injuries and death by gunfire. These officers average possibly one dangerous situation in 500 assignments.

Newark police officers, New York City police officers, and other officers in the nations big cities face a dangerous situation an average of one in every twenty-five assignments.

TRAFFIC VIOLATORS

Pulling over traffic violators is one of the most dangerous situations that a police officer will encounter. Officers have to take certain precautions to avoid and diminish the chances of a fatal encounter.

Officers in small towns in the suburbs are at a greater risk. They have no idea at all that the guy they have pulled over can be wanted for an armed robbery. An officer stops a motorist for running a red light. The officer assumes that this is a routine traffic violation. The officer has his guard down and he writes out a traffic summons. An average of thirty-two to forty officers are killed every year because they fail to take proper precautions.

The essential habit to develop and the first procedure for police officers to execute is to call your radio dispatcher and request a record check of the car's plate number. If you are working the night shift, keep your high beams on and your search light on the driver. Do not leave your vehicle until the radio dispatcher record checks the plate number. Wait until the dispatcher advises you on the status of the car. You want to know if the vehicle was reported stolen. You want to know if the car was used in a rash of robberies. Remember that if the car record checks with no report of a criminal status that does not necessarily rule out that the car was not used in a crime. Keep in mind that the car could have been robbed at gunpoint or stolen an hour ago. The victim could be at home sleeping. The victim also might have been shot and dumped on the roadway by the assailant. Use extreme caution and wait for a backup unit before you approach the vehicle.

All police officers have to remember that when you are in uniform, you are always prone to be a target to a criminal. Even when you are off duty, use extreme caution.

Always conduct yourself with a good attitude and professional courtesy. It is not advisable to pull over a driver unless you are still in full uniform when you are off duty. Department regulations state that officers should take their uniform off when they finish their tour of duty. Unfortunately more officers are killed taking a police action while they are off duty. Use discretion when you are involved in off duty police action.

If a motorist violated a traffic light or another type of traffic violation, do not get involved in a heated argument if they struck your car. Make sure you properly identify yourself as a police officer when you are off duty.

FATAL OFF DUTY MISTAKES

I want all police officers to remember this tragic event that took place in 1991 in New York City. Remember this story and think twice before you overreact to a situation.

In Queens, New York City, in a quiet little community, a bizarre event occurred to an off-duty New York City police officer.

In May 1991 an off-duty police officer was involved in a motor vehicle accident. A heated argument ensued between the two drivers. The other driver, a male in his thirties, alleged that the off-duty officer was intoxicated. He further stated that the driver (officer) was very arrogant and that he never showed a police badge. The driver told the police officers that he never identified himself as a police officer. The complainant alleged that the driver (officer) threatened him. "He scared me to death to the extent that I feared for my life," the complainant said to the police. "The driver was nuts. Suddenly he became enraged and I observed him reaching for a gun from the side of his waist," he continued. "The driver (officer) reached for a gun and I reacted by pulling out a knife. I stabbed the driver multiple times in the chest to protect my life."

The officer lay in the street critically wounded. Police later identified the victim as a New York City officer.

The driver who critically wounded the off duty officer fled the scene on foot. He turned himself in to the New York City police the next day.

The police officer died of multiple stab wounds at the hospital. The other driver filed charges of terroristic threats and said he killed the assailant in defense of himself. His lawyer presented the case to a grand jury.

The grand jury weighed the evidence in the case. They presented the prosecutor's office with a no bill verdict. The driver who stabbed the off-duty officer was not guilty of a criminal offense. The jury ruled that it was the off-duty officer who was a menace to the defendant and that self-defense acquitted him.

The outcome sent shock waves to all law enforcement officers. The New York police officers were completely shocked and outraged by the decision.

This bizarre case sent a message to all police officers. When you are off duty use extreme caution when you are involved in an accident. Use a tactful approach with good demeanor. Always identify yourself as a police officer and present your badge and identification card. Conduct yourself as a professional police officer and call for police car. Don't abuse your authority. Do not provoke a situation that can lead to a heated dispute.

A short time after this incident occurred, Newark Police Director Claude Coleman issued a police memorandum. In the letter he cautioned officers to act accordingly when they are involved in an off-duty incident. He advised police officers to be aware of the aftermath of what can happen to a police officer. As a police officer you have to conform to the guidelines of the police rules and regulations. The story of the tragic death and the grand jury decision handed down was pointed out and stressed by Director Coleman.

If you have been drinking do not take any police action when you are off duty. You can very easily become a victim yourself. Your presence of mind is faltering. Your inability to react to a dangerous situation can lead to a fatal mistake. Don't let your negligent ineptness escalate into a traffic aftermath.

When you are drinking out of the city limits where you are employed, keep your gun at home if you are going to consume several drinks. Your gun will be a hindrance rather than a defensive weapon. An assailant can overpower you quite easily if you are in an intoxicated state. As a police officer you only have a split second to decide the fate of a armed suspect. An officer has to be physically fit and sober at all times. There are no second chances afforded to us.

One very important part of a police officer's career is to focus on the intangible sequence of encounters you will have to deal with. Officers are killed tragically every year because of inadequate training. Some officers fail to remember that your best friend can turn out to be your worst enemy.

One good example to focus on is this situation: Officers are dispatched to a robbery in progress. When you arrive at the scene the first suspect you encounter is a good friend that you grew up with. You graduated from grammar school and high school with this guy. You were very close friends for years. During those split seconds that you recognize each other, a dangerous liaison can happen at any moment. Your first response is "Hi Tom, what are you doing here?" Suddenly he draws a gun from his jacket. One or two split seconds pass and you freeze in your decision to draw your gun. By the time your mind reacts to the reality that he might shoot you, it will probably be too late to react and defend yourself. He now has the big advantage.

You have to enforce the law. Your best friend is a criminal and he will gun you down. He does not want to go to jail. This guy you grew up with is no longer your friend. You're the man in blue and he is the foe.

Those cops and robbers games you played as children are now for real. It is no longer a kids' game. You have to drill into your head that you represent the law. Officers stand out like a traffic light when they wear a blue uniform. Police officers are trained to focus in on how a suspect thinks when he is caught in the act of a crime. He is going to try every avenue of escape possible to elude you. An officer must realize that a suspect is a threat to his life.

You arrive at the scene of a crime. You recognize the suspect as a close friend you grew up with. Your friend only recognizes you as the enemy. Having the knowledge of knowing how the criminal thinks may save your life someday. Now you are prepared and ready to react differently if you encounter your close friend at the scene of a crime. When you arrive at the scene of a crime. Your gun should be pointed at the suspect. If he is armed with a gun, take cover and be ready to shoot him if it is your only means of defense.

Another major mistake that officers make is their attitude toward ethnic groups. Having an attitude of prejudice can lead to a fatal mistake. An officer cannot under any circumstances show any kind of favor or prejudice toward any race.

What you have to drill in your head and always remember is the stone cold fact that a white, black, yellow suspect whether male or female will kill you faster then you can blink an eye if you hesitate to react accordingly. Your split decision reaction can be the difference between life and death in all given situations. If your attitude tells you that a black suspect will kill you faster than a white suspect, someday that attitude may cost you your life.

Sometimes officers fail to react to a situation as a professional. You will rarely, if ever, get a second chance. If you make a mistake and hesitate to react quickly, bang—you're dead.

Your reaction time in all given situations is vital to your survival. It will determine whether you will live or die.

The officers mentioned in this chapter made unfortunate fatal mistakes that cost them their lives. If we can learn and remember their mistakes, someday they may save your life.

I grew up in Irvington, New Jersey. Over the years I became very good friends with most of the police officers in Irvington. In my late teen years I joined the Irvington Junior Police. I coached the kids in basketball and baseball for ten years. During those years, Officers Roberto and Garaffa became very close friends of mine. During their career they became legends as highly decorated police officers.

I find it very difficult to write about Officers Anthony Garaffa and Otto Roberto. I knew that Tony and Otto would want all officers to learn from their mistakes. It brings tears to my eyes to tell the tragic events that led to their fatal untimely deaths. The story recalls tragic memories to all Irvington police officers and their family members who loved and respected them. I remember seeing police cars passing the location of Fortieth Street and Springfield Avenue. As the weeks passed after Officer Garaffa died, I observed Irvington police cars would flash there red light on in respect for a fallen hero.

The incident occurred on a late Summer day on August 9, 1984. Officer Garaffa was dispatched to Fourtieth Street and Springfield Avenue on a burglary in progress. A canine unit was also sent to the location as a backup unit. Ironically his regular partner, Officer Jimmy Mannart, was on vacation. Officer Garaffa worked alone on this night.

When Officer Garaffa arrived at the scene, there were no signs of a burglary. Officer Garaffa observed a white male walking toward the corner of Fortieth Street and Springfield Avenue. Officer Garaffa got out of the police cruiser and approached the suspect. Garaffa observed a large brown bag in his arms.

Garaffa recognized the suspect. He was later identified

as Ted Rose. They grew up together in Irvington so they recognized one another. Garaffa relaxed when he confronted Rose. This is an extremely dangerous position to leave yourself in.

As I reminded officers earlier in this chapter, your best friend can become your worst enemy. The fatal encounter that caused the untimely death of Garaffa should be remembered by all police officers.

No one was at the scene to give an account of the confrontation that occurred between Rose and Garaffa. I can only surmise what actually happened that fateful night.

Officer Garaffa asked Ted Rose, "What do you have in the shopping bag?" Rose replied, "I have some fireworks in the bag. I bought a bunch of rocket launchers." Officer Garaffa told the suspect (Rose) to drop the bag to the ground. Rose hesitated to obey the officer's command. Officer Garaffa again stated, "Ted, drop the bag to the ground." Officer Garaffa must have instinctively sensed that something was wrong.

Suddenly with Officer Garaffa left in a vulnerable position, the assailant (Rose) raised his arm with the bag cradled and elevated and positioned directly in front of Garaffa. Rose had a sawed-off shotgun concealed in the shopping bag. Evidently when Garaffa saw the barrel of the shotgun pointing at him, Officer Garaffa did not have his gun drawn on Rose. There is no need to elaborate on what could have changed Garaffa's fate. In a split second Rose raised the bag and fired at point blank range of approximately ten feet from Garaffa.

The officer suffered a critical gunshot wound to the chest. Officer Garaffa never knew what hit him. The shotgun blast knocked him out instantly. His internal organs were severely wounded.

The backup unit arrived at the scene minutes later. The officer requested an ambulance immediately. The assailant was arrested a few minutes later.

Officer Garaffa was rushed to the hospital. Unfortunately the doctors could not stop the massive internal bleeding.

Officer Anthony Garaffa was a highly decorated medal of honor policeman. He was loved and respected by his peers, family members, and all of the Irvington police officers. I will never forget his willingness to be there for a victim.

Officer Garaffa was well-known for his relentless pursuit of justice. His great personality and fun-loving attitude will be remembered by all. He always took the time to be there for a troubled teenager. The tragic event of August 9, 1984 will be remembered by all of us. We will greatly miss a one of a kind brave officer. God bless you, Tony. My deepest sympathy is extended to his family members.

We can't turn back the clock and correct the fatal mistake that Officer Garaffa made. What is important now is that we have learned from his tragic demise. I can only stress to all police officers that you have to always be on guard. Don't assume a routine situation at any given time. This emphasis should especially be focused on when officers arrive at the scene of a potential crime. An officer has to treat all suspects with his guard at the ready. You cannot react to a situation differently because of a person's color or creed. Remember again that your best friend can some-day turn out to be your worst enemy. Always treat a sus-pect as a potential threat to your life when a serious crime is committed.

When you arrive at a crime scene and you have the prob-able cause to draw your gun, don't hesitate to have your gun drawn on a suspect. If your decision to shoot at an armed suspect freezes, there are no second chances. Forget about those movies about a suspect who has a gun in his hand. The officer has his gun pointed at the suspect. The officer yells out, "Drop your gun or I will shoot." Those split seconds will cost you your life.

Don't give the assailant an advantage. While you are warning him to drop the gun, he can plug you with several bullets in your chest. Assailants that are armed with a deadly weapon have every intention to blow you away.

If Officer Garaffa had his gun drawn on the suspect and had taken cover behind the car, the outcome would proba-bly have turned out differently.

Unfortunately could of, would of, should of, is not going to bring back any of the 10,000 officers who were killed by fatal mistakes over the years. This chapter and the officers who died valiantly will serve us all by our learning from their fatal mistakes.

The trial of Ted Rose, the assailant who killed Officer Garrafa, leaves a bitter taste in my mouth. I remember when he had his trial. He was sentenced to the electric chair. The State Court overruled his death sentence of a lethal injection. Irvington Police Officers and Garaffa's family were very upset that Rose's sentence was commuted to life in prison.

I recall another Irvington police officer who was gunned down in February 1969. I can still vividly remember the untimely death of Officer Otto Roberto.

Otto and his partner were working the afternoon shift. They were assigned to work in a police cruiser. On this afternoon it was very quiet in the streets.

Officer Roberto's partner decided to have his hair trimmed at a barber shop on his lunch break. Officer Roberto left his partner at the barber shop and decided to resume patrolling the area.

Officer Roberto observed a robbery in progress. He notified the radio dispatcher that he was pursuing a robbery suspect. Officer Roberto apprehended the suspects. As he was searching the suspect, another assailant shot him at point blank range in the chest. Otto pursued the suspect for several blocks with a severe gunshot wound. Suddenly Otto collapsed and died from massive internal bleeding.

Once again another officer is killed in the line of duty. Witnesses at the scene stated that officer Roberto never had an opportunity to shoot the assailant. Police officials surmized that Otto might have known the suspect from his childhood years. Those timely seconds of reaction cost Officer Roberto his life. Witnesses said Officer Roberto never had his gun pointed at the suspects.

Officer Roberto was a highly decorated, well-liked individual. He had a muscular body. He had a friendly personality. He had a special love for teenagers and understood their problems.

The possibility that Officer Roberto was acquainted with this suspect who shot him is real. Otto had a friendly demeanor with hundreds of teenage residents.

Doctors at the hospital stated that Officer Roberto's decision to run with a critical gun wound caused massive internal bleeding.

We can all learn and remember the fatal mistake that Officer Otto Roberto made. For those officers who are fortunate enough to have a partner, try to stay with your partner and don't assume that you can be a hero on your own. Having the advantage of two officers working as a team will diminish the risk of being one of the more than 150 officers killed each year in the United States.

Three Newark police officers who were killed in the 1970s were not known very well by me. However, I was working when they were killed in the line of duty.

Police Officer Jack Snow was assigned to the traffic division. When he was off duty he moonlighted as a check-cashing courier.

On one hot day in the summer of 1976, Officer Snow was working his routine assignments in the traffic bureau. Officer Snow received a phone call from Police Officer D'Elia. His car broke down and he asked Snow to cover his bank runs to Kearny. Officer Snow obliged and he proceeded to the bank in Kearny, New Jersey. Officer Snow has done this routine hundreds of times.

As Officer Snow approached the bank, he was unaware that a robbery had occurred minutes before his arrival.

The bank robbers saw Officer Snow's police cruiser. Officer Snow had his side window rolled down. Suddenly at point blank range Snow was shot multiple times. Officer Snow was pronounced dead at the scene.

The robbers were hunted down in the thick marsh and captured after several hours of an intense search. The assailant were sentenced to life prison terms.

Officer Snow was taking an extremely high risk. He was picking up a large amount of money. He transported between $50,000 to $75,000 on a daily basis. The grim reaper was always hovering over Officer Snow. He made his trips to Newark via Kearny a routine trip with no problem. Fate and an untimely place and location cost Snow his life.

There are hundreds of police officers everyday who moonlight for check-cashing stores. I did it myself for ten years. I transported $30,000 a day twice a week. Sometimes I would do the routine three times in a day. The last time I did a run was the day Officer Snow was killed. I realize that the courier job should be the responsibility of Well Fargo and other courier agencies that are manned by three armed guards.

In 1978, Police Officer Artie Williams won a large amount of money in the New Jersey Pick-it Lottery. People around the neighborhood got wind of his great luck and his winnings. One of his friends gave the information to the wrong person.

A burglar broke into Williams' apartment while he was sleeping. Suddenly Artie woke up and saw the suspect taking his money. Officer Williams retrieved his service revolver. Williams chased the suspect to the stairway in the apartment hallway.

Officer Williams had the suspect cornered and he confronted him. The suspect pulled a gun from his jacket. Officer Williams pointed his gun at the assailant. Officer Williams fearing for his life fired one shot at the suspect. The bullet traveled three feet and fell to the floor. The suspect fired several shots at Artie Williams.

Officer Williams, a veteran Newark police officer, was pronounced dead on arrival at University Hospital. Detective Lieutenant Charles Whitner and Detective Utsey arrested the suspect a few days later. He is serving a life sentence.

Ballistic tests showed conclusively that Officer Williams' bullet was a dud.

The tragic death that occurred to Officer Artie Williams prompted the Police Director to revise department policy. Lieutenant Nicholas Sapieza was in charge of the Newark Police Pistol range. On several occasions prior to Williams death, Lieutenant Sapieza reported that the ammo used by officers was weak. Officers now are required by state law to qualify twice at the pistol range. Lieutenant Sapieza has instructed range instructors to double check that all police officers change their ammo twice a year.

Lieutenant Sapiera was solely instrumental in convincing the City of Newark to change guns and ammunition. In 1991 all Newark police officers exchanged their .38 six shot revolvers. Officers are armed with a thirteen shot 9 millimeter semi-automatic Smith and Wesson guns.

If Officer Williams had been armed with a 9 millimeter gun, the burglar would have been killed instantly.

Another veteran Newark police officer was killed in the line of duty at a Newark bank. Officer John Gottfried was assigned to the Emergency Bureau. He walked down to the Howard Savings Bank, which was around the block from the Emergency Bureau on Raymond Boulevard and University Avenue.

On November 28, 1980 Officer Gottfried went to the bank to cash his check. The weather outside was miserable. There was a heavy rain coming down at a steady pace. John borrowed a raincoat from another officer. John was wearing a yellow raincoat with black lettering on the back of the raincoat. The letters printed two inches in size read: Newark Police Emergency Bureau.

The Howard Savings Bank was being robbed by three black males and one teenager. Officer Gottfried walked into the bank and did not know it was being robbed.

Officer Gottfried stood out like a green traffic light. They observed a cop dressed in uniform wearing a police raincoat with the logo "Newark Police Emergency Bureau." Gottfried never had a chance. Suddenly the assailants were pumping bullets into the officer. Gottfried was lying on the floor mortally wounded. He was still alive with several bullets in his chest. One of the assailants pumped several bullets into his head. When I arrived at the scene John was dead lying in a pool of blood. I was sick to my stomach when a witness stated: "The officer was shot multiple times in the chest. One robber walked right up to him and pumped several shot at close range into the officer's head."

Homicide Detectives Charles Conte, Charles Whitner, and Richard Fanning, along with other members of the Robbery and Homicide Squads arrested the suspects who were members of the New World Organization. They are presently serving life term sentences. Officer Gottfried murder was brutal and I will never forget it.

As a police officer we can learn from the fatal mistake made by Officer Gottfried. When you go to a bank observe what is going on before you enter the bank. When you are off duty and are still in uniform, wear a jacket to cover your uniform. Officer Gottfried's death was basically contributed to by simply being at the wrong place at the wrong time.

In September 1984 an Essex County police officer pulled over a traffic violator near 280 in East Orange. The officer did not know that he was wanted for a robbery that occurred earlier in the day. The officer approached the vehicle to ask the driver for his driving credentials. The driver had a sawed-off shotgun in his lap. Suddenly the assailant blasted one shot into the officer's chest at point blank range. The officer died at East Orange General Hospital.

Another officer is killed by not following an important procedure. The plate number on the car should have been record checked. The officer should have waited for a backup unit to assist him.

Hundreds of police officers have been killed during routine traffic stops.

On December 21, 1981 one of New Jersey's highest decorated state troopers was savagely gunned down on Route 80 near Sparta, New Jersey. Trooper Phillip Lamonaco, 32, the state trooper of the year in 1979, was shot to death, when he stopped a car with two men along a rural stretch of Route 80 in the Warren County community of Knowlton Township. The two assailants, Thomas Manning and Richard Williams, were convicted of the crime. They were in a car bearing Connecticut plates.

Trooper Lamonaco was shot nine times by the assailants. A violent gun battle ensued when Lamonaco observed that the suspects were armed. A routine traffic stop ended in the tragic aftermath of a slain trooper. State police policy contributed to the death of Trooper Laonaco. Troopers have to be paired, as the odds are against them. Recently State Troopers have been allocated partners on the evening and night tours of duty.

In 1992, two New York City detectives were gunned down at point blank range. The suspect was being transported back to jail after his arraignment. He was in the back seat of the unmarked police detective car.

The detectives had the suspect handcuffed to a radiator in the Prosecutor's Office in County Court. The suspect observed a detective open his cabinet. The detective locked his gun in the six foot steel cabinet. The suspect managed to gain access into the cabinet and he stole the gun from the detective's locker.

The detectives should have never left the prisoner alone. The other detective should have never left his gun in his locker, especially with a convicted prisoner left alone in the room. The detectives should have searched the prisoner before they placed him in the car, especially since they left him alone.

This story is just another tragic mistake made by our brother officers. Police officers are not perfect, we are prone to making mistakes just like anyone else. The big difference is basic, we cannot afford to make a fatal mistake. Our profession does not give us a second chance. When an officer makes a mistake, it will cost him his life.

Minutes before shooting two New York City police officers in the washroom of a Brooklyn police stationhouse, a prisoner told a cellmate that he "had nothing to live for" and intended to "do something," Police Commissioner Raymond Kelly said.

In late April 1993, a drug suspect killed himself after seriously wounding two police officers by wrestling control of an officer's pistol inside the bathroom.

The shootings took place at 6:34 P.M. in a first-floor bathroom of the Seventieth Precinct on Lawrence Avenue in the Parkville section.

The wounded officers, Mary Capotosto, twenty-nine, and Robert Noblin, twenty-five, fortunately came through surgery at Kings County Hospital after being shot. They both remained in critical condition and doctors said it was too soon to know whether they would pull through.

After shooting the officers, the prisoner, Danny Cook, used the officer's last bullet to take his own life.

The suspect, Danny Cook, twenty-seven years old of Brooklyn, was arrested at 1:25 P.M. for possession of cocaine and heroin and was about to be taken to central booking in downtown Brooklyn when he asked the officers to go to the bathroom.

Officer Mary Capaposto who had been guarding him, got Officer Robert Nublis to escort him to the bathroom.

Inside the bathroom, Cook somehow grabbed Nublis' .38 caliber revolver and shot him twice in the torso. Cook was 6'2" and 230 pounds, outweighing the 5'8" Noblin by fifty-five pounds. Both officers should have been in the bathroom.

Officer Capaposto heard the shots, ran into the bathroom unarmed and was shot in the head.

Capaposto had checked her gun while fingerprinting the other prisoner. She rushed in unarmed and shouted: "He's got the cop's gun. Drop the gun. Drop the gun."

Cook, who had fired at Noblin four times, shot Capotosto

in the head, then killed himself. No other gun was fired. About ten other officers were in the stationhouse at the time.

Police officers can learn from the near fatal mistake that consequently occurred to Officers Noblin and Capotosto. I have taken hundreds of prisoners into the bathroom to make a nature call. There is no reason why a prisoner can't take a leak with the handcuffs on his wrists. If he has to use the toilet let your partner hold your gun and wait for him to finish his nature call. There also should be steel bars on the bathroom window.

The biggest problem with police departments is that there have to be certain procedures set to safeguard our lives. Routine procedures turn into fatal mistakes.

New York City officers as well as other departments have routinely taken thousands of prisoners to the bathroom without handcuffs. The procedure continued because there was never any flaws to report. I don't think you will ever again read about New York City Officers shot by an un-cuffed suspect in a bathroom.

Obviously you have to use extreme caution when you have handcuffs off of a prisoner booked for homicide, rape or possesion of heroin. A prisoner wanted on a traffic war-rant is less likely to attack you.

Fortunately for Officers Noblin and Capotosto, they have recovered from their injuries quite well.

I recall the trial of a Raritan Township man whose car struck and killed a twenty-four year old outstanding offi-cer, Trooper Thomas J. Hanratty of Elizabeth, New Jersey. The accident that claimed his life was on Route 78 near Summit, N.J. in the westbound lanes and occurred on April 2, 1992.

Hartmann, whose car struck and killed a state trooper (Thomas Hanratty) on Route, acted recklessly by drinking alcohol after taking cough medicine and then getting be-hind the wheel of his car, Prosecutor Rubin said.

Union County Assistant Prosecutor Ann R. Rubin told a jury in Elizabeth that forty-one year old John H. Hartmann, Jr., "made a decision to drink" several beers at lunch on April 2, 1992 after taking cough medicine, despite warnings on the label to avoid alcoholic beverages.

Rubin said the accident, which claimed the life of Trooper

Hanratty, was the "result of a combination of the defendant's consumption of alcohol and misuse of cold medicine."

One of the witnesses who testified said that after the fatal accident she asked Hartmann what had happened, and he responded, "I coughed."

On March 10, 1993 Hartmann was on trial before Superior Court Judge William L. E. Wertheimer. He was charged with manslaughter and death by auto. The incident occurred in Summit after the officer had given directions to a motorist who was lost.

As a police officer we know that the criminal justice system has its flaws that unfortunately favor the defendant. Such was the case when Judge Wertheimer rejected a state motion to enter into evidence a record of Hartmann's drunken driving arrest on April 1, 1988, when his blood level was determined to be .223.

A person is considered to be driving while intoxicated if his blood alcohol level is .10 or higher.

Hartmann's blood level following the incident in Summit was .05, which is below the legal limit for intoxication, according to state officials.

The laws are not stiff enough. If Hartmann had his license suspended for two years and he served a one year jail sentence. Maybe his arrest of April 1, 1988 would have turned the clock in a different direction on April 2, 1992. I truly feel that Trooper Hanratty would be alive today if Hartmann had served a one-year jail term.

The tragic death of Trooper Hanratty happened in a nightmare few seconds.

Hanratty, a member of the State Police for three years, had stopped a motorist for a motor vehicle violation along Route 78 west near the exit for Route 24, when another driver stopped to ask the trooper for directions.

Trooper Hanratty was walking back to his cruiser when suddenly he was struck by Hartmann's 1991 Hyundai on the shoulder of the roadway.

A passing motorist stopped and used the radio in Hanratty's cruiser to call the State Police barracks in Sommerville for help. Trooper Hanratty was airlifted to University Hospital in Newark, where he died twenty minutes later of massive head trauma.

Hartmann, a burglar alarm installer and repairman, remained at the scene following the accident.

In emotional, sometimes tearful testimony, witnesses in the case began recounting what they had seen at the time of the incident.

One of the witnesses, Terry Jones of Warren Township, was traveling eastbound on Route 78 on her way to Union Township when she saw Hanratty on the shoulder of the westbound lanes. She said she saw the officer walking from behind his cruiser, apparently on his way to get into his vehicle, when Hanratty suddenly "made a quick motion as if to get away."

Jones said the officer "put his hands up" and looked as if he were going to "jump on his car, and then he went into the air." She estimated Hanratty was thrown about eighteen feet. Jones said she immediately pulled her car over, ran across the highway and knelt down by Hanratty.

"The first thing I did was put my hands on him and pray for him," she said. "His head was very injured and cracked."

Members of the trooper's family, including his parents, Thomas and Francis Hanratty of Elizabeth, wept during the testimony. Hartmann's relatives sat quietly behind the defendant.

Jones said she had retrieved Hanratty's shoes and shattered service revolver from the roadside and remained at the scene until the helicopter arrived.

Assistant Union County Medical Examiner, Shiego Kondo, testified at the court trial. Kondo said that Trooper Hanratty suffered extensive skull, brain and other injuries, including two broken legs.

Detective David Alston, an undercover State Police narcotics officer, recalled how he happened on the scene while en route from Newark to the Sommerville barracks. Stuck in traffic because of the accident, Alston said he heard the words "trooper down" over his portable radio, and he made his way to the scene in his unmarked car.

Alston, who knew Hanratty, said he failed to recognize his friend immediately "because he had blood all over his face."

State Police Detective Sargeant Paul Sinckler, who also

responded to the scene and was the officer who drove Hartmann to the Somerville barracks, testified that the defendant appeared to be "very distraught" at the scene.

The defendant began weeping as Sinckler recounted how
Hartmann appeared to have "dry heaves" and was on the
verge of vomiting. He said Hartmann claimed that Hanratty had stepped into the roadway and that he never
meant to hit the trooper.

Patricia Zennario of Toms River, the lost motorist Hanratty had aided, testified she had taken the wrong exit off
the Garden State Parkway and found herself on westbound
Route 78. She said she saw Hanratty's patrol cruiser with
its flashing lights and pulled in behind his car on the shoulder of the roadway.

Zennario said Hanratty went to the passenger side of her
car and gave her directions to get back to the Parkway. She
said the trooper was on his way back to his police vehicle
when he turned and looked back at oncoming traffic.

Zennario said Hanratty suddenly had a "startled look on
his face and he turned around and started running." She
said she turned around saw "a small car" coming at her
at an angle. "It whooshed by me and struck the officer,"
Zennario said.

She said the trooper "just went straight up in the air. He
looked like a little doll flying up in the air." She said the
trooper fell back to the ground on his head.

Zennario said she saw Hartmann's car travel up the highway a short distance, veering back and forth on the roadway before coming to a stop.

A jury in Elizabeth deliberated for nearly fourteen hours
over two days before finding John Hartmann, forty, innocent of manslaughter and death by auto charges.

Superior Judge Wertheimer did find that Hartmann had
an open container of alcohol in his vehicle, his second conviction on the charge.

He ordered Hartmann to serve ten days of community
service at a local cemetery, in addition to imposing more
than $450 in fines.

The verdict stunned members of Hanratty's family and
friends. The verdict upset state troopers and police officers
across the United States.

"It's like I lost a son for nothing," said his father, Thomas

Hanratty Sr. "This sends the wrong message out to other troopers, firefighters, police officers and emergency medical personnel, that they can be killed and the people responsible go unpunished."

He said the verdict "will not bring my son back. His mother and I will always look at his picture and cry."

I personally found the verdict appalling. Trooper Hanratty was in full uniform and Hartmann negligently killed him. "How could this jury ever find him innocent? This is a travesty of justice," Officer Moravek said.

The defense attorney argued that the fatal incident was "a tragic accident that could have happened to any one of us."

He told the jury that Hanratty could have contributed to his own death by being "perilously close" to the roadway when he was struck.

The jury also heard testimony from witnesses who said Hanratty was on the shoulder of the highway when he was struck by Hartmann's 1991 blue Hyundai.

Blood and urine tests indicated Hartmann consumed more than a single beer but that his blood alcohol level at the time he struck Hartmann was approximately .06, which was well below the legal intoxication of .10.

A state trooper testified that he found an unopened sixteen-ounce can of beer and a cup containing beer residue underneath Hartmann's vehicle during an inspection of the accident scene.

All the troopers who were present when Hartmann was asked to undergo physical sobriety tests at the State Police barracks in Somerville testified that he did not appear to be intoxicated.

Hartmann gave state police investigators a statement hours after the incident and said he had taken his eyes of the road to glance into his rear view mirror. When he looked back, he saw Hanratty standing in the roadway. Hartmann said he applied his brakes and swerved to avoid hitting Hanratty.

Other witnesses testified they never saw Hartmann reduce his speed, or hit his brakes, until he pulled to a stop after hitting Hanratty.

The trooper was thrown about eighteen feet into the air and more than 150 feet down the roadway by the impact.

He suffered head, brain and internal injuries and he tragically died twenty minutes later in University Hospital in Newark.

Trooper Hanratty, a resident of Bailey Avenue in Elizabeth, was stationed at the Somerville barracks. He was a nephew of former Elizabeth Police Director Joseph Brennan and former Elizabeth Police Chief John Brennan.

Hanratty was the first New Jersey trooper to be killed in the line of duty since January 1987, when Trooper Theodore Moos from the state police barracks in Belmar was also struck by a vehicle.

In April 1993, a Route 78 West section was named after a fallen trooper. The three-mile section of the interstate, which cuts through Springfield Township, Summit, Mountainside and Berkeley Heights, will be officially known as the "Trooper Thomas Joseph Hanratty Section of the Lightning Division Memorial Highway."

A plaque commemorating Hanratty's service will be erected along the roadway as part of the Legislature's resolution, which was signed by Governor Florio.

"Trooper Hanratty was the best of what we have in our state," said Florio, flanked by members of Hanratty's family, including his father, Thomas Sr., and mother, Frances, during the brief Statehouse ceremony. "Unfortunately, his life will always be an unfinished story," the Governor added.

While the memorial is "obviously a very small gesture," Governor Florio said he is hopeful it will become a testament to "our tremendous pride and loyalty" in state troopers and a reminder to drivers.

"We hope they will become even more aware of the other people on the road and, in fact, become more concerned of everyone else's well-being," said the Governor.

"We want drivers, obviously, to grasp the deadly problem of drinking and driving."

Trooper Hanratty, was a graduate of the State Police 112th Class in 1989, and was twenty-four years old when he died.

In addition to naming the section of the highway after Hanratty, officials also announced they would create a scholarship fund in the trooper's name.

The Governor also said that state troopers "will always carry" the legacy of those who died in the line of duty.

The story of Trooper Hanratty's death and the trial that followed was intently detailed for a meaningful purpose. We can all have our own opinions on how Hartmann's trial should have been judged.

Based on all the testimony and evidence presented to the jury, I found the verdict handed down as ludicrous. The jury slapped all police officers in the face.

I share my deepest sympathy along with that of thousands of our brother officer in Trooper Hanratty's mom and dad's grief. His memory will linger with us always.

Hanratty's death is another reminder to all of us who are dressed in blue and are sworn to fight crime and serve the public.

Police officers are prone to being killed at any given minute of the day. If the Attorney General with the backing of President Clinton does not make a mandatory death sentence for assailants that kill police officers, we will continue to be a statistic of 150 officers killed each year.

I'm sure all police officers, especially highway patrol officers, will approach motorists from the passenger side when they are pulled over on the shoulder of the road.

Motorists can make our job less hazardous by pulling over to the extreme right of the shoulder. Police cruisers should also be positioned five feet to the extreme right of the shoulder. Trooper Hanratty's fatal mistake has taught us a lesson in safety when entering and exiting our police cruisers.

On October 15, 1991 a national police officers memorial was dedicated. Officers who sacrificed their lives and died valiantly can be found among the 13,267 names currently engraved on the walls of the national law officers memorial, which is dedicated to all federal, state and local law enforcement officers in the United States. The memorial is located in Washington, D.C.

As I close this tragic chapter on police officer's fatal mistakes, another officer is added to the list. Fortunately this officer will get a second chance to correct his mistake.

On March 23rd, 1994 a Newark Police narcotics detective reacted to a dangerous situation that has killed hundreds of officers in the past ten years.

As you read this chapter you realize how important it is to learn and understand the Attorney General guidelines involving reasonable belief, probable cause and the risk involved in a deadly force situation. Proper use of probable cause and deadly force is coordinated.

An off-duty Newark police officer was shot in the knee as he intervened in an armed robbery at a convenience store.

Detective Michael Days, thirty-two, suffered a flesh wound when he tried to stop a gunman who was fleeing from the Quick Stop Supermarket at 329 South Eleventh Street, at 10 A.M., said Detective Daniel Collins, a police spokesman.

Daye, who was in street clothes, stopped at the store at Thirtieth Avenue to buy a newspaper, Collins said. He was walking into the store when the gunman stepped outside past him.

"I stopped to buy the *Star-Ledger,* and as I was walking toward the store, the man walked past me real quick," Daye said from home after surgery on the four-inch wound that snaked down the side of his left knee.

"As he walked by, I saw a black thing in the waistband of his pants," Daye said. Daye could have reacted instantly if he had knowledge and proper training regarding "probable cause." As a police officer, Daye was justified using the Terry act to pat down the individual.

Then the owner walked out and Daye, noticing his agitation, asked what the problem was.

"He told me that the guy walking away from us had robbed him," Daye said, adding he realized the black object he had noticed was a gun.

Daye identified himself as a policeman and yelled for the gunman to stop.

"He turned and said something and fired a shot," Daye said. "I had already pulled my badge out when he turned. But I didn't have a chance to get cover."

Officers who are afraid or are unsure if they are justified to point their weapon at a suspect can learn from Daye's near fatal mistake. Pull your gun out first and if you have the time pull out your badge. Don't give the assailant the advantage. You will only have a split second to decide in the use of deadly force. The assailant should have been killed when he pointed the gun at Daye. Let us not forget that we are trained to shoot the target in a mass zone. You cannot quality at the police range if eighty-five percent of your bullets are not fired in the mass zone. I don't like to go to police officers' funerals. At the time of this writing, it was just a week ago on March 18 that I attended New York City Police Officer McDonald's funeral.

When you have to control a situation where the fear of your life is at stake, always draw your weapon out when you are confronting a suspect. If your not sure of the Attorney General's guidelines in a dangerous situation always remember this: "It is better to have a jury of twenty-three grand jury members reviewing your actions than to have six pallbearers carrying your casket down the stairs of the funeral home."

After being shot, Daye crawled to his car and called for help.

"I just wanted them (police) to catch this guy," Daye said, adding he thought of his nine-year-old son, Tyrone, and his mother Shirley, as he waited for help. "I was hoping I'd be all right for their sake."

The gunman fled in a brown Toyota parked on South Twelveth Street. He had stolen $150 from the store and a portable radio.

"I'll be taking a few days off," Daye said, adding he had to wait until the doctor's discharge him. "But I'm ready to go back to work," Daye said. He is a five year veteran, calling the job as a police officer "the best in the world. Especially in the narcotics squad."

Officer Daye's courage, fortitude and dedication is to be commended. He will be presented with a class "A" valor award. I'm sure his next encounter will have a different result.

Another nightmare has been imbedded into my mind and thousands of officers across the country. When I read about N.Y. Police Officer Shawn MacDonald's fatal encounter with two robbery suspects it truly struck me personally. It was as if a lightning bolt passed violently thorough my body and soul.

It was just a short time ago on June 17th, 1993 (Refer to Chapter 23) when I left my assigned post. A citizen came into Police Headquarters and stated he was just robbed by six robbery suspects. I left my post immediately and contained the assailants by ordering the suspects to drop to the ground. They were ordered at gunpoint and we awaited for backup units before they were patted down and handcuffed.

I was fortunate that on this occasion as well as other dangerous situations that I was not killed.

Officer Shawn Macdonald, twenty-six years old and assigned to the Forty-fourth Precinct in the Bronx, was gunned down and killed on March 16, 1994. He was the first officer killed in New York City in 1994. He served the City of New York gallantly for 1 and a $1/2$ years. Macdonald leaves behind a wife and two young children.

Once again we can and will learn from the fatal mistake that has occurred here.

Officer Macdonald was informed by a citizen that a robbery in progress was occurring at a store near his assigned post.

MacDonald was detailed to an abandoned building that was a hazard to anyone who would enter it. His assignment was to keep intruders out of the building.

Macdonald left his post and did not hesitate to respond to the scene of a robbery.

Macdonald displayed the kind of courage, bravery and fortitude that we all hope we are capable of attaining. He did not fear for his life and truly showed the confidence that he could apprehend and contain the suspects without incident.

We are the "Blue Warriors" of the cities and towns, sworn to protect the property and lives of the citizen. This is the job we chose; there are no guarantees.

Officer Macdonald chose to be called a "Blue Warrior" to excell "Above the line of Duty." No one ordered Macdonald to leave his assignment and take the extreme risk he chose to undertake. Let us all remember Shawn as a bona fide hero who sacrificed his life to prevent these robbery victims from being killed by the assailants.

Macdonald displayed his ability as a "Blue Warrior" and he will always be remembered as a member of New York City's Top Cops.

We can only speculate as to why Macdonald chose to handcuff these suspects. He placed himself in an extremely dangerous and vulnerable position.

We can't turn back the clock and bring him back to life. However we can learn from his fatal mistake.

We cannot second guess and do not have the right to question why he took this type of evasive action. We were not there and do not know what took place.

Every situation is different and maybe he had no other options available. Let us all as brother Police Officers respect his bravery & courage. Let us remember his mistake and learn from it.

Let us adjust our training methods.

Your options in this type of dangerous situation are few, but here are a few actions that will prevent other officers from receiving an Inspector's Funeral.

1. Use extreme caution when entering the store and have your gun position in a combat form.
2. Hold the suspects at gunpoint. Position yourself so that they cannot shoot at you from point blank range. Order the suspects to drop to the ground, belly down, and hands and arms in from of their bodies. Use your weak hand to transmit from your radio. Keep your gun and eyes fixed on the suspects at all times. If the suspect moves his hand and draws a gun, *don't* give him the order to freeze. If you observe the gun, the fear of your life is imminent; fire shots at him in the *mass zone* as you are trained at the police range.
3. *Do not search or handcuff suspects when you are alone.*
4. If you have to handcuff the suspects because the situation has left you with no alternatives, A. Order the suspects to lay face down with their hands gripped behind their heads. Place them five feet apart horizontally. Keep your gun in your strong hand. Pat down the first suspect with your gun fixed on his head approximately 2 feet from it so he can't grab it. Do a pat down from top to bottom and handcuff him using your weak hand. Handcuff his left wrist and than his right wrist. Keep the cuffs on tight and he should be secured with his hands secured from his back. Now go and do the second suspect; however, keep an eye on the second suspect when you are cuffing suspect one. It is always a good policy to keep two pair of handcuffs on you at all times.

Officer. Macdonald received a full inspector's Funeral

with thousand of officers from across the U.S. paying their last respects to a fallen hero. He received the city's highest honor, The Medal of Valor Award, which was presented to his wife.

May god rest his soul in peace. On behalf of the Newark Police Department we extend our deepest sympathy to Officer Shawn Macdonald's family.

22 Learning the Intangible Dangers

Police officers have to focus on the intangible dangers involved in a domestic violence altercation. Thousands of officers are seriously injured during the violent fights that occur during family disputes. They occasionally escalate into full blown heated fights between next of kin and husbands and wives. Hundreds of people involved in these confrontations are killed by gunfire and knives.

Police officers have to use extreme caution. They have to be alert and ready for any given situation to arise. Police officers always have to gain control of the situation. Most importantly keep your attention on both participants involved.

Officers have to be aware of the new state laws enforced in 1992. These new laws have strengthened police powers involving domestic violence arrests. In the past officers tried to adjust family altercations. Officer now have to use good discretion when they handle a domestic violence situation.

Using the State Attorney's domestic violence guidelines, officers are now enpowered to be the complainant if the victim refuses to have her husband arrested. If there is any evidence that she has been assaulted by her boyfriend or husband, officers at the scene are required to execute the arrest of the assailant.

Police officers are reminded that if you have an assignment regarding domestic violence, if the complainant (victim) shows you a court restraining order, the husband or boyfriend has to be arrested for violating the order.

These new domestic violence laws were passed for an important reason. The State Attorney General wants women to be protected from their spouses.

The plight of the battered wife is a sad reality. Somewhere in the United States a woman is assaulted by her spouse once every fifteen seconds.

As a police officer one of the most important factors for you to have knowledge of is probable cause. It is extremely important to know when to execute proper action when you are involved in a probable cause situation. Learning all the aspects of of probable cause will determine your decisions in thousands of assignments throughout your career in law enforcement.

Always remember that probable cause is a strong asset to use as a co-pilot. It will guide you to use good discretion in a given situation. It will back up your judgment for the reason why you reacted to a particular situation. It will provide you with the justification as to why you acted as you did on a particular assignment.

Remember that you should always have the advantage over all situations that are dangerous to you and your partner.

When you are dispatched to the scene of an assignment involving a suspicious person with a gun: For example a black male, 5'10", 157 pounds, age thirty to thirty-three. He is wearing a green shirt, brown pants, white sneakers. He has brown hair and a mustache.

When you and your partner arrive at the scene, you observe a black male fitting the description broadcast by the dispatcher. Don't make the fatal mistake that has over the past ten years caused the death of hundreds of police officers.

Always remember that you have the probable cause to take your gun out of the holster and have it pointed at the suspect. Don't walk within ten feet of the suspect and order him to put his hands over his head and freeze. Using that kind of technique can cost you your life. You want to eliminate every possibility of getting into a shootout at point blank range. You can avoid it by taking cover behind a car, tree or house. There will be occasions in your career when you will have no cover. When that situation occurs, it will be your split second decision that will determine your fate.

The key element is gaining control of the situation. With your gun drawn on the suspect the advantage will be in your favor.

By taking cover in a tense situation you will diminish the chance of the suspect having the opportunity to shoot you and your partner. It will also avoid an imminent deadly shootout that can cause stray bullets to kill an innocent person.

Once you have control of the situation, order the suspect to lie flat on the ground. Order the suspect to be on his stomach with his arms and legs spread apart. If there is a building where the suspect was caught, order him to place his legs spread apart and to keep his hands placed on the wall. Your partner should search the suspect from top to bottom. It is imperative that you search his body area between the legs where his testicles and butt are. Use caution when you are searching his pockets or jacket. The suspect could have a tainted needle. You want to avoid getting pricked by a tainted needle. While you are patting down the suspect, your partner should be two feet from your left side and his gun should be pointed at him at all times. If the suspect is armed he can reach in his pocket in a split second and blow both of you away. Keep your eyes on him constantly. If the suspect has a weapon or drugs, a complete search is justified.

Call for a backup unit if you are working alone. Don't search a suspect alone without another officer present.

After completing a pat down of the suspect, if he has no weapons or drugs found in his possession, record check the individual and execute an interrogation report. Keep a record of your interrogation sheets for future reference.

Occasionally during your career, an arrogant person will be upset that you detained and patted him down. He will complain that you violated his rights. He will write your commanding officer a letter. He will say that you had no right pointing a gun at him. He will tell your Captain that you had no right to search him.

This situation occurs to thousands of police officers who are doing their job. The essential procedure that you executed is going to save your life.

Remember that you were dispatched to the scene of a man with a gun. You observed a man fitting the description. You had the probable cause to have your gun drawn on the suspect.

After completing your search and record check of the individual, if he is in the right now, be cordial with the individual. You can explain to him that you were dispatched to the scene warning of a man with a gun. Unfortunately he fit the description of the suspect.

Veteran police officers in Newark will recall a highly decorated detective who retired from the Newark Police Department. His name was Detective Dave Toma. He was a well-known detective who used hundreds of disguises.

I recall that on a few television shows, Toma always boasted about how fortunate he was in regard to drawing his gun. Toma said he rarely had to draw his gun in his police career.

Dave Toma was fortunate that he rarely had to take his gun out of his holster. However, I don't know how many situations he was in when he should have pointed his gun at a suspect. How many times did Toma risk his life by not drawing his gun on a suspect possibly armed with a gun?

The breed of young criminals today would not permit Toma to survive. There is no second chance on the street today. An armed suspect will blow you away in a second. Try approaching an armed suspect without your gun drawn. Sooner than you think we will be giving you a full inspector's funeral.

I have been a member of the Newark Police Department for twenty-four years. I have confronted hundreds of extremely dangerous situations. I have drawn my weapon hundreds of times on different situations. I have taken my gun out of my holster when I approached a potentially dangerous situation thousands of times. If you have the probable cause to draw your weapon, don't hesitate to have your gun at the ready to use. Those split seconds can make the difference.

There are too many officers dead today because they were afraid that they would face departmental charges for taking their gun out of their holster.

I'm asking all police officers to carefully read about and understand probable cause and the procedures on the use of deadly force. If you are not sure when you can use deadly force, the split second that you hesitate in a deadly confrontation will cost you your life.

Another key element to survival when you approach a potentially dangerous situation: Use good discretion and always have a clear head at all times. Don't take your family problems to work with you.

If you have the probable cause to have your gun out of its holster to be used in a split second, dangerous situation, do not hesitate to have your gun drawn and ready to fire at point blank range. Reasonable belief and probable cause is the key element.

Always refresh your memory in reference to your City and State Regulations regarding the proper use of deadly force.

I have observed hundreds of police officers over the years who have responded to burglaries in progress. Eighty percent of these officers never drew their weapon. When an officer gets out of his police cruiser, he should take his gun out of the holster. A police officer needs to have that split second advantage when he is surprised with a burglar with a deadly weapon.

A knife or gun is a deadly weapon to be confronted with. An assailant can cut you to pieces with a knife.

The reason why I stress that all police officers have their gun drawn when approaching a situation that justifies the possible use of deadly force is that those precious seconds that you save are the advantage you need when you confront an armed suspect. By the time you get out of the car and observe a suspect with a gun, a volley of bullets can be in your chest.

Remember the view and reaction that the suspect observes. You are in uniform and he reacts to a police officer who has caught him in the act of a crime.

When a suspicious person is in the area where a crime has occurred, the probable cause involved in the situation empowers you to have your gun drawn. What is essential is that you do not overreact to a situation.

A person in the area where a burglary occurs does not necessarily make the person the actual burglar. It does empower you to have the probable cause to draw your gun on the potential suspect. The key element in a possible dangerous situation is to have complete control. Police officers do not have the luxury of assuming a situation. There is always a remote possibility that the suspect is an innocent person in the wrong place at the wrong time.

CONCEALED WEAPONS

Before you and your partner get into your police cruiser, open the rear doors and carefully check the seats. You may be surprised to find a gun, razor, or knives embedded there by suspects. Be extremely careful during the search. A tainted needle can be wedged in the seats. Getting pricked by a tainted needle can lead to serious infection.

Officers will ask how did this gun get in this police car? Probably a sloppy search by another unit on a previous tour of duty. Chances are the officers did not properly search the prisoner. The suspect arrested may have had the weapon, perhaps a gun concealed between his legs and it was snuggled, tightly wedged into his testicles and butt. While he was being transported to the precinct to be slated, the suspect planted the gun in the seats. The suspect avoids being charged with possession of a gun.

There are a lot of police officers who are searching their prisoners incorrectly. Officers are reluctant to search the area of a man's testicles and butt. If you are one of the thousands of officers that has this attitude, I strongly suggest that you do a complete search on all suspects arrested. A failure to execute a top to bottom search can lead to your death.

DEADLY FORCE

As a police officer it is essential that you have all the knowledge of intangible factors involving the proper use of deadly force.

In a twenty-five year career, a police officer in a small community will usually not be involved in a fatal shooting. One member of the entire police force will shoot and kill an armed suspect. The statistic increases as you step into the cities. In Newark, New Jersey, with a force of 1,100 police officers, less than 100 police officers will be involved in a deadly shootout in their career. Narcotic Detectives are involved in more shootouts than any other division.

In twenty-four years of service in the Newark Police Department I have been involved in three deadly shootouts. I know how important it is to have the proper knowledge involving deadly force. Having only a split second to make a decision. Knowing when you can use deadly force will someday save your life.

The basic rules of thumb involving deadly force: The cops shoot with deadly accuracy when your life is on the line. Don't shoot at a suspect who is fleeing the scene.

Trying to take out an armed suspect who is holding a hostage: Those situations occur in the movies. Realistically you are not going to risk shooting the victim. Call your command for a sergeant to have a marksman take out the assailant. There are too many intangible risks involved in a shootout. You do not want to have a stray bullet hit an innocent person.

I truly feel that we have watched too many police movies and television police series. How many movies have you seen where the suspect has the gun pointed at a police officer. The officer shouts out. "Freeze this is the police, drop your weapon." If that is your way of controlling a dangerous situation, "Bang you're dead."

Hundreds of police officers are dead today because they gave the assailant the advantage. By the time you order the suspect to freeze and drop the gun, he will fire his gun at point blank range. Multiple gunshot wounds will be in your chest seconds before you have the opportunity to defend yourself. (I'm asking of one favor from every police officer reading this book. Please wear a vest.)

When an armed suspect has a gun pointed at you, he

has signed his own death with a noose clinged around his neck. Shoot the suspect in the zone that you are trained at the police range. You are not trained to shoot a suspect in the leg or hand. An assailant will blow your head off. If you think he is aiming for your arm or legs, you are sadly mistaken. Forget about those cops and robbers movies.

If your first shot brings down the suspect there is no need to fire more than one shot. If a suspect is high on drugs it will take several shots to bring him down.

You might consider yourself an excellent shooter. It is an entirely different ballgame when you are in a potential shootout. An officer cannot be instructed or advised on how many shots he should fire from his gun. There are intangible factors that have to be considered. If you are within ten feet of an armed suspect, two shots should bring down an assailant. If you are fifteen to twenty feet from an armed suspect you would fire several shots at the suspect. You can only hope that one of those bullets will bring the suspect down.

One of the most important elements that you always want to remember: If there are innocent bystanders who are several feet in back of the suspect, try your best to take cover and avoid a shootout. An officer does not want an innocent person killed by a stray bullet. If there are no options, make your first shot a deadly bullet that disarms the assailant.

DEADLY HERO

Don't try to be a hero, heroes are born everyday. As a police officer you will have plenty of situations in your career that will reward you as a hero.

Police officers are all true heroes who have dedicated their lives to protect the lives and property of all people.

It is important for all officers to realize that a knife or razor is a deadly weapon that can endanger your life with the same capability as a gun.

When a situation arises involving a suspect armed with a large knife, small knife or a machete in his hand, hold your ground if the suspect is in a menacing position to attack you. One warning with your gun pointed at him from point blank range of ten feet is sufficient. A distance of ten feet is as far a limit that you can safely hold your ground. One warning to drop the weapon justifies your reaction to an extremely dangerous situation. Don't take the position that you can disarm the assailant. The assailant can very easily slice you to pieces.

One stab wound to your chest can become fatal. Don't risk being a dead hero. If you are a first degree black belt, obviously you don't need a gun to disarm him.

When your warning fails prepare to defend your life. The assailant has made his move to seriously hurt you. Shoot the assailant with as many bullets as it justifiably takes to bring him down. If the assailant is mentally unstable or high on drugs, several shots will have to be on target to stop him.

In 1993, two Newark police officers were confronted by a mentally disturbed brute. He was continuously beating up his mother. He was a husky, exceptionally strong person who could overpower three men in a blink of an eye.

When the officers arrived at the scene, the suspect was armed with a large machete. He charged forward swinging the machete at the officers. He was warned to drop the knife. When the assailant came within ten feet of the officers, both officers fired several shots at the assailant. An autopsy revealed that the assailant was shot thirteen times. Incredibly only one shot critically wounded the man.

When an assailant is threatening you with a baseball bat use extreme caution. One blow to your head and your brains will be scattered on the ground. Only you can decide if the danger of your life is imminent.

If the assailant is mentally disturbed he will not obey your order to drop the bat. Suddenly the assailant will attack you with the bat. He has the capability of killing you at will.

Every situation that you face will have a different approach. Your discretion and the probable cause surrounding the circumstances will decide the assailant's fate.

The use of deadly force is one of the toughest reactions an officer has to make. An officer has only a split second to decide whether a suspect will live or die. The proper use of deadly force has a fine line. The threat of your life is a key element.

The most important rule of thumb to remember regarding the use of deadly force: Do not shoot at an assailant unless there is an imminent threat to your life. Exhaust all means possible to avoid shooting an unarmed suspect.

Only you can decide if shooting a suspect will save your life. Anyone who attempts to rob an officer of his gun is a danger to the officer and to the society we live in. His intention are of deadly proportions.

Every situation that you encounter will have a different outcome involving the use of deadly force. Read and learn all the intangible circumstances involved in the proper use of deadly force.

I have been fortunate enough to publish my story for all to read. I could have been killed on several occasions during my career. I was fortunate that the bullets fired at me in those deadly shootouts never hit their mark.

No doubt that one of the key factors why six pallbearers aren't carrying my casket to a grave. The knowledge I have grasped combining probable cause and the proper use of deadly force saved my life.

Having my gun out of my holster when I exited the police cruiser: those vital seconds made the difference.

23 Officers Can Make a Difference

Working at Newark Police Headquarters the past six years I have absorbed a great deal of knowledge by digesting over 200,000 crimes committed. Learning the criminals unique "modus operandi" and passing it onto the public is essential. The chapter "Preventing you from becoming a Victim of a Crime" points that out in detail. Having knowledge of a criminal's technique will someday save your life.

I have gained the respect of victims who have reported crimes at headquarters. You learn a valuable presence of mind by showing the victim that you are sincerely concerned for his welfare.

Recently a victim asked me for help in regard to a restraining order. The story is detailed in a chapter on domestic violence.

I was rewarded with the news from Lieutenant Beard that the assailant was arrested for aggravated assault with intent to kill, violation of a restraining order and terroristic threats.

Realizing the reality that the victim's life would be safe-
guarded. Taking the time to make an effort to effect the
arrest of the stalker. Going above the line of duty makes
the job of a police officer worth its weight in gold.

I recall another incident in May, 1993. A fifteen year old
Jersey City teenager came to police headquarters for help.
She reported that her twenty-six year old boyfriend choked
her in a fierce stranglehold and punched her several times
in the face. She feared for her life and pleaded with me not
to arrest him.

I asked her why she did not want him arrested. She hysterically blurted out, "If I sign a complaint and have him
arrested, he is going to kill me."

I advised and assured the victim that under the new domestic laws in the State of New Jersey. If you choose to
relinquish the charges against him, the police officer's can
sign the complaint against him.

Given that advice the victim took a deep breath and
calmed down. She was astonished when I told her that we
would arrest him on our own complaint.

I advised the suspect that if he had a beef about being
locked up, "You can confront me for affecting your imminent arrest. Your girlfriend is no longer the complainant."

I went to the men's room on a nature call. When I returned the victim had left the building. I said to the suspect,
"Where did your girlfriend go?" He replied, "She told me
that she was going to walk to Penn Station and take a train
to Jersey City."

Assistant Identification Chief Michael Sassone (Newark
Police Identification Bureau) was sitting with me at Police
Headquarters. I asked Mike if he would go with me in my
car to find the victim. I told Mike that I was deeply concerned that the young girl might be raped or killed by an
assailant. At 4:00 A.M. the risk of becoming a serious crime
victim is great.

Chief Sassone and I conferred about her welfare. We did
not rule out the possibility that her boyfriend would lash
out on her for reporting the incident to the police.

Chief Sassone and I knew that we were violating police
rules and regulations by leaving our assigned post. However we both agreed that the safety of the victim was our
first priority. Calling for a police unit would not help us. I

did not want precious minutes wasted. She was left in a vulnerable position.

My discretion told me to take a police action and concern about breaking rules was secondary to finding the victim. I truly felt that my concern for a juvenile would justify my actions. I submitted a Captain's report on the entire sequence of events.

Our only thought was to make sure that the young lady would not become another tragic victim of a dangerous society.

Chief Sassone and I got in my car and proceeded to find the teenage victim. After about five minutes of intently looking for her, Chief Sassone observed her walking east on Market Street near the corner of McCarter Highway.

I got out of the car and talked with her. "Young lady, you're going back with us to Police Headquarters. I'm going to call your mother up and have her take you home. When we find your boyfriend, he is going to be arrested." We observed the suspect walking on Edison Place near McCarter Highway. The suspect was transported by East District Officers to Police Headquarters.

I notified the teenager's mother in New Jersey. She was elated when I advised her that her daughter was in police custody. She came down to police headquarters. She advised me the suspect was forbidden from seeing her. She had a friend drive her down to pick up her daughter. The suspect was slated at the east district and charged with assault. He also had a open bench warrant.

The mother of the child was extremely thankful for the concern we showed on behalf of the safety for her child.

I personally thanked Assistant Chief Michael Sassone for backing me up. On several occasions in his twenty-five year career Mike Sassone has held robbery suspects that he observed commit a crime. He is a credit to the Newark Police Department. His exemplary courage has shined through on many occasions.

On April 7, 1993 Mrs. Candice Hall came into police headquarters emotionally distraught. She asked me where can I obtain a marriage annulment. I found it strange that a person would ask for an annulment on a Saturday afternoon.

My first instinct was that she must be a battered wife, victim of an abusive husband.

Mrs. Hall stated, "Last night my husband Vincent Guinyard punched me several times in the face and chest. He put a gun to my head and said he was going to blow my head off."

I advised Mrs. Hall that she needed more than an annulment. I executed a terroristic threat with intent to kill report. "Your husband has to be arrested as soon as possible." "My husband is outside sitting on the grass by the City Hall annex on Franklin Street," Mrs. Hall said.

I was surprised when she told me that her husband was outside. I called the target team detectives upstairs, no one was there.

I asked Detective Walker and Issac to back me up. I advised them that the victim's husband was outside and armed with a gun.

We observed the suspect (Guinyard) sitting on the rail adjacent to the City Hall side entrance on Franklin Street.

When Detective Issac and I got within 100 feet of the suspect, Guinyard saw us approaching. I was in uniform so Guinyard knew we were coming for him.

Guinyard fled west on Franklin Street. We pursued Guinyard across the intersection of Broad and Franklin Streets. Guinyard jumped over a fence on Hill Street.

We lost sight of Guinyard for five minutes. We split up in three directions. Detective Issac apprehended the suspect at Washington Street and Court Street. A passing motorist trapped Guinyard in an alleyway.

We failed to find the gun that Guinyard had ditched. An East District Unit arrived at Police Headquarters. Guinyard was slated at the East District and charged with terroristic threats, aggravated assault with intent to kill and possession of a gun.

We were fortunate to apprehend the suspect. More than likely he would have killed his wife when she arrived home. Guinyard was angry that his wife double-crossed him. Guinyard came down to City Hall to get an annulment. He never gave it a second thought that his wife was having him arrested.

Mrs. Hall took a deep breath and a sigh of relief was

evident. She was absolutely elated when I advised her that we apprehended and arrested her husband.

On another occasion a Newark resident Khayyam Bey, twenty-two years old, walked into Police Headquarters at 3:51 A.M.

"Officer I'm turning myself in, I just killed my girl-friend," Bey said. I questioned the suspect, "Sir how do you know that you killed your girlfriend?"

"I strangled her until she was no longer breathing. Her face has turned dark blue. She is dead, officer," Bey said. Although Mr. Bey was highly intoxicated and appeared to be a sick individual, I believed that he was telling me the truth. I handcuffed Bey and advised him of his rights.

I called Lieutenant Norvilas and advised him of the situation. "A Police unit and a supervisor is responding to your location, Officer Moravek," Norvilas said.

Sergeant Robert Gerardo and Officers Headd and Michael Irasella arrived at police headquarters. Sergeant Gerardo talked with the suspect. He confessed that he strangled his girlfriend.

Bey led the officers to her body in their Society Hill condominium. When the suspect, Bey, arrived at the condominium with the two patrol officers and Sergeant Gerardo, they were met by his mother, Michelle Bey, who was watching the little boy.

Officers had been to the condominium at 3:13 A.M. on a domestic violence call but left twenty minutes later when no one answered the door, Sergeant Evans said.

The defendant told police he had been watching television with Daniels and the toddler when an argument erupted and Bey strangled her to death.

Bernadette Daniels, twenty-five of Vaughn Drive, the mother of an eighteen-month-old boy, was found dead on her bed about 4 A.M. said Sgt. Alonzo Evans, a police spokesman.

I have come to realize that over the twenty-four years that have passed by, the most rewarding part of police work is giving support to the victims of crime—showing compassion, understanding, and the willingness to care for their well-being. The victims will deeply appreciate your concern for them.

On July 29, 1989, I received one of the nicest letters from

a victim's mother. The letter was sent to Police Director Claude Coleman and to the editor of the Newark Star Ledger. I was amazed when I realized that their are people who truly appreciate when an officer extends himself to a victim of a crime.

On July 28, 1989 a young lady named Vicki Plowden approached the front desk at Newark Police Headquarters. She was distraught and upset as she cried while telling me the incident that occurred to her.

Miss Plowden was involved in an auto accident that could have been fatal. The driver of the other vehicle became violent. "He threatened to pour gasoline on my car if I didn't leave, Miss Plowden said."

Her voice was trembling as she told me that for three hours she waited for the police to arrive at the scene. To her dismay the police never arrived.

She was extremely upset as she told me what occurred to her on the evening of July 27, 1989 at 11:00 P.M.

"I walked into police headquarters and explained the situation to the desk officer. Officer Victor George was very rude and abrupt. He told me that he did not have an accident book available to execute a report. He ended the conversation by advising me to go home and call for a police car to respond to my house," Miss Plowden said. Miss Plowden told me an incredible story that would have scared the living daylights out of anyone.

Plowden was involved in a terrible nightmare that could have easily cost her life. She displayed courage when the other driver threatened to pour gas on her car.

An Internal Affairs Investigation was ordered by Police Director Coleman. The investigation into the response time discovered the police car was sent to the wrong location. Miss Plowden gave the radio dispatcher the wrong address.

Director Coleman apologized to the Plowden family. Officer George should have been sensitive to the terrible ordeal Miss Plowden experienced. Officer George should have notified his desk lieutenant to have an officer bring an accident book to his desk, Director Coleman said.

Director Coleman transferred Officer George to the Record Identification Bureau the next day. Officer Marty Kimball was assigned to the desk.

I apologized to the distraught young lady. "I will do

everything possible to regain your confidence in the Newark Police Department," Moravek said.

I made out an accident report and an 802 terroristic threats report. I notified the south district detectives of the victim's report.

Miss Plowden left police headquarters with a smile on her face.

I was elated when later detectives both told me that the Plowden family wrote a letter to the Newark Star Ledger and to Director Coleman.

The letter read as follows:

"OFFICER COMMENDED FOR KINDNESS."

Dear Editor:

On July 27, 1989 my daughter was involved in an automobile accident which could have been fatal because the driver of the other car threatened to throw gasoline on her. She called the police and waited a couple of hours and no one responded to her call.

Later that evening, about 11:00 A.M., she went to police headquarters and explained the situation to an officer who was very rude and abrupt, and told her he did not have any police reports available and to go home and wait for a radio car.

On July 28, 1989, my daughter returned and explained what happened to Police Officer Moravek. He immediately expressed concern and apologized to my daughter about what had occurred. He gladly took all the information and was deeply concerned. While sitting there, another lady commented on how nice and pleasant Officer Moravek is to everyone.

Thank God for Officer Moravek. He should be commended for his efforts and his kindness shown toward his fellow man. We need more people like him. We, the Plowden family, salute him and thank him for being concerned about a human being who was in distress. We will never forget him. He will always be remembered in our prayers.

Mr. and Mrs. Thomas Plowden,
Newark

After reading this letter and the newspaper article I was numb. Our best achievements as police officers is when people like the Plowden family take the time to show their appreciation in a letter.

I would choose to receive five letters a year from victims of a crime. A letter of gratitude is appreciated more than a class "A" valor award.

As you have witnessed in this chapter, officers can make a difference when they go that extra yard. There are thousands of situations that you will encounter.

Your decision to react to the circumstances involved can unknowingly save the life of a domestic violence victim.

On May 30, 1993 a distraught woman walked into police headquarters. Mrs. Ewok had fear in her eyes as she told me her ordeal.

"Officer Moravek, my husband began to choke me on the corner of Franklin Street and Mulberry Street. We were at dinner earlier and my husband became violent. He said he would kill me if I went to the police station. He said he would kill me and my seven-year-old daughter if I divorce him," Mrs. Ewok said.

Twenty minutes later after I was completing my report charging Mr. Ewok with assault and terroristic threats.

Suddenly a man came into police headquarters. "Officer Moravek, that's my husband and he is going to kill me," Mrs. Ewok blurted out.

Within seconds, I handcuffed the suspect, Austin Ewok. "Mr. Ewok, you have the audacity to come into police headquarters to kill your wife in front of me."

Mr. Ewok was advised of his rights and slated at the East District by Officer Roberto. The judge set a "no bail" on his charge of terroristic threats.

When a complainant reports that they have been threatened and they fear for their life, I notify the detectives to make every effort to arrest him as soon as possible. When a victim states that her estranged husband is at home, she is given the option of going to a home for battered women in Belleville.

On a hot humid night of June 17, 1993 at 10:50 P.M. a victim of a strong-arm robbery approached the front desk at police headquarters.

"Officer Moravek, I was just robbed by four black males and two black females. Two black males were kicking me in the legs and chest. The other two males were holding me down. They took my $17 green card. Officer, this happened two minutes ago by the bank on Broad and Green Street," Mr. Gavin T. Sears said.

I asked the victim if he could identify the suspects. Sears said yes. "In which direction were the suspects fleeing?" I asked.

"They are walking south on Broad Street, between Franklin and Walnut Streets," Sears said.

I notified the police dispatch that a strong-arm robbery had occurred at Broad Street and Green Street orchestrated by four black males and two black females. The dispatcher said he had no one available. I notified the Lieutenant that I needed a unit.

I requested that the dispatcher have a backup unit converge on Walnut and Broad Streets. The suspects should be in that vicinity, walking south on Broad Street.

Fortunately as I was running out the door, two off-duty officers were walking up the stairs. Officer Salters stated, "We're going to the Record Bureau to pick up a copy of a police report." I'd never met either officer. They properly identified themselves as Newark Police Officers from the west district.

"Officer Simmons and Officer Salters, would you back me up on a dangerous venture? I wanted to collar six robbery suspects that just robbed Mr. Sears on Broad and Green Streets. The suspects are four black males and two females. They are walking south on Broad Street. Mr. Sears stated they did not show any weapons. We have to be extremely careful, they might be armed with weapons," I said.

Officer Anthony Simmons and Officer Keith Salters never hesitated to oblige me.

Both officers simultaneously said, "Let's go, Moravek, and try and collar them."

We carefully canvassed the area along Broad Street. When we got to Broad and East Kinney Street, we observed three black males.

Mr. Sears yelled out in an excited voice. "That's the guys that robbed me." Officer Moravek asked him again, "Mr. Sears, are you sure they are the robbery suspects?"

"Yes, I'm sure these are the guys that robbed me," Mr. Sears said.

We drove the car slowly east on E. Kinney Street. When we passed the suspects we all got out of the car seconds apart.

With my gun firmly gripped in my right hand I took a combat position.

"You're under arrest, don't move, slowly walk to the wall and keep your hands behind your back," I sternly ordered. With our guns pointed at point blank range we had the suspects contained. If they were armed, chances were slim that they would make a move for their guns. We surprised them and had the situation under control. We avoided a deadly shootout. The quick containment of three of the robbery suspects was successful.

We caught the three other suspects a half a block east on E. Kinney Street.

Officer Salters and Simmons searched the suspects for weapons.

Mr. Sears positively identified the four black males. Mr. Sears did not want to press charges against the two females. They did not harm me, Sears said.

Within minutes after requesting for an assist officer, five units arrived. Captain Brennen was on the scene and he ordered the officers to take the prisoners to the East District.

Officers Simmons and Salters slated the four suspects on a charge of strong armed robbery. The two females were interrogated, record checked and released. I know how dangerous it is to attempt to contain six robbery suspects. Two chapters from the wild west district in the early 1980s can attest to that fact. I was involved in deadly shootouts twice by myself.

"I'm glad you guys are with me. I really didn't want to confront six robbers by myself," I said to Officers Salters and Simmons.

Officers Anthony Simmons Id 6962 and Officer Keith Salters Id 6967 are a credit to the Newark Police Department. Their dedication to duty was exemplified when they risked their lives to apprehend six robbery suspects.

We were fortunate that none of us were seriously injured. If they have been armed with guns and had committed other robberies with possible homicide charges pending, we would have been involved in a deadly shootout.

Officer from the east district and the detectives and other officers from the north, west and south districts heard of the excellent teamwork that prevailed.

The extra effort that we can extend to the victims of crime

is what being a cop is all about. We the police officers of Newark and across the nation can make a big difference.

I personally thanked Officers Anthony Simmons and Keith Salters. I extended my thanks to Captain Brennen and the east district units that arrived in a few minutes after an assist officer was requested. My sincere gratitude to all of you.

Officers Simmons and Salter were not obligated to risk their lives. I of all the officers involved did not have to leave my post.

I could have written out the police report and have the units in the east try to apprehend the suspects.

We are undermanned by a shortage of 400 police officers. I understand that the entire country is under fire. We the police officers who are sworn to enforce the laws have to put out an extra effort. If I can do it, so can you.

I didn't have to risk my ass to venture out into the streets. Those officers that know me, expect me to go above the line of duty.

I can't change the dedication that I have for the city I work in. I'm asking all of you to be exemplary officers.

Mayor Sharpe James is fortunate to have a staff of Director Celester, Chief O'Reilly, Golba, Santiago, Gesuado, Captains Arky, Tassie, Fanning, Borrelli, DeFilippo, Edwards, Gauthier, Rankin, Cefalu and Inneo. They are the backbone that has instilled in all of us the desire to make the effort.

Eighty percent of the officers in Newark wear the badge proudly. Unfortunately not everyone on this job is dedicated. However, eighty percent is an outstanding number.

I personally respect and admire the courage, dedication and fortitude you display. Where your uniform proudly and always be careful.

24 Great Balls of Fire

I find it only fitting that we change the pace of this book. We're going to bring down the intensity. This chapter is unique, and everyone will enjoy the outcome. I recommend that all women who are in a dangerous situation, by all means, use this method of defense.

A brave young lady handled a dangerous situation this way, she literally had the audacity to grab the suspect by his balls and control the situation at hand.

"Attack Victim Grabbed Thug by the Balls." The story was in the *New York Daily News*. The story was written by Mike Royko.

This is an incredible story about a brave woman. In twenty-four years of police service, I have never heard of anyone taking a bully by the horns.

Curtescine Lyold should be awarded the Woman of the Year award. She is a one in a million individual who came out on top of the situation.

Lloyd is a middle-aged nurse who lives with an elderly aunt in rural hamlet of Edwards, Miss. near Jackson.

This is her story, most of it taken from a court transcript.

One night, Lloyd was awakened by a sound. She thought it was her aunt going to the bathroom.

Suddenly a man stepped into her bedroom. He declared his intentions, which were to rob her and commit sexual assault. Of course, he phrased it far more luridly.

Then he took off most of his clothing and jumped into bed.

Lloyd: "I got it. I grabbed it by my right hand. And when I grabbed it, I gave it a yank. And when I yanked it, I twisted his testicles at the same time."

"He hit me with his right hand, a hard blow beside the head, and when he hit me, I grabbed hold to his scrotum (testicles) with my left hand and I was twisting it the opposite way. He started to yell and we fell to the floor and he hit me a couple of more licks, but they were light licks. He was weakening some then."

With Lloyd still hanging on with both hands, squeezing and twisting the fellow's pride and joy, they somehow struggled into the hallway.

"We were going down the hallway, falling from one side to the other, and we got into the living room and we both fell. He brought me down right in front of the couch and he leaned back against the couch, pleading with me.

"He said, 'You've got me, you've got me, you've got me, please, you've got me.' I know damn well I got you.

" 'Please, Please, you're killing me, you're killing me,' he said, 'I can't do nothing. Call the police, call the police!'

"I said, 'Do you think I'm stupid enough to turn you loose and call the police?' He said, 'Well, what am I gonna do?' I said, 'You're gonna get the hell out of my house,' He said, 'How can I get out of your house if you won't let me go? How can I get out? I can't get out.' I said, 'Break out, you son-of-a-bitch. You broke in, didn't you?' And I was still holding him.

"He said, 'Oh, you've got me suffering, lady, you've got me suffering.' I said, 'Have you thought about how you were going to have me suffering? He said, 'Well, I can't do nothing now.' I said, 'Well, that's fine.'

Lloyd, still twisting and squeezing, dragged the lout to the front door. When he finally unlocked the door, he screamed, "I'm out, I'm out."

But Lloyd, now confident that she had the upper hand and a full grasp of the situation, said, "No, damn it, I'm taking your ass to the end of the porch. And when I turn you loose, I'm going to blow your fuckin' brains out, you nasty, stinking, low-down dirty piece of shit, you.

"And when I did that. I gave it a twist, and I turned him loose. And he took a couple of steps and fell off the steps and he jumped up and grabbed his private parts and made a couple of jumps across the back of my aunt's car.

"I ran into my aunt's room, got her pistol from underneath the nightstand, ran back to the screen door, and I fired two shots down the hill the way I saw him go. And then I ran back in the house and dialed 911."

The police came and examined the man's clothing. Inside the trousers was written the name Dwight Coverson. They found Coverson, twenty-nine, at home, in considerable pain and wondering if he could ever be a daddy.

A one-day jury trial was held. As Coverson's court-appointed lawyer put it: "The jury was out ten minutes. Long enough for two of them to go to the bathroom."

And the judge gave him twenty-five years in prison.

Three years to the day I started writing this book, I finally completed my manuscrupt. I wanted to end the book with a humorous story about a courageous victim of a crime. Everyone can relate to her ordeal. We can laugh at the incredible spunk this lady has. I hope all women can be brave enough to use Lloyd's technique.

Unfortunately life does not bear us with laughter all the time. I am writing Chapter 25 reluctantly. I truly wish I could change the events of June 3, 1993.

25 Terror in the Halls of Justice

The reality of life sets in with no illusions as I reluctantly write a chapter that should never have needed writing. Unfortunately I cannot change the outcome that occurred on June 3, 1993. I am in dismay, I feel a deep emptiness inside, while I write this story.

I am dedicating this chapter and the entire book in memory of a true dedicated "Blue Warrior." Detective John Sczyrek Jr. will be remembered by all of us.

When I heard from Officer Frank Fontana that Detective Sczyrek was shot and killed at the Essex County Courthouse, I said to Fontana. "How, Frank?" "He was assassinated by a drug dealer," Fontana sadly said.

"Oh my God, no. I gotta get down there, Frank. I'll talk to you later."

I drove down to the Essex County Courthouse. WINS radio reported that officers were still looking for suspects. At the courthouse I met Officer Robert O'Connor, and an off-duty West Orange Police Officer, Raymond Rosania. Officer O'Connor was a former U.S. Marine and recipient of 2 class "A" valor awards.

He was one of the first officers on the scene.

"Moravek, they killed one of my best friends and a brother officer. They shot Sczyrek in the back of the head. Two of the suspects have been caught. They're looking for a third suspect," Officer O'Connor said.

O'Connor gave me a big hug and a kiss on the cheek. He had tears streaming down his cheeks as he told me the story of what had occurred.

"I'm going to the Prosecutor's, Bob, I'm volunteering my off-duty hours, I'm not going home until we catch all the scumbags that are involved," I said.

I talked with Lieutenant Gagliano and Captain Inneo. "I want to go on the raids with your squad, Captain, I'm not going anywhere till we have all the suspects."

"All right Moravek, glad to have you aboard. Have a seat with the other narcotics detectives," Captain Inneo said.

Officer Rosania was sitting on the chair with the Narcotics Detectives.

Detective Lieutenant Vincent Gagliano is the head field supervisor of the Narcotics Division. He immediately responded to the crime scene with Narcotics Detective Captain Jerry Inneo, Commander of the Narcotics Division.

"Lieutenant Gagliano, I want to introduce you to Officer Rosania. He has volunteered his time to assist us in capturing the suspects. His brother is Anthony Rosania from the Newark East Squad Detective Bureau," Moravek said.

On the third floor of the Essex County building, Sergeant Tamburello and Detectives Nick Scaglione, Daren Coley, Ellia Aquino, Jimmy Kneipp, Renaldo Perez, Larry Kates and Billy Thomas all sat in silence. Tears were flowing down our cheeks, we were all in a state of shock. We waited patiently for hours, Captain Inneo was going to brief us on the situation at hand. The remainder of the narcotics squad sat down in the Prosecutor's reception area. Detectives Michael Petrillo, Nicholas Scaglione, Jerry Buglione, Rocco Buglleone, Juvo Gianella, and Abdul Hesanall had this eerie look on their faces. The pain we all felt inside was worse then having someone pierce a sword right into our hearts.

An investigation into the assasination of Detective

Sczyrek was immediately put into effect by the Newark Police Director William Celester and Chief Thomas O'Reilly. Homicide Detective Captain Dzibella, Internal Affairs Captain Purcell Goodwin, Internal Affairs Detective Lieutenant Edward J. Adelman, Detective Lieutenant Anthony J. Plinio and Detective Lieutenant Eugene Nicholson, Homicide Detectives Anthony Ambrose and Carmine Demaio were at the scene of the crime.

Detective Lieutenant Nicholson immediately roped off the crime scene where the shooting occurred. Combining Newark's finest with the Prosecutor Detectives, we all knew that our top notch detectives would break the case wide open.

We were all on standby waiting for orders to be issued.

"We will be conducting raids on locations in the city to apprehended suspects if so ordered by Captain Inneo. Wait here patiently and I will get back to you," Lieutenant Gagliano said.

After five hours of waiting for a decision, Captain Inneo entered the reception area and spoke to all the officers involved. "Our primary investigation has been completed. All suspects in this case are secured in this building. Thank you all for your dedication to duty. Special thanks to Officers Raymond Rosania and Officer Otto J. Moravek for responding here from their homes and off-duty," Captain Jerry Inneo said.

SHORTCOMINGS IN SECURITY

Although the security in the Essex County Courthouse is a disgrace, no security in the world could have saved Detective Sczyrek's life.

It is a tragedy that security is always beefed up after officials realize that they have failed to execute proper safety precautions.

It was a travesty to see a provisional Sheriff Officer shot in the chest by an assailant. Sheriff Fontoura should have foreseen the extreme danger facing an unarmed officer. Where was the Deputy Sheriff who guarded the judge?

When the shot was fired in the court hallway, Officer Ralph Rizzolo Jr. dashed out of the courtroom and was shot.

I find it appalling that Chief Prosecutor Clifford Minor

and Deputy Chief George Dickscheid permitted an unarmed officer to work in the courts. Provisional officers and regular officers that are unarmed cannot and should not be given the responsibility of working security in the courts. Unarmed officers have to be assigned to working on the inside behind the desk.

Essex County officials installed metal detectors recently. However, they should have been there years ago. The terroristic explosion at the World Trade Center implemented tighter security.

Fontoura has asked county officials to hire an additional eighty officers to secure the safety of the County Court House.

Rest assured that Sheriff Fontoura is by far the best Sheriff the County of Essex has ever had. As a captain, lieutenant sergeant and Newark police officer, Fontoura always excelled in the field. Recipient of many valor awards, Fontoura always displayed courage and professional service to the citizens of Newark.

Deputy Chief George Dickscheid recently retired from the Newark Police Department. Dickscheid was my Commanding Officer for six years. I have the highest praise regarding his accomplishments during his twenty-five years in Newark. He exemplified the best as Captain of the West District.

Unfortunately they had to take the heat for the lead culprits. The Essex County Board of Trustees, the appropriations committee are the inside people who call all the political shots. They are responsible for the misguided setup.

LITANY OF SHOOTINGS

The violence that is occurring in the courts the past eighteen months should eventually force the hands of justice.

The litany of shootings and killings point up shortcomings in court security. The blatant point blank range shootings of Officers Ralph Rizzolo Jr. and John Sczyrek Jr. are a prime example of Essex Counties Sheriff Department's extremely poor Intelligence Unit.

Taxpayers shell out thousands of dollars for the safety of their loved ones. The County Intelligence Unit failed to obtain the knowledge of the North Carolina connection that was involved in the assasination of Sczyrek. They also failed to conclusively report to Sheriff Fontoura the extreme danger of having provisional officers working in the courtroom unarmed.

Effective Intelligence Units can make a big difference. On June 24, 1993 the FBI Intelligence unit uncovered a plot by eight suspects. They planned to blow up the Lincoln and Holland Tunnels and the United Nations building. Extensive police work and an effective use of personnel is the key to a good intelligence unit.

Rage and Violence

There was a time when courthouse violence was unheard of. That time has long passed as we live in an era of blatant terrorism.

Such incidents are increasingly becoming a fact of life, despite beefed-up security at courthouses around the United States.

Rage and violence are a fact of life in the once-sacred "halls of justice."

Here are some of the recent violent episodes that have occurred across the United States.

Ellie Nessler shot and killed Daniel Driver, accused of molesting her eight year old son at a mountain church camp, during the hearing at the Toulumne County Courthouse in California on April 2, 1993. Nessler pulled a handgun out of her purse as she approached the witness stand to testify.

Gilbert Ortiz, twenty-three, opened fire inside the Bronx courthouse February 24, killing a woman and wounding a man before being shot and wounded by a court officer. Ortiz wore a bulletproof vest into the building, which also holds offices for the borough president and the district attorney.

John T. Miller, fifty, of Ohio walked into the Child Support Collection Unit inside the Schuyler County building, which also houses the county courthouse, in Watkins Glen, N.Y. in October 1992 and opened fire with a semi-automatic hand-gun. When the shooting spree was over, he had killed four collection unit employees and himself. In a brief standoff with authorities he said caseworkers had ruined his life because of their efforts to collect child support from him.

Jeffrey Erickson, a former police officer on trial for bank robbery, slipped free of handcuffs in a Cook County courthouse garage in Chicago July 20, 1992, grabbed a gun from a guard and killed two other guards before fatally shooting himself.

Lawyer George Lott fatally shot two lawyers and wounded two judges and a prosecutor at the Tarrant County Courthouse in Fort Worth, Texas, on July 1, 1992. Lott surrendered at a TV station, saying he was angry over his divorce and a child molesting charge brought against him by his former wife.

District Judge Lawrence Jahnke was shot and seriously wounded by Reuben Larson during a hearing on failure to pay child support in Grand Forks, N.D., May 5, 1992.

Kenneth Baumruk shot and killed his estranged wife, Mary Louise Baumruk, and wounded their attorneys while waiting for a divorce hearing to begin in Clayton, Mo., also on May 5, 1992.

Carolyn Francis Logan shot and wounded brother-in-law Phillip Dale Byrd while arguing at the Colbert County Courthouse in Alabama May 4, 1992.

Shirley Lowery was stabbed and killed by Benjamin Franklin in the Milwaukee County Courthouse March 9, 1992. Lowery had gone to the courthouse to seek a permanent restraining order against Franklin.

Abdulla H. Awkal killed his estranged wife and brother-in-law in the Family Conciliation Services office of the Cuyahoga County Courthouse in Cleveland January 7, 1992.

Cop "Assassinated" in Halls of Justice

On June 3, 1993, in Newark, N.J. an Essex County Courthouse was turned into a bloody battleground when an assailant (al-Damanay Kamau) "assassinated" Narcotics Detective John Sczyrek Jr., who was to be a key witness against the assailant's two cousins on trial at the Essex County Courthouse.

As terrified people in the courthouse yelled and dived for cover, the gunman (Kamau) suddenly critically wounded a deputy sheriff, Ralph Rizzolo Jr who courageously ran out of a nearby courtroom after hearing the shot fired.

Kamau also pegged shots at two other officers as he ran down to the eighth floor. He then took another elevator to the first floor and ran out of the courthouse.

Another great security job of Fontoura's sheriff officers: Kamau was able to escape right out the front door. It is amazing that the officers on the first floor are not all armed. Fontoura and Dickscheid have to take the weight for their decision to have unarmed officers guarding the entrance doors. There is no excuse for having provisional officers handling security in the courthouse.

Newark Police Director Celester has armed Newark police officers guarding all municipal judges. Proper security measures must be implemented.

The detective from Newark's Narcotics squad, John Sczyrek Jr., thirty years old, had just come up from the prosecutor's office on the fourth floor and was about to enter an eleventh-floor courtroom.

The suspect, Philson, twenty-five, of Newark, nonchalantly walked up to him and passed him. Suddenly in a split second, Kamau pulled out a gun and from point blank range Sczyrek was shot in the back of the head. Sczyrek collapsed at the courtroom door. Detective Sczyrek never had a chance of survival. He died instantly from the gun shot wound. The fatally wounded officer never had a chance to defend himself.

Provisional Sheriff's Officer Ralph Rizzolo, twenty-four, was unarmed when he confronted Kamau. Suddenly when Kamau saw Rizzolo, he went into a "combat crouch" and shot him in the chest.

The bullet penetrated into Rizzolo's chest and ledged in his arm. Rizzolo had surgery performed on him at University Hospital. He was released a few weeks later and has recovered from his wound.

Kamau raced down a stairwell and fired at another deputy sheriff broadcasting on his walkie-talkie. Security staffers sealed the courthouse.

It must be repeated. Sheriff Fontoura and his staff underestimated the dangers of having a security staff of armed and unarmed officers. You are not going to arrest an armed suspect with an unarmed sheriff officer in pursuit.

Suddenly the suspect burst from the ground-floor stairwell, and guess what happened when an unarmed security officers confronted him. Kamau ran directly toward the entrance and exit door. Does it amaze you to know that Philson ran past an unarmed security officer and out the door, getting off a shot at the officer as he started to give chase?

Al-Damanay Kamau, also known as Eddie Lee Philson, of Newark, was captured near the intersection of Branford Place and Market Streets.

During an intense search and questioning of suspects, Tanesha James, an Essex County probation officer, was charged with conspiracy. She admitted to smuggling the gun by going through the employee's entrance, which does not have detectors. For obvious reasons pending the outcome of the subsequent trial, I will not reveal the location where James exchanged the gun. James did give the gun to Kamau somewhere on the floors of the Essex County Courthouse.

Superior Court Judge Serena Perretti was not injured during the wild shooting melee, which took place in the hallway outside her courtroom on the eleventh floor.

The shootings occurred about eleven A.M., as Sczyrek was waiting to testify in an evidentiary hearing involving Daryl Hill and Charles Oliver, both of Newark. The two were on trial before Perretti on drug and weapons charges.

Al-Damanay Kamau is believed to be a cousin of one of the two drug defendants. An investigation into a link of conspiracy is pending.

Kamau told relatives in North Carolina a week before the assasination that he was going to shoot the detective and the judge because he thought his cousin was not receiving a fair trial.

When Newark police officers found out about the North Carolina connection and the planned assassination, they all were extremely upset.

Police Officer Johnny B. Doe said it best in a very distraught emotional voice: "It just goes to show you Moravek, Fontoura, Dickscheid, Minor and the rest of their staff should hang their heads low and resign their positions. What kind of an Intelligence Unit are they running up there? Minor puts out a statement to the press that he found out a week later that Kamau's family members had knowledge of the assassination, weeks before the shooting. If that is an Intelligence Unit, we are in trouble."

"Unfortunately Bobby their intelligence unit is deplorable, it has to be restructured. They didn't do the job and they should hang their heads in disgrace. They cost us the life of a promising young detective. We can never replace an outstanding cop that was so intently dedicated to fighting the elements."

"They better get their heads and asses wired together. Heads are going to roll. This investigation into their security laxness is far from over," Officer Doe said.

Sczyrek had made an undercover purchase of about $20 worth of heroin from Hill and Charles Oliver, and police then arrested the two. The accused shooter was in the apartment where the arrests were made but was not charged due to a lack of evidence. Eddie Lee Oliver Kamau assasinated Sczyrek in "cold blood." Philson came into the courthouse with a mission. This individual came into the building with the express purpose of assassinating this police officer.

Chief Prosecutor Minor, Sheriff Fontoura and Director Celester said Oliver shot Sczyrek, a thirty-year-old father and seven-year police veteran, in the corridor on the eastern end of the eleventh floor.

Sheriff's Officer Rizzolo heard the shot, came out of a courtroom at the other end of the floor and was shot as Kamau ran toward him. Suddenly Kamau stopped, pulled a gun from his waistband and shot the unarmed Rizzolo once in the chest. Kamau then ran down a stairway on the western side of the building.

Sheriff's Officer Tom King entered the stairway on the tenth floor. Suddenly Kamau fired at him, missing his head by inches.

King called in an alarm on his walkie-talkie and pursued Kamau down the stairs, losing him on the way.

When Kamua reached the courthouse lobby, he walked nonchalantly toward an exit and was stopped by a security officer who told him the building has been sealed off and he could not leave.

Suddenly Kamau bolted past the officer and into the courtyard between the courthouse and the Essex County Hall of Records.

The unarmed security guard, Jacinto Rivera, gave chase. Suddenly Kamau wheeled around and fired at him, fortunately the shots missed Rivera.

Kamau fled through the parking lot on the north side of the Hall of Records, dropping the gun and his jacket in a patch of grass near a guardrail.

Officer Rivera is a Marine Corps graduate and is presently in the U.S. Marine Corps Reserve, he is also currently waiting to enter the Newark Police Academy.

As a former Marine I congratulate him for his bravery.

Rivera and Sheriff's Officer Fred Apicelli chased Kamau down the Market Street hill. Three other sheriffs in a patrol vehicle spotted Kamay in the parking lot of Burger King restaurant at Market Street and University Avenue and ordered him to halt.

The assailant stopped but ignored the officers orders to spread eagle on the ground. At that point, Rivera and Apicelli ran up and Kamau was subdued and handcuffed.

Kamau was transported back to the Essex County Prosecutor's Office. He was slated and charged with murder, attempted murder, aggravated assault and weapons offenses.

During intense questioning by detectives, he initially told investigators he had not done the shootings, but had merely carried the gun out of the building.

Detective Sczyrek, of Belleville, was killed instantly, Rizzolo, twenty-four, also of Beleville, was shot once through the chest, with the bullet passing through a lung, exiting his body and lodging in his arm.

Newark Police Director William Celester said Sczyrek had been assigned to the Narcotics Division for eleven months. He called Sczyrek one of the division's most active officers.

The trial of Hill, twenty, and Oliver, twenty-three, was adjourned and reset for the last week of June, 1993. The two were jailed in lieu of $1 million bail each.

Sheriff Fontoura said he ran up the stairs from his second-floor office after hearing the radio call about the shootings. When he arrived on the eleventh floor, he saw Sczyrek's body in the corridor and heard Rizzolo crying out.

"He said, 'Sheriff, I'm in pain.' I said, 'That's good,'" Fontoura related, explaining he told the officer that meant he was alive and could make it through.

Minutes after the shootings, there were dozens of officers from different forces on the eleventh floor. The eastern end of the corridor was blocked with yellow crime scene police tape, as investigators combed the area for evidence.

Newark Police Detective Lieutenant Eugene Nicholson, Internal Affairs Division, carefully roped off the crime scene area and preserved it.

The assistant prosecutor handling the Hill and Oliver drug case, Carolyn Murray, said Detective Sczyrek had just helped carry bundles of papers into the courtroom when he went out into the corridor and was shot. Judge Perretti was not on the bench at the time of the shooting.

She said when she and others in the courtroom heard the first shot, officers ordered them to get down and went to block the door.

"It was just shocking to everyone," Murray said. She called Sczyrek "a gentleman" as well as an excellent officer.

One woman outside the courthouse when Kamau ran from the building said she saw him pull a gun.

"It was one of the most frightening experiences of my life," she said. "The guard at the door, Officer Rivera, told him to stop but the man in the green suit just kept walking very fast. Then I saw him reach under his jacket and I could see him pull out a gun," said Yolanda Melvin, an employee of the Essex Bail Bond Agency.

"The officer called for him to stop again and the man turned around and fired a shot. It didn't look as if he shot at him; it looked like a warning shot to me. Suddenly, he started running and threw a gun into the bushes," she said.

"I heard the gunshot and I was terrified, but there was nowhere to run. They had sealed the building, so I couldn't get into the courthouse. I definitely got a good look at him. He was a good-looking man. He had a nice face but had some lower teeth missing," she said.

Officers quickly recovered Kamau's jacket and a large-framed revolver, a .357 Magnum, from the parking lot.

New metal detectors were installed in the courthouse in March 1993. Everyone in the building except court employees and jurors must pass a magnetometer that beeps when it detects metal, including pens and keys.

"Nothing is foolproof," said Sheriff Fontoura. "This is an example of how vulnerable we are. If someone is bent on assassinating someone, there is no security system I know of that is foolproof."

Fontoura failed to admit that along with his staff they have made a mistake. They have a flaw in their security system and a month after the shooting no one is apologizing to the public. The courthouse should be dedicated in Sczyrek's name.

Hundreds of thousands of dollars were spent on a metal detector system. If a suspect enters the doorway of the metal detector, does Fontoura expect unarmed security officers to disarm an assailant armed with a gun? We already have read about how Kamau had no problem escaping from the courthouse.

He could have left a trail of blood with several innocent people killed. Other officers could have been killed when Kamau escaped. Fortunately a bloody confrontation never occurred.

The failure of Sheriff Fontoura's officers to contain Kamau in the building is a joke. Kamau should have been gunned down when he attempted to escape from the courthouse. You cannot have unarmed officers trying to arrest an assailant!

The assassination of Detective Sczyrek was very difficult to handle. When confirmed reports leaked out that Probation Officer Tanesha James smuggled a gun into the courthouse and gave it to Kamau, we all bowed our heads. We were double-crossed by one of our own.

The Luck and the Omen of Thirteen Years Turned Deadly

For thirteen years I, along with 1,000 other officers, have been lucky.

We have been rammed by stolen cars and dragged along the ground, stabbed with ice picks and even shot several times at point blank range. We all survived until June 3, 1993. This day will go down as the darkest day in the history of the Newark Police Department.

Narcotics Detective John Sczyrek, had just left the men's room and reentered a hallway on the eleventh floor of the Essex County Courthouse to testify on a drug case when a cousin of a man he arrested on a $20 undercover drug buy in the summer of 1992. Suddenly Kamau walked up behind Sczyrek about eleven A.M.

Kamau quickly pulled out a .357 Magnum from beneath his jacket. In a flash of a second Kamau put the large caliber .357 revolver just a few inches behind Sczyrek's ear and pulled the trigger, killing the detective instantly.

A seven-year, highly decorated veteran of the force who lived in Belleville, New Jersey, Sczyrek was married and was the proud father of a two year old daughter. John and his wife were expecting another baby in July 1993.

When other lawmen arrived at the eleventh floor corridor, they found a nightmarish scene of blood-spattered walls and growing pools of blood: two fallen heroes lay in a deadly confrontation, one dead and one wounded.

Outside the hospital, a Newark police officer and a friend of Sczyrek's broke down in tears as Newark Police Director William Celester, Police Chief Thomas O'Reilly and Sheriff Fontoura left to inform Sczyrek's family of his death.

As news of the shooting crackled over police radios across the city, grieving fellow Newark police officers remembered the slain narcotics detective as a dedicated officer and devoted family man.

"John was the kind of cop you always wanted watching your back," said one of his former partners, Detective Rocco Bulione. He had tears in his eyes as he spoke with high praise of Sczyrek.

"We lost a good and dedicated police officer. Something like this takes a piece of all of us with it. It hurts," said Sheriff Fontoura of Detective Sczyrek.

"I was supposed to testify with John on this case. John told me he would call me on the air if they need me to testify," said Narcotics Detective Ellia Aquino. "Officer Moravek, my heart is torn apart. John was a one in a million dedicated detective; he worked so hard to get into the narcotics division," Detective Aquino said.

Officer Robert O'Connor, who graduated from the Newark Police Academy and was at Sczyrek's wedding, broke down when he said to me, "Moravek, John's death has taken a piece of our hearts from all of us."

"John was one of my partners when I was assigned to the narcotics division," said Newark Police Detective Derek Glenn. "He was my backup and he was very enterprising and enjoyed police work. He took a very creative approach to the job. He was a damn good cop."

"He was one of our better narcotics officers," said Police Director Celester, who had to pause to compose himself during the interview sessions. "He was well-liked by everyone in the department."

Newark Mayor Sharpe James mourned Sczyrek, calling him "an outstanding police professional and devoted husband, father, and son. Our hearts go out to the Sczyrek family."

"He was a good cop, a quiet kid, very reserved, very bright," said Rocco Malanga, president of the Policemen's Benevolent Association. "He only came on the job in 1986 and he made it to the narcotics bureau already."

He was highly decorated during his years of service, receiving numerous commendations from the city and numerous command citations. "He's even been PBA Officer of the Month twice since he came on the job," Malanga said.

On the narcotics squad only eleven months, Sczyrek rose quickly through the patrol ranks to detective. John's father is a retired Essex County police officer who served for more than thirty years on the job before retiring.

"This is just tragic, he was such a terrific guy," said fellow Detective John Mauriello. "He had a wife and a kid, and he loved his work. I remember years ago when he couldn't wait to get into narcotics, and now this."

"This senseless and barbaric act warrants full prosecution of the individuals involved and shows the need of passing the Brady bill for removing handguns from our society," Mayor Sharpe James said.

"There are only a chosen few who have displayed the courage and dedication to duty of Sczyrek's caliber," I said. "He was always so energetic and when he came to work he was mentally and physically ready to make a good narcotics collar. I still see him coming through the door," I said sadly with tears dropping from my eyes.

Sczyrek is the twenty-eighth officers shot and killed in the line of duty since the city incorporated. The first officer died in 1954. Officer John Gottfried was the last officer killed on November 28, 1980.

Narcotics Was His Goal to Attain

By all accounts, John Sczyrek was one of the saviest narcotic Detectives on the Newark Police force.

He had the look—including a dirty blond ponytail and an earring—and the street smarts to survive as an undercover cop in the dirtiest of worlds, drug dealing.

But it was all worthless in a courthouse corridor when he was shot in the head.

"Who ever would have thought that an undercover cop would be shot in the courthouse," said Sczyrek's commanding officer Detective Captain Jerry Inneo.

Captain Inneo said the thirty year old officer seemed to have a knack for his work.

"You'd never make him for a cop" and he had collared "tons" of undercover drug buys and arrests.

"He was not afraid of anything," said Captain Inneo. "He did any job you asked him to do. He was a cop's cop."

Sczyrek was following in his father's footsteps when he joined the department.

Captain Inneo said the rookie cop had come to him six or seven years ago when Inneo was the executive officer for the department's east district, "and I could see right then that he had the makings to be a great police officers. I immediately put him into plainclothes."

Then, his voice halting briefly, he added, "I recommended him and his partner to narcotics two and a half years ago, that's what makes this so tough."

On Monday May 31, 1993, Sczyrek spoke of his fears of being killed on the job.

I remember showing Detective Sczyrek one of the last chapters in this book "The Blue Warrior," dealing with seven police officers who were killed in the line of duty and the mistakes they had made.

"You're so right," Sczyrek as told me. "When you come on the job, all those cops and robbers games you played as kids you can't do when you're confronting someone on the street. You can't treat them as if they're your best friend."

FINAL SALUTE TO A FALLEN HERO
The ride to Nutley, New Jersey filled our hearts with remorse. Detective James Golden drove Deputy Chief Michael O'Connor's car. Chief O'Connor sat quietly in the front seat. Sergeant Fairchild and I sat in the back. We left police headquarters fifteen minutes before the procession of hundreds of police cars and motorcycles. O'Connor was Sczyrek's Commanding Chief.

In a lifetime a police officer will never see a show of respect and brotherly love like that displayed in Nutley, N.J. on June 7, 1993.

The painful story of the assassination of Detective John Sczyrek Jr. had to be written and read and remembered by police officers throughout the United States.

Every officer has been stabbed in the back by this nightmare that has turned out to be a terrible reality of life. We are all vulnerable to the realization that we can be killed at anytime, anyplace.

FOURTEEN THOUSAND STRONG

Thousands of police lined Nutley Streets to mourn Detective Sczyrek.

More than 14,000 law enforcement officers from around the world joined John Sczyrek's family and friends on June 7, 1993 in Nutley, N.J., to pay their respects to an officer assassinated in cold blood.

The officers came from as far away as Ireland and as close as Irvington, New Jersey. There were police cars from California, Houston, Texas, Phoenix, Arizona, Dade County, Florida, North and South Carolina, Maryland, Maine, Virginia and Washington, D.C. New York City had over 200 police officers, Jersey City had over 100 officers; I can go on forever. The Nutley residents were in awe as they watched 14,000 police officers march in a solemn procession.

The officers filed by unison side by side in rows filled 200 deep.

We all stood at attention in front of the Holy Family Church as the Alleluia Chorus was sung brilliantly. In the midst of the quiet warm morning came the sound of an angel. Mrs. Lynn Adelman's voice rose high above the rafters. It echoed majestically through the entire church grounds. Mrs. Adelman's vibrant voice sent chills vibrating throughout my body. She sang "Let there be peace." There wasn't a dry eye to be seen. The tears streamed down my cheeks.

As the casket of slain Newark Police Detective Sczyrek was carried up the stairs, every police officer stiffened his back and brought his hand to the brim of his hat to salute the procession as it went up the church stairs.

The pallbearers were Narcotics Detectives Nick Scagleone, Daren Coley, Ellia Aquino, Jimmy Kneipp, Renaldo Perez and Police Officer Robert O'Connor.

Leading the procession directly behind the casket were Sczyrek's immediate supervisor, Detective Lieutenant Vincent Gaglione, Narcotic Division, Commanding Officer, Detective Captain Gerard N. Inneo, Commanding Deputy Chief Michael O'Connor, Detective Sergeant Thomas Cetnar III, Detective Sergeant Jackie Tamburello and Detective Sergeant David McCummings.

The tolling church bell was replaced by silence, broken only by the blare of emergency sirens in the distance.

HANDS OF THE LAW

During his eulogy, Monseignor Louis Fimiani, who had married Sczyrek and his wife in Holy Family Church five years before, contrasted the detective's hands with those accused of killing him.

"On Thursday morning, a hand took a gun into a courthouse in Newark, N.J. and very deftly transferred that gun from one hand to another one," Monseignor Fimiani said. "This hand, at a given moment, pulled the trigger to fire the mortal blow that felled Detective John Sczyrek."

"What potential evil the human hand is capable of," said the pastor. "It can deal in drugs, entice the young, entice the innocent to believe that crime will bring them a better way of life.

"How different another pair of hands, strong and massive, the hands that belonged to John Sczyrek," Fimiani said.

"They are hands that fought evil, hands that fought crime, hands that put fear in others as needed," said the pastor. "Yet these same hands somehow tenderly and lovingly said to his daughter Shannon: Daddy will fix it.

"These same hands embraced [his wife] Cheryl in love and were extended to many of us in fellowship and brotherhood. These were massive, strong hands, tender, loving hands," Msgr. Fimiani said.

From the Book of Wisdom, Monseignor Fimiani read the passage that promises that God holds the souls of the just in his hands, and no torment shall touch them.

"He is holding the soul of this just man," Fimiani promised the friends and family gathered to bid farewell to Sczyrek.

Sergeant Mark Whitley, Sczyrek's former partner, spoke

of the man whom he met in the police academy in 1986 and grew close during the years they worked together until they "reluctantly parted company last in 1992."

Sergeant Whitley took deep breaths of air as he spoke sincerely of his friend. Holding back the tears was tough as the "Sarge" continued his eulogy.

"At times he was unapproachably distant and strong, like when he was working with a crowd. At times he was sweet and gentle, like when he was holding his precious daughter Shannon," Sergeant Whitley said.

"When a brother officer fell on hard times and needed help, he was always there to organize a benefit," Whitley said of his friend, a member of the executive board of the Fraternal Order of Police, Lodge Twelve, and a state and national delegate to the FOP. He was also a member of Nutley Elks Lodge No. 1290.

"We will all miss him," Whitley said, adding "I will always love you and remember you."

To all the Newark officers at the funeral, about 1,000 strong, and those who were unable to attend, he said that they will never really fathom the "magnitude of our loss. No one loved his fellow officers more deeply or wore the uniform more proudly than John Sczyrek."

He called on the officer's friends and comrades to share their stories about John with his wife, daughter and family. And he thanked the thousands of other officers at the church for attending the ceremony, sacrificing their personal time to be there.

"Having grown up in a police family, he knew that officers rally around and support each other in times of need," Sergeant Whitley said. "He always wanted to be a cop. He grew up around cops, his father was an Essex County police officer and he always talked about him as a hero."

Sergeant Whitley took a couple of deep breaths.

He reminded everyone that "today we buried a great man, a great cop. He always talked about the need for being careful, never relaxing his guard.

"But for one moment, he relaxed, let his guard down in an environment where he felt safe," Sergeant Whitley said. "If he had been given a sliver of a chance to defend himself, he would be here today."

With those last words Sergeant Whitley left the podium.

We all bowed our heads and said a final prayer before we left the church.

Mrs. Adelmann sang another song that touched all of our hearts. I could not stop my tears. As officers proceeded to leave the church Mrs. Adelmann was singing "God Bless America" and "Battle Hymn of the Republic." It was a touching farewell tribute to a true hero.

The church mass lasted over two hours.

As the pipers and bagpipes and drums played, 14,000 officers gave Detective Sczyrek a final salute as his casket was slowly carried down the church stairs and placed into the hearse.

Hundreds of police vehicles, seventy motorcycles and the city's mounted squad accompanied Sczyrek to the cemetery, driving first around the community where he grew up, stopping in front of his home in Belleville and the schools where he studied as a boy.

Nutley residents lined the curbs, commiserating with the family. They told me that they had never seen so many police officers gathered in one community.

The entire East Coast has never seen such a huge gathering of police in tribute to one fallen hero.

School children, let out of class for the afternoon, stood on the sidewalks with their hands over their hearts as the motorcade passed by.

Chills and goose bumps invaded my entire body as I watched in awe. Heartwarming best describes my view of observing from the procession of the motorcade. The entire town of Nutley and Belleville payed homage to a local hero.

The highlight of the drive back home was seeing children standing straight and tall with their hands crossed over their hearts.

In the sun-dappled cemetery, flags flew in the stiff breeze and the trees bowed as the wind drowned out the priest's words and the music from the bagpipes and drums of the Police and Fire Emerald Society of Essex County.

As the pipers disappeared over the ridge, their wailing notes fading in the distance, and the family drove away in black limousines, Newark's finest lined up and filed past Sczyrek's coffin, saying one last prayer, one last good-bye, saluting, genuflecting and touching, one last time.

A Sincere Salute in Memory of our Brother Police Officers of the City of Newark Police Department who made the Supreme Sacrifice in the Line of Duty.

Thomas Adubato
Robert Anderson
Maxwell Badgley
Joseph Baumann
Richard Burns
Edward Dehmer
Howard Downes
Benjamin Ellsden
John Gaffney
John Galler
Charles Gerstner
John Gottfried
John Gutekunst
Joseph Hagel
Leslie Haskins Jr.

Frank Irvin
Robert La Motta
Theodore Laux Sr.
Thomas Lyons
John McGovern
Cedric Pettersen
Patrick Ryan
John Sczyrek Jr.
Albert Seltzer
Frank Shannon
John Snow
Frederick Toto
Arthur Williams
Jack Woomer

The following pages contain the names of honored members of the Newark Police Department.

Honorable Police Chiefs

Chief Anthony Barris
Chief John Golba

Chief Thomas O'Reilly
Chief Charles Zizza

Honorable Police Directors

William H. Celester
Claude M. Coleman
Charles Knox

Charles Redden
Dominick Spina
Hubert H. Williams

Honorable Deputy Chiefs

Charles Cefalu
Thomas Chrichley
Daniel Del Bagno
George Dickscheid
John Dunsmuir
Nicholas Gesualdo
George Hemmer
Thomas Henry

Thomas Martin
John Mosca
Michael O'Connor
Gerald Patella
Robert Rankin
Joseph Santiago
Christian Voltz

Top 20 Captains

Richard Arkey
George Bagnall
Otis Barnes (Retired)
Perry Borrelli
Frank Cefalu
James Cosgrove
Vincent DeFillippo
John W. Dooley
David Dzibella
John Edwards

Luther Engler
Richard Fanning
Robert Gauthier (Retired)
Thomas Grill
Thomas Hunt
Gerald Inneo
John Kossup
Michael Pocchio
Joseph Rox (Retired)
Stephen Tassie

Top 20 Lieutenants

**Lt. Edward J. Adelman
Lt. Phillip Aquino
Lt. William Capra
Lt. Barry Collicelli
Lt. William Damiano
**Lt. Archibald Davidson
Lt. Gus Dimino
Lt. Vincent Gagliano
Lt. Ciro Mangione
**Lt. Edward Norvilas

Lt. James O'Connor
Lt. Anthony Perillo
**Lt. Anthony J. Plinio
Lt. Eugene Posella
Lt. Kenneth Rox
Lt. Nicholas Sapienza
**Lt. Daniel Szizer
Lt. Joseph Tutela
**Lt. Thomas White
**Lt. Charles Whitner

*Denotes promotion to next rank.
**Asterisk denotes promotion to Captain

Top 20 Sergeants

**Sgt. John Scott Bey	Sgt. Richard Maquire
Sgt. Vincent Bongermino	**Sgt. Brian Morris
Sgt. John Catalupo	*Sgt. James C. Nelson III
*Sgt. Luciano Collazo	**Sgt. Frank Padilla
Sgt. Daniel J. Daly	*Sgt. Michael Parris
*Sgt. Samuel DeMaio	**Sgt. Joseph Pollaro
*Sgt. James J. Dupont	Sgt. Kenneth Santora
*Sgt. Alonzo Evans	**Sgt. John G. Watral
Sgt. Alfred Hawkins	Sgt. Mark A. Whitley
Sgt. John M. Jurgensen	Sgt. Joseph Wilke

*Asterisk denotes Promotion to Detective
**Asterisk denotes promotion to Lieutenant Detective

Top 20 Detectives

*Det. Anthony F. Ambrose III	Det. Gary Miller
Det. Gerald Buglione	Det. Edward H. Moravek
Det. Rocco Buglione	Det. Anthony Mullarkey
Det. Nicholas Casale	Det. James Nance (Retired)
Det. Chuck Conte	Det. Michael Petrillo
*Det. Carmine P. DeMaio	Det. Louis Portella (Retired)
Det. Elbert Eutsey	Det. Anthony G. Rosania
*Det. Mario Genzone	Det. Nicholas Scaglione
Det. Juvo Gialanella	Det. William Thomas Jr.
*Det. Paul A. Lorenc	(Officer of the year (1993)
Det. Michael Marelli	
(lieutenant)	

*Asterisk denotes promotion to Sergeant Detective

Top 20 Veteran Police Officers

*Stanley Belchik	(4 "A" Valor Awards)
Alphonso A. Caruso	(2 "A" Valor Awards)
**Alan R. Cappetta	(2 "A" Valor Awards)
*Joseph Catalupo	(10 "B" Valor Awards)
*Robert D'Angelo	(2 "A" Valor Awards)
*Robert J. Fisher	(2 "B" Valor Awards)
**Marty Goldman	(4 "A" Valor Awards)
*Joseph Grosso	(4 "B" Valor Awards)
*Charles S. Kaiser	(2 "A" Valor Awards)
*Dennis Kihlberg	(3 "B" Valor Awards)
*James Kneipp Jr.	(3 "B" Valor Awards)
Michael LaMotta	(2 "A" Valor Awards)

Top 20 Veteran Police Officers (continued)

John A. Malanga	(4 "B" Valor Awards)
Joseph Mauriello	(3 "A" Valor Awards)
**Otto J. Moravek	(4 "A" Valor Awards)
*Robert O'Connor	(3 "A" Valor Awards)
Raymond Schaefer	(2 "B" Valor Awards)
*Willie Stroud	(3 "B" Valor Awards)
*Michael Thomas	(4 "B" Valor Awards)
*Nate Thompson	(3 "B" Valor Awards)

*Asterisk denotes promotion to Detective
**Asterisk denotes Promotion to Sergeant

Top 20 Rookie Officers (5 Years or Less)

*Mark Ausby	*Lawrence Kates
Nicholas Baglione	Christopher Kossup
*Irving Bradley Jr.	*Yvette Lopez
*Carmine Buonsanto	Fred J. Masucci
*Al Burroughs	*Anthony Moraes
*Lillian Caban	*Vincent A. Ucci
Michael T. Cavallaro	*George Vasquez
Michael Cirasella	*Vinnie Vitiello
*Derrick J. Eutsey	*Robert Wise
Joseph Juliano	*Steven Yurik

*Asterisk Denotes Promotion to Detective

The below listed Newark Police "Blue Warriors" deserve honorable mention for the courage and fortitude they have dedicated to the City of Newark, N.J.

P.O. Richard Allen
P.O. Foster Badgley
Lt. John Beard (Retired)
Sgt. Ralph G. Boswell
Det. Noreen Britt
Sgt. Sam Clark
Lt. Gayton Collonello
Capt. Frank Donnelan
Det. Matthew Donnelan
Lt. Charles Dukee
Det. Anthony Esposito
Sgt. Allen Fairchild

Capt. John Feind
Lt. Joe Ferrullo
Sgt. Vincent Gayder
Lt. Barbara George
P.O. Greg Gillhooly
Det. Betrice Golden
Det. Pat Hannorhan
P.O. Daniel Helber
Lt. Michael Hughes
Lt. Tom Hughes
Sgt. Leslie L. Jones Jr.
Sgt. Stephen A. Magna
Sgt. Robert A. Marelli
P.O. Neil C. Minovich
P.O. Darren Nance
Sgt. Robert O'Dwyer
Sgt. Michael Parris
Det. Dan Piccotelli
Sgt. James F. Post
Sgt. Dennis J. Reilly
Sgt. Joe P. Reilly
Lt. Dario Rizzitello
Lt. Frank Rogers
Sgt. Harry Romeo (Retired)
Sgt. Sal Russamanno
Lt. Carmine Russo
Lt. Robert Russo
Lt. Charles Schaefer
Sgt. Thomas Scull
P.O. John Siino
Sgt. Sam Siino
P.O. Vincent Siino
Det. Harvey Simmons
Lt. Dan Tauriello
Sgt. Charles Wilson
Sgt. Steve Wyrwa

Class "A" Awards Recipients 1992

BELLEVILLE
Joseph Bagonis
Mattia Bernardo
Leonard Burrell
Robert Charles
Thomas Gazzo
John Martucci
Dante Pasquale
James Paterno

BLOOMFIELD
A. Mongiello - Det.
A. Nigro
M. Bardi
R. Tonic

EAST ORANGE
Keith Benson
Ned Duke
Edward Giles
Berkely Jest
Nicholas Martinez
Russell Musal
Harry Osterhoudt
Laderrick Perry - Det.
Morris Rhodes
Harvey Rison
Roland Smith
Horace Watson
Kenneth Welshman
Darryl Wright
Rose Wilson - Det.
Benjamin Mondesir
Lori Lee Bernard
    Antonovich - Lt.
Lafayette Hamlett - Det.
Eugene Motsch
James Pitts - Det.
Benjamin Powell 3rd
Barry Jackson

ESSEX COUNTY
SHERIFF
Bart Vallaro - Det.
Gary Nash - Det.
Gerard Tucci - Det.
Keith Cummings - Det.
Joe Hefferson - Det.
Darrell Miller - Det.
Gary Madera - Sgt.
Calvin Thomas - Det.

ESSEX COUNTY
PROSECUTORS OFFICE

James F. Mulvihill
Peter J. Francese
John S. Redden
Norman W. Menz, Jr.
Louis E. Greenleaf
Charles H. Acocella
Joseph A. Martino
William A. Walsh
David Martinez
Richard P. O'Malley
Ruben T. Contreras
Vincent F. Byron, III
Louis A. Carrega
Stephen E. Bright
Patrick V. DeFrancisci
Henry Ferer
William F. Isetts
Stephen R. Praschak
Frank A. Racioppi
William B. O'Connell
Henry L. Dillon
Louis A. Portella
John C. Arnold
James A. Delissio Jr.
Joseph Duker
David Kircher
Sheila Hobson

IRVINGTON
Bobby Goines
Crawford Whiting
John Van Bavel
Janet Ribeiro
Robert McHugh
Peter Burgess
Charles Burghardt
Michael Daniluk
Kim Williams
William T. Edgar - Sgt. / Det.
Scott Hildebrand - Sgt.
Gene Nigro - Det.
Donald Doriety - Det.
Richard Herzer - Det.
Nicholas Gargas - Det.
Ralph Collura
Pasqual DelVecchio
Michael Healy
Patrick Brennan
Catalino Santiago
Marshall Reiter
Roman Melenka
Phillip Gregory
Anthony Velez
Joseph Monticello

Charles Hutcheson
Gary Christie - Det.
Leonard Mazauskas
Robert J. Passafiume - Sgt.
Michael Tomich
Aaron Graves
Michael Walker
Frank Cunningham
George Venturi - Lt.
Phillip Rucker
Michael Mellilo
Joseph Manderski
Diomedes Valenzuela
Melvin Shamberger
Ladimir Tavares - Det.
Barry Halpern - Det.
John Molisso - Det.

ARSON
INVESTIGATORS
Gerald Highsmith
Richard Restaino
Fred Shackleford
Eugene Poole

NEWARK
Gene Etchison
Manuel Carillo
Joseph Hadley Jr.
Vanessa Davis
John Matos
Carmine Buonsanto
Anthony Iemmello
Joseph Juliano
Samuel DeMaio - Det.
Vincent Cordi - Det.
Daniel Helber
Joseph Wilke
Anthony Morales
John Leszkowicz
Nick Baglione
Labeeb Abdullah
Paul Lorenc - Det.
Charles Conte - Det.
Richard Williams
Peter Biggiani
Anthony Perillo - Sgt.
Gregory Millstein
Joseph Conzentino
Steven Yurik
Manuel Carrillo - PO
Robert Russo - Sgt.
Pedro Zamora Jr. - PO
Yvette Lopez - Det.

Charles Cefalu - D / C
David Letts

NUTLEY
Joe Russonella - Det. Lt.
Joseph Villano - Det.
William Lopa - Det.
Jack Barry - Det.
Robert DeBello - Det. Sgt.
Gail Ferrara
John Rhein

MAPLEWOOD
Joseph Guglielmo

MONTCLAIR
Thomas Oates - Capt.
John Gilligan - Det.

Robert Rowan - Det.
Manford Ayers - Det.
Rocco Miscia - Lt.
Phillip DeFrank

ORANGE
John Wade
Vincent Vitiello
Hareem Simms
Todd Mosby
Edward Smith - Lt.
Michael Gannon - Sgt.
Joseph Cosentino - Det.
William Cieri
Brian David
Joseph McNair - Lt.
Joseph Pallitto
Steven Crumpton
Tracy Wright

Anthony Carpiniello
Michael McManus
Carlos Gonzales
Chris Dunn
Willie Coley
Judith Rothenberger
Kevin Sooy
Thomas Iadiorio
James Chechele
Joseph Pagano
James Cullen

SOUTH ORANGE
Barry Ring - Lt.
Michael Bolger - Sgt.
Randy Garrett - Det.
Mark Garrett
Donald Wallsckleger

Class "B" Awards Recipients 1992

BELLEVILLE
Arthur Connolly - Det.
James DelGrosso - Det.
Ronald Edwards - Det.
Michael Giuliano
James Giuliano - Det.
Patrick Goldrick
Joseph Larceri
Daniel Ward
Anthony Wieners - Det.

BLOOMFIELD
J. Caron
E. Clark
D. Davis - Sgt.
S. DiDomenico
D. Druker
S. Sunn
E. Dwyer
T. Fano
M. Frazzano - Sgt.
C. Goul
J. Graney
W. Jones
D. Maisto
A. Micelli
C. Priolo
J. Pulido - Sgt.
D. Robinson
M. Rozek
R. Russomanno
J. Sierchio

J. Velez

EAST ORANGE
Michael Allman
Archie Alston - Sgt.
Joseph Ash - Det.
Timothy Bradley
Richard Carroll - Det.
Steven Carter
Michael Chwal
Frank Cocchi - Sgt.
Delacy Davis
Andrew Dielmo
Lawrence Flanagan
Kevin Gilsenan - Sgt.
Charles Hall
Michael Johnson
Ernest Jones - Det.
Tyrone Kelly
Gary Kelshaw - Det.
John Legates - Sgt.
Richard Leon
Michael Livett - Sgt.
Alfonza Marina - Det.
Timothy O'Keefe
Michael Person
William Phillips
Barry Porterfield
Benjamin Powell II
Tyrone Reynolds
Eric Robinson - Lt.
William Robinson

Robert Sauthoff
Christopher Scott
Steven Simms - Det.
Freddie Townes
Victor Tucker
Santiago Salicrup
Gregg Masi - Det.
Anthony Cox
Carlos Gonzalez
Anthony Tortorella
Edward Smith - Lt.
James Melchinonda - Capt.
Lawrence Roche - Sgt.
George Holmes
Daryl Butler - Det.
Joseph Cosentino - Det.
Edgar Pinckney - Det.
Ben Moore
Thomas Coen
Pat Russo
John Young
Louis Castro - Det.
Richard O'Malley - Lt.
Joseph Pallitto
Brian David
Nicholas Liotti - Sgt.
John Wade
Chris Dunn
Frank Scura
Pat Uggierio
Paul Palmere
Kevin Sooy

**ESSEX COUNTY
SHERIFF DEPT.**
William Capko
Michael Bettin - Det.
Joe Hefferson - Det.
Nicholas Cerreto - Det.
Fernando Franco - Det.
Robert Oliver - Det.
Calvin Thomas - Det.
John Ferrara - Det.
Arthur Paradiso - Det.
Michael Culey - Sgt.
Don Hurley - Det.
Arnold Bernard - Det.
Santo Aodica Sr. - Det.
Dennis Kihlberg
Donald Bartel
Marion Coleman
Gary Matthews
Michael Fogeio

LIVINGSTON
William Eppell
Anthony Orefice
Andrew Borschuk
Carl Bloch - Sgt.
Stephen Yannotti
Dennis Doriety
Robert Williams - Sgt.
Lawrence Kroll -Lt.
Eugene Olson - Sgt.
Joseph Ottobre - Sgt.
Theodore Pankiewicz
Sean Halpin - Sgt.
Michael Daminao - Lt.
Lee R. Schroeder - Det. / Capt.
Craig M. Hanschuch - Det /
Sgt.
Douglas S. Weber - Det. / Sgt.
Jack Hickey - Det.
Stan Chciuk - Det.
Drew Hoeke - Det.
Anthony Dippold - Det.
Brian Rabbitt - Det.
William Hain - Capt.
William Brennan
Richard Flinn

MAPLEWOOD
David Green
Patrick J. Coyle - Sgt.
David A. Cross
Vincent J. Cuozzo

Lawrence A. Frank
Thaddeus J. Gnida
Kevin C. Graham
Michael Marucci
Michael J. Mault - Det.
Stanley Rosa

MONTCLAIR
Perry Mayers - Det.
John Leverich
Donald Williams
Vincent J. Cuozzo
Lawrence A. Frank
Thaddeus J. Gnida
Kevin C. Graham
Michael Marucci
Michael J. Mault - Det.
Stanley Rosa

MONTCLAIR
Perry Mayers - Det.
John Leverich
Donald Williams
Charles Lavery
David Sabagh
Sean Carlesimo
Kenneth Miscia
Wayne Desmet
Agustin-Arencibia
William Morrison
Frank Gowen

NEWARK
Neil Minovich
Mario Martin
Keith Issac - Det.
Jose Valentin - Det.
Fred Masucci
James Post
Leonard Breaux
Otto Moravek
Felix Rodriguez
Robert Lee Williams
Steve Rivers
Efrain Velazquez
George Vasquez
Rafael Ramos
Vincent Vitiello
Sean Gaven
Fiore Purcell
Edwin Mendez
Charles Congelosi
Nichola Casale - Det.
James Wynn - Det.

Frank Huff - Det.
Michael Johnson - Det.
John Scott Bey - Sgt.
Joseph Melvin
Rene Lisojo
Israel Caraballo
Manuel Carrillo
Carlos Hernandez
John Witsch - Lt.
Carmine Cosenza - Det.
Michael Thomas
Willie Thomas
Victor Cugliari
Gerard Vella
Fredy Pierre
Kevin Moore
Anthony Fiumefreddo
Michael Chirico
Thomas Delloiacovo
Joseph Zieser
William Sanchez
Michael LePoint
Darren Price
Bill Brady
Nicholas Scaglione - Det.
Ilia Aquino - Det.
Ronald Soto
Vincent Bongermino
Dwayne Wilkins

ROSELAND
John Matheis
Kevin M. Kitchin
Christopher Vanadia

SOUTH ORANGE
Kyle Kroll
Edward Schmidt
Joseph Bradley
Michael Bradley
Eric Moore
James Chelel - Sgt.
Patrick Zazzaro
Robert Raddi
Steven Davenport
Mark Prial
Hugh Ames
Paul Jones - Det.
Thomas Andrew - Capt.
Paul Aulisio - Capt.
Steven Palamara
Richard Padalino - Lt.
James Russell

Class "C" Awards Recipients 1992

BELLEVILLE
Thomas Agosta - Det.
Jack Baumgartner
Gerard Campanella
Gerard Corbo
George Geyer
John Hood - Det.
Nicholas Krentz - Sgt.
Paul Long
John Mailot - Lt.
Frank Marino
James Melillo
Anthony Passarella
Anthony Romandetto
Thoma Rossi - Sgt.
Rory Scheumeister
Scott Sim - Sgt.
Joseph Simonetti - Capt.
Gary Souss
John Towey
Joseph Trabucco
Anthony Tucci
Anthony Weedo
Joseph Zarrillo

BLOOMFIELD
W. Abendschoen
S. Antonsson
T. Bianco - Sgt.
M. Behre - Sgt.
C. Chiarello
E. Clark
E. Clark
M. Cooper
S. Dunn
S. Dunn
K. Dybus
K. Dybus
T. Fano
T. Fano
R. Gilsenan
R. Gilsenan
C. Goul
J. Graney
W. Jones
D. Maisto
G. Mastroeni - Det.
G. Mastroeni - Det.
S. Messina
S. Messina
C. Priolo
D. Robinson
A. Servedio
J. Sierchio
T. Smith
A. Zachares
A. Zachares
L. Zawinstowski - Sgt.

ESSEX COUNTY
POLICE
Joseph Castagnino - Det./Lt.
Richard E. Levens
Anthony Ruggiero
Stephen DeRosa
Michael Cali
Joseph Spero
Matthew Palardy
Dominic Bertoldi
Richard Potts
Louis Mignone
Rocco Montesano
Thomas Filan - Sgt.

EAST ORANGE
Clarence Brown
Derrick Brown
Eugene Digiacomo - Sgt.
Bruce Doriety
Brian Dyer - Sgt.
Kevin Green
Richard Gregory
Keith Hinton
John Jackson - Lt.
Hurley Jones
Michael Kasper
Karl Keene
Philip Major
Frank Michetti
William Moore
Raymond Neves
Floyd Newton
Hosia Reynolds
Robert Shaw
William Shirden
James Smith
John Thornton
Carl Turner
Mercedes Vega
John Zimmerman

ESSEX COUNTY
JAIL
Thomas Darcy - Lt.
Stanley McClroy
Bassett - Sgt.
Edgar Barcliff
Thomas Kincade

ESSEX COUNTY
SHERIFF
Christopher Imperiale
William Capko
Nicholas D'uva
George Shanaphy - Sgt.
Ignacio Mendez - Det.
Vincent Mercandante - Det.
Nicholas Vinci - Det.
Michael Bettin - Det.
Gary Madera - Sgt.
Thomas McColgan - Det.
Donato Nisivoccia - Det.
Ronald Tutela - Det.
Marion Coleman
Daniel Rinaldi - Det.
Santo Modica III - Det.
David Hughes - Det.
Anthony Melia - Det.

IRVINGTON
Richard Wilkins
Kuzma Uchin
Michael Isselin

LIVINGSTON
George Banzhaf
Andrew Glassman
David Drylie
Matthew Foley·
Stephen McSpirit
Timothy Dunmyer

MAPLEWOOD
James J. Bordino III
David G. Breen
Charles A. Cataldi
John Cheasty - Sgt.
Paul Conlon
David A. Cross
Lewis DeMelo, Jr.
Robert M. Dombrowski,
Jr. - Det.
Jose A. Matinez - Sgt.
Michael A. Marucci
Thomas A. Perna
John A. Perna
John P. Plesnik
John P. Tutunjian

MONTCLAIR
Michael Oates - Sgt.
Roger Terry

Edward Gowen
Robert Ramundo
Theodore Ryan
Edward Hancock
James Marinaro
John Beyer

NEWARK
Gene Etchison
Richard Moreno
Joseph Bezak
Reynaldo Diaz
Joequan Jenkins
Stanley Guthrie
Robinson Rodriguez
Javier Rivera
Luther Lyle
Robert Braswell
Juan Gonzalez
Gregory Hamilton
James Chieppa
Kenneth Holloway
Wilberto Rivera
Elby Roberts
Umar Abdul Hakeem
Samad Washington
Joseph Matozzi
Michelle Whitted
Roy Wheeler Weaver
Anibal Nieves
Frank Faretra
Robert Sarappa
Pdrito Cruz
Eversley Sifontes
Kenneth Hubert
Julio Valentin
Antonio Perez
Michael Daye
Keith Rubel
Kevin Gaven
Nick Maresca

Kevin Johnson
Louis Smith
Gilbert Rodriguez
David Burgos
Donald Stokes
Neftalis Mendez
Michael McDuffie
Tracy Rayner
Anthony Simmons
Chester Soloweij
Terrez Toldens
Kenneth Koonce
Joseph Grosso
Edward Philson
Darren Gilbert
Kirk Rubel
John Sino
Kyle Brown
Tyrone Moore
James Wright
Keith Sheppard
Jeri McQueen
James Watson
Thomas Candura
Hubert Clark
Derek Lawz
Samuel Mendez
Gerard Piacenza
Matthew Spencer
Niles Wilson
James Arroyo
Jose Montalvo
Joseph Forlenza
Michael Knight
Reginald Merritt
Larry Blake
Matthew Donnellan
Reinaldo Arocha, Jr.
Michael Cirasella
Landre Johnson
Brian Johnson

Hernandez Thomas
David Santiago
George Ramos
Juan Gonzalez
Oscar Davis
Shawn Garrett
Stephen Cornick
Mark Hill
Miguel Marquez
Marion Solomon
Phillmon McFadden
Jose Tavres
Manuel Lorenzo
Frank Perez
Hubert Clark
Anthony Caruso
Vincent Ucci
Nathan Headd
Samuel Gonzalez
Genaro Ortiz
Keith Salters
Anthony Rggiero
Crystal Rollins
Joseph McGinley - Det.
James Cullen
Ronald Wright
Eiugene Muhammad
Jose Pereira
Israel Caraballo
Victor Diaz
Joseph DaRocha
Richard Cuccolo

ROSELAND
Durande Williams
Robert Masiello

SOUTH ORANGE
McFadden
James Russell
William McMillan

Class "A" Valor Award Recipients 1993

Det. Anthony Ambrose
Det. Reinaldo Arocha
Lt. George Bagnall
Det. Harry Boger
Det. Irving Bradley
PO William Brady
PO Frank Bristol
Det. Sam Bristol
PO David Burgos
PO Carmine Buonsanto
PO Joe Cantalupo
PO Michael Chirico
PO Derrick Clemons
PO Joe Conzentino
PO Pablo Cruz
PO Thomas Delloiacovo
Det. Carmine DeMaio
PO Renaldo Diaz
Det. Victor M. Diaz
Det. Jack Eutsey
PO Frank Faretra
PO Richard Flounoy
PO Joe Gallant

Det. Rafael Garcia
PO Anthony Gayder
PO Vincent Gayder
Det. Michael Gillens
PO Antonio Gonzalcz
PO Roger Harris
Det. Noreen Britt Headen
PO Cesar Hernandez
Det. Abdul H. Hasan
PO Mark Hill
PO Carmine Horvath
PO Keith Hughes
PO Milton Jacobs
PO Landre Johnson
PO Joe Juliano
PO Michael Lalley
PO Michael La Motta
PO Joe Lobardo
Det. Paul Lorenc
Det. Miguel Marquez
PO Mario Martin
Sgt. Milton Medina
PO Lawrence Mellilo

PO Neil Minovich
PO Kevin Moore
PO Otto J. Moravek
PO Calvin Parkman
PO Dennis Reilly
Det. Anthony Ricca
PO Javier Rivera
PO Elby Roberts
Sgt. Carmine Russo
PO Keith Salters
Det. Thomas Scull
PO Keith Sheppard
PO Anthony Simmons
Det. Willie Stroud
Det. Steven Tassie
PO Michael Turner
PO Joe Watson
PO Roy Wheeler Weaver
PO Ulysses Whetstone
PO James Wright
Det. Steven Yablonsky
PO Steve Yurik
PO Angelo Zamora

Class "A" Award Recipients Spring 1994

Richard Allen
Frank Bristol
Carmine Buonsanto
Derrick Clemons
Joseph Conzentino
Frank Faretra
Vincent Gayden
Roger Harris
Keith Hughes
Joequan Jenkins
Rene Lisojo

Lawrence Mellilo
Joseph Melvin
Calvin Parkman
Fedy Pierre
Carmine Russo
Kenneth Terry
William Thomas, Jr.
Sim Timmons
Joseph Watson
Steven Yurik

Class "B" Award Recipients Spring 1994

Reinaldo Arocho
Mark Ausbey
Barry Baker
Garry Baker
Larry Blake, Jr.
William Brady
Paul Braswell
David Burgos
Miguel Carrillo
Tracy Childress
Reynaldo Diaz
Vincent Filippone
Richard Flounoy
Jose Gonzalez
Cesar Hernandez
Orlando Hurtado
Landre Johnson
Kevin Johnson
Andrew Jones

Joseph Juliano
Mario Martin
Horace McGloster
Mario Medina
George Mendez
William Mitchell
Dennis Reilly
Keith Sheppard
Eversley Sifontes
Anthony Simmons
Mathew Spencer
William Tartis
Michael Turner
Julio Valentin
Gerard Vella
Vincent Vitiello
Samad Washington
Ulysses Whetstone
James Wright

1994 Law Enforcement Officer of the Year
Lorenzo Marchese
Essex County Corrections PBA Local 153

1994 Unit Citations
Belleville
Nutley
East Orange
Essex County Prosecutors Office
Irvington P.D.
FBI Task Force

Class "A" Awards Recipients Fall 1994

BELLEVILLE LOCAL #28
Off. Gerard Corbo
Off. Rory Scheumeister
Off. Joseph Trabucco
Off. William Palatella
Off. Frank Parillo
Off. Anthony Tucci
Off. Richard Giordano
Off. Patrick Goldrick
Off. Robert Charles
Det. Michela Guliano
Det. Robert Capeco

BLOOMFIELD LOCAL #32
Off. C. Chiarello
Off. S. Dunn
Off. M. Falco
Off. T. Fano
Off. D. Gury
Sgt. M. Leonard
Off. S. Messina
Off. A. Nigro
Off. M. Rozek
Off. T. Smith
Off. E. Sousa (4)
Off. J. Testa (3)
Off. G. Trapp (3)
Off. G. Wiegand
Off. A. Zachares

EAST ORANGE
Off. Earl Graves
Sgt. Edward Jene
Off. Berkely Jest
Off. Tyrone Kelly
Off. Eric Lewis
Off. Richard Leon
Off. Joaquin Martinez
Lt. Kevin Morgan
Off. William Phillips
Off. Santiago Salicrup
Off. Jimmie Sheard
Off. William Shirden
Off. Timothy Sullivan
Off. Kenneth Welsman

IRVINGTON
Det. Sgt. William T. Edgar
Det. Sgt. Robert Passfiumo
Sgt. Scott R. Hildebrand
Sgt. Scan Halpin

Det. Ladimir Tavares
Det. James De Angelis
Off. Michael Mellilo
Off. Joseph Monticello
Off. Michael Walker
Off. Edward Dimaggio
Off. Livio Cioffi
K9 Off. Stephen Yannotti
Off. Mark Manderski
Off. Peter Burgess
Det. William R. Eppell
K9 Off. Frank Cunningham
Det. Michael Healy
Off. Patrick Brennan

LIVINGSTON
Sgt. Edward Kelly
Off. George Banzhaf

MILLBURN
Off. John J. Laverty, Jr.

MONTCLAIR
Off. Phillip De Frank
Off. Charles Shaw
Off. Edward Gowen
Det. Robert Smith
Off. James Marinaro

NEWARK
Lt. Vincent Gagliano
Off. Christopher Kossup
Off. Labeeb Abdullah
Off. Michael Turner
Off. Robert Boyer Jr.
Off. Tyrone Moore
Off. Charles Hummel
Off. Israel Caraballo
Off. Clifton Burchett
Off. Reynaldo Diaz
Off. Ricardo Feliciano
Off. Ronald Pomponio
Off. Scott Sayre
Off. Kirk Rubel
Off. Gregory Gilhooley
C/O Carmine Caprio
C/O William Buchanan
Constable Antonio Liguori
Sgt. Vincent Bongermino
Det. George Mendez

Off. Reinaldo Arocha
Off. Gerard Vella
Off. Vicent Vitiello
Off. Anthony Arce
Off. Hector Majias
Off. Michael Chirico
Off. Timothy Hague
Off. Robert Williams
Off. Hector Rodrigues
Off. Lucinda Simmons
Off. Joseph Gallant
Off. Edwin Gonzalez
Off. Paul Caricella
Off. Angelo Sciara
Off. Anthony Kerr
Off. Vincent Ucci
Off. Steven Rivers
Off. Leonard Breax
Off. Vivian Attoyo
Off. Keith Jordan
Off. Michael La Torre
Off. Hetibrto Ballester Jr.
Off. Steven Yurik
Off. Dominick Di Andrea
Off. Kevin Herder
Off. David Cuccolo
Off. Dwayne Wilkins
Off. Cheryl Washington
Off. Joseph Hadley
Off. Michael Beasley
Off. Anthony Gibson
Off. Kevin Lassiter
Off. Charles Good
Off. Araseliz Ocasio
Off. Robert Williams
Off. Jose Velez
Off. Gerry Guanci
Off. James Hill
Off. Sandro Colon
Off. Darrel Major
Off. Dennis Reilly
Off. Julio Valentin
Off. Edward Lang
Off. Alfreddy Fletcher
Off. David Robinson
Local #3
Off. William Brady
Off. Hector Rodriguez
Off. Miguel Carrillo
Off. Jose Gonzales
Off. Keith Rubel
Off. David Burgos

Off. Reynaldo Diaz
Det. Jose Valentin
Off. Vincent Fillipone
Off. Horace McGloster
Off. Reinaldo Arocha
Off. Ronald Pomponio
Off. Joseph Hadley Jr.
Off. Robert E. Dunn Jr.
Det. Frederick Mitchell
Off. Otto Moravek
Det. Richard Moreno
Det. Jose Pereira
Det. Michael Daye
Det. Alfred Burroughs
Det. Anthony Moraes
Off. Jose Rosa
Off. Reinaldo Bosque
Off. Glenn Singleton
Off. Teddy Malamug
Off. Vincent Corti
Off. Gregory Millstien
Off. Michael Cavallaro
Off. David Pearson
Off. Luis Ortiz
Off. Joseph Darocha
Off. Paul Carnicella
Off. Rene Lisojo
Det. Joseph Bruno Jr.
Det. Nicholas Colombo
Det. David Burgos
Off. Barry Baker
Off. Garry Baker
Sgt. Nicolas Maresca
Off. Steven Yurick
Off. Robert Lee Williams
Off. Joseph Penevolpe
Off. Toms Ciccone
Off. Neil Minovich
Off. William Tartis
Off. Emmanuel
   Rodrigues
Off. Carlton Perry
Det. William Thomas
Off. Jose Gonzale Jr.
Off. Wilfredo Torres
Off. Luther Fatman
U.S. Agent Douglass
   Farrell
U.S. Agent James
   Sullivan
Off.Geoffery Luckey
Off Heriberto
   Ballester Jr.
Off. Delvis Matos
Off. Joseph Melvin
Off. Joseph Penevolpe

Off. Robert Williams
Off. Frank Lucas
Off. Willie Caldwell
Off. Marion Reynolds
Off. William Rodriguez
Off. Manuel Carrillo
Off. Wilfredo Medina
Off. Lorenzo Valentine
Off. Sandro Colon
Off. William Zois
Off. Marcus Thomas
Off. Calvin Parman
Off. John Cuccolo
Off. Anthony Lucarelli
Det. Anthony Moraes
Det. Michael Lalley
Det. William Funk
Det. Nick Scaglione
Det. Tracy Childress
Det. Richard Cuccolo
Off. Milton Jacobs
Det. Marilouise Dorch
Off. Hector Corchado
Det. Arlen Alvarado
Off. Fred Masucci
Off. Robinson Rodrigues
Off. Wilfredo Gonzales
Off. Wilberto Rivera
Off. Scott Sayre
Off. Michael Palermo
Off. Patrick Dimcola
Off. Raphael Berubez
Off. Darrel Major
Det. Reinaldo Perez
Det. Patricia Kines
Off. Michael Walski
Off. Glen O'Neil
Off. Scan Gaven
Off. John Melillo Jr.
Off. William Maldonado
Det. Joseph Watson
Off. Arthur Wohltman
Off. Luis Delgado
Det. Vincent Pabon
Off. Rafael Ramos
Off. Michael Branon
Off. Jose Negron
Off. Michael Latorre
Off. Giulio Cavallaro
Off. Samuel Cerasiello
Off. Thomas Ciccone
Off. Gregory Hamilton
Off. Cheryl Washington
Off. Murad Muhammad
Off. William Conley
Off. Anthony Agular

Off. Exequiel Leyva
Off. Darrell Major
Off. Garnet Person
Off. Ronald Polhill
Off. Labeeb M.
   Abdullah

NJ TRANSIT POLICE
Sgt. Samuel Wike
Sgt. Charles Thomas
Off. James Finnegan
Off. James Rodgers
S/A Tim Sharkey
Sgt. Eggers

NUTLEY
Sgt. Robert
   Malanga
Off. Mark De Litta
Off. Robert Kordas
Off. Brian Jernick
Off. Paul Edwards
Off. Gail Ferrara
Off. Kevin Watts
Off. Christopher Lamond
Off. David Moran

ORANGE
Off. Christopher Dunn
Off. William Cieri
Off. John Young
Off. Steve Crumpton
Off. Shawn Harris
Off. Andrew Berkery
Off. Arlo Webster
Off. Brian David
Off. Joseph Martin
South Orange
Off. Mark Prial
Off. Frank Lipere

WEST ESSEX
Off. John Delotto
Off. Louis Cammarata
Off. Martin Brennan
Sgt. James Moye
Off. Chuck Voelker
Sgt. Glenn Donker
Cpl. William Coughlin
Cpl. Michael Moran
Off. Michael Bramhall

WEST ORANGE
Sgt. Robert Stock
Ptlm. Robert Stock
Ptlm. Vincent Pecora

Ptlm. Richard Potts
Ptlm. Patrick Yorke
Ptlm. Raymond Rosanie
Ptlm. Robert Martin
Ptlm. John Fagan
Ptlm. Bilal Muhammad

**ESSEX COUNTY
CORRECTIONS**
Off. Larry Stewart

**CALDWELL
ESSEX CITY JAIL
ANNEX**
Off. Ronald (Duke)
Simms
Off. Steven Sweigart

**ESSEX COUNTY
POLICE**
Off. John Donfrio
Off. Joseph Sauchelli

Off. E. J. Pollara

**ESSEX COUNTY
SHERIFF**
Det. Ronald Tutela
Det. Pedro Quinones
Det. Anthony Ricca
Det. Peter Surdi
Det. Nicholas Vinci
Det. Ignacio Mendez

Class "B" Award Recipients Fall 1994

BELLEVILLE
Off. Joseph Zarrello
Off. James Melillo
Lt. Nicholas Krentz
Off. Frank Malfatto
Det. Kevin Smith
Sgt. Charles Padula
Off. James Sochaski

BLOOMFIELD
Sgt. M. Behre
Off. C. Chiarello
Off. S. Ciccone
Sgt. D. Davis
Off. D. Drucker
Off. S. Dunn
Det. S. Gerhauser
Off. R. Gilsenan
Off. C. Goul
Off. M. Horton
Off. W. Jones
Off. J. Krentz
Off. W. Luke
Lt. J. Marcey
Off. C. Priolo
Sgt. J. Pulido
Off. D. Robinson (2)
Off. J. Ross (2)
Off. M. Rozek
Off. J. Sierchio
Off. P. Spatola
Off. J. Testa
Off. T. G. Walsh (3)
Sgt. J. Decker
Off. S. Messina
Off. J. Velez
Off. D. Maisto

EAST ORANGE
Lt. Joseph Angelo

Off. Richard Bell
Off. Keith Benson
Off. Phyliss Bindi
Off. Troy Bowers
Off. Timothy Bradley
Det. Clarence Brown, Jr.
Det. William Butler
Off. Reginald Butts
Sgt. Frank Cocchi
Off. Kevin Coleman
Off. Angel Cocepcion
Det. Anthony Cox
Off. Frank Deherde
Sgt. Eugene Digjhcomo
Off. Lawrence Flanagan
Off. Daniel Francis
Det. William Garvin
Off. Edward Giles
Off. Keith Gillespie
Off. Kevin Green
Off. Charles Hall
Off. Joseph Hammond
Off. Dwayne Harris
Off. Bart Haverty
Det. Isaiah Jackson
Off. Michael Jackson
Det. Ernest Jones
Off. Hurley Jones
Det. Gary Kelshaw
Det. James Kelshaw
Off. Carl Kyer
Off. Paul Lobur
Off. Phillip Major
Off. William Mango III
Det. Alfonza Marina
Det. Paul McCusker
Off. Benjamin Mondesir
Off. Derrick Moses
Off. Frank Niciaro
Off. Timothy Okeefe

Off. Christian Patrick
Off. Elliot Petty
Det. James Pitts
Off. Benjamin Powell III
Off. Wanda K. Powell
Det. Phillip Reed
Off. John A. Robinson
Det. Willie Rowe
Off. Alejandro Sanchez
Off. David Sealy
Det. Elaine Settle
Off. Andres Soto
Off. Roland Smith
Off. Horace Watson
Det. Michael Williams

IRVINGTON
Ptlm. Steven Schulz
Ptlm. Robert G. Gizenski
Capt. Michael Chase
Ptlm. Robert McHugh
Ptlm. Melvin Shamberger
Ptlm. Roman Melenka
Ptlm. Kim Williams
Ptlm. Michael Isselin
Ptlm. Anthony Velez
Det. Richard Herzer
Det. Edward Almutis
Ptlm. Pasqual Delvecchio
Ptlm. Dominic Mercadante
Ptlm. Lonnie Friedman
Ptlm. James Clyburn
Ptlm. Gerald Malek

LIVINGSTON
Det. Sgt. Craig
M. Handschuch
Det. Sgt. Douglas Weber
Cpt. William Hain
Det. Jack H. Hickey

Det. Stanley J. Chciuk
Det. Drew Hoeke
Det. Anthony Dippold
Off. William Brennan
Off. Christopher Reinhardt
Off. Kenneth Hanna
Stuart Lukowiak
Off. David Drylie

MILBURN
Off. Thomas Paranzine
Off. Paul Jackson
Off. Ronald Lipp
Off. Joseph Johnson
Off. Joseph Leone
Off. Horace
  Giambattista Jr.
Off. Peter T. Eakley

MONTCLAIR
Off. John Beyer
Off. Mary Donenghi
DLT. Robert Sobers
Det. Wayne Desmet
Det. Scott Roberson
Capt. Eugene Carey
Lt. Robert Duncan
Off. Kenneth Miscia
Off. Stephen Graybush
Off. Charles Hancock

NEWARK
Off. Kevin Herder
Off. Robert Clark
Off. Michael De Maio
Off. Angelo Sciara
Off. Pal Carnicella
Off. Edwin Mendez
Off. Calvin Parkman
Off. Glenn Singleton
Off. Milto Jacobs
Off. Emmanuel
  Rodriguez
Off. Kevin Rhodes
Off. Patrick Di Meola
Off. Michael Palermo
Off. Antonio Cardoso
Off. Phil Litterio
Off. Leonard Breaux
Off. Steve Rivers
Off. Juan C. Munoz

Off. Wilfredo Mercado
Off. Pedro Zamora
Off. Dominic Di Andrea
Off. Willie J. Thomas
Off. John Matos
Off. Gary Bean
Off. Geoffrey Lucky
Off. Luther Bean
Off. David Burgos
Off. Reinaldo Perez
Off. John Siino
Off. Keith Jordan
Off. Cheryl Washington
Off. Rodney Barron
Off. Cliffs Spencer
Off. John Cuccolo
Off. Anthony Lucarelli
Off. Pedro Neves
Off. Nick Baglione
Off. Edwin Gonzales
Off. Roger Harris

NJ TRANSIT
Lt. Richards
Lt. Tarasevitsch

NUTLEY
Off. John Miterko
Off. Aaron Morrison
Off. Phil Keseling
Off. Bob Cassie
Sgt. Steve Rogers
Lt. Raymond Hackett
Det. John Rhein
Det. Jack Barry

ORANGE
Off. Willie Coley
Off. Thomas Coen
Det. Michael Crowley
Off. Willie Brown
Det. Jerome Anderson
Off. Michael Juliano
Off. John Wede
Off. Steve Crumpton
Off. Brian David
Off. Arik Webster
Off. John Young
Off. Joseph Martin
Off. Vincent Vitiello
Off. James Chechele

Off. Thomas Iandiorio
Off. Christopher Dunn
Off. Todd Mosby
Off. Orlando Soto

SOUTH ORANGE
Sgt. Charles Hooey
Off. William Pillus
Off. Patrick McKell
Off. Donald Wallschleger
Off. Maura Lynch
Off. James Sutula
Off. James Cuccinello
Off. Paul Clohosey
Off. Randy Garret

VERONA
Sgt. Martin Santuoso

ESSEX CTY.
CORRECTIONS
Off. Alexander Brandt
Off. Jose Gradaille
Off. Clifford Hollis
Off. Lorenzo Marchese
Off. Paul Nardone (2)
Off. Louis Pastena (2)
Off. Neil Simeone
Off. Milton Vaughn
Off. Salvatore Vitale (2)
Off. Jeff Wood

ESSEX CITY,
SHERIFF
Det. John Balsamo
Det. Edward O'Mara
Lt. Gary Madera
Det. Cyrus Littles
Det. Robert Greene
Sgt. John Ferrara
Det. Fernando Franco
Det. Steven Serritella
Det. Eduardo Moreno
S.O. John Mongiello
Det. Fred Apicelli
Det. Vito D'Alessio
Det. Ant Demeo
Det. Michael Scardine
Det. Richard Colabelli
S.O. Mark Cosenzo
Det. Frank Laminitti

Class "C" Award Recipients Fall 1994

BELLEVILLE
Off. George Geyer
Off. Anthony Wieners
Off. Nicholas Tribley
Off. Carmen Cerreto
Off. Gary Souss
Off. Anthony Passarella
Off. Brendan Dullaghan
Lt. John Mailot
Off. Joseph Bagonis
Off. Joseph Tramaglini
Sgt. John Towey
Off. Vincent Masi
Off. Thomas Gazzo
Off. Stephen Xenios
Off. John Martucci
Off. Mattia Bernardo
Capt. Robert Estelle
Sgt. James Del Grosso
Off. Anthony Weedo
Det. Craig Mack

BLOOMFIELD
Off. M. Cooper
Off. A. French
Off. C. Goul
Off. R. McGoldrick (2)
Off. A. Nigro
Det. C. Raszetnik
Off. J. San Silverino
Off. P. Spatola
Off. John Alston
Off. Albert Bey
Det. Troy Boone
Sgt. Michael Brown

Off. Raymond Brown
Sgt. Ralph Cafone
Det. George Casale
Off. Trent Clark
Off. Tyrone Crawley
Det. William Davis
Off. Christopher Dehagara
Sgt. Brian Dyer
Det. Hillard Edmond
Det. Aron Evans
Sgt. Norwood Hikson
Det. Thomas Koundry
Capt. Michael Kula
Sgt. John Legates
Lt. John Marchewka
Off. Nicholas Martinez
Sgt. Joseph Matrale
Sgt. Jack McGarry
Off. Frank Michetti
Off. Gregory Natson
Off. Paul Nigro
Det. Edith Ottley
Off. Michael Person
Det. Alexander Pettiford
Off. Donald Preston
Sgt. Richard Senft
Det. Steven Sims
Off. Shawn Stacevicz
Sgt. Carl Stoffers
Det. Victor Tucker
Off. Mercedes Vega
Det. Eric Washington
Off. Ronald Watson

GLENRIDGE

Off. David Butterfield
Off. Edward Johnson
IRVINGTON
Sgt. Robert G. Sizenski
Sgt. Charles Angello
Ptlm. Marshall Reiter
Ptlm. Thomas Chakeras
Ptlm. Michael Yannuzzelli
Capt. George Venturi
Ptlm. Joseph Misale
Ptlm. Tracey Bowers
Ptlm. Kenneth Wiazlo
K9 Off. Charles Burghardt
Ptlm. Phillip Gregory
Sgt. Joseph Mustacchio
Sgt. Barry Halpern
Sgt. Myron Prokopiw
Ptlm. Edwin Villafane

MILLBURN
Off. Robert Ronceray
Sgt. Steven Laverty
Lt. James Miller
Off. Michael J. Palardy Jr.
Off. Bernhard Neuhaus
Off. Edward Staeger

MONTCLAIR
Off. Alan Cumming
Off. James Lalor
Off. Richard Pinck
Off. John Carlo
Off. Wilhelm Young
Off. Jack Gilligan
Off. Donald Williams

Congratulations to the 134 "Blue Warriors" who were selected for their courage, dedication and fortitude. These police officers were selected for their achievements throughout their careers.

The officers selected apprehended thousands of criminals during their career. They were awarded numerous Valor Awards and hundreds of Command Citations. They excelled "Above the line of duty."

I consider all of Newark's finest as "Blue Warriors." The young officers of today have a tough challenge ahead of them. These officers will perform "Above the line of duty" as Newark's finest "Blue Warriors."

I salute and respect all of the "Blue Warriors" across the United States who have dedicated their lives to protect the lives and property of the citizens of our country.

I look forward to writing my next book *The Blue Warriors: Medal of Honor*. Twenty-five of Newark's highest decorated officers will be written about.

A special salute to our Commander in Chief, President Bill Clinton, who in September 1994 had a bill passed by Congress that will effectively hire 100,000 additional police officers to fight crime in the streets.

Epilogue

To all the police officers who have read this book: I hope you enjoyed the exciting chapters. We all can learn from some of the sad tragedies that occurred. I know that Chapter Twenty and especially Chapter Twenty-Two will someday save your life. We can all learn and remember from other police officers' mistakes. A message to the officers that joined the Police Department because they needed a job or liked the money that the City of Newark or any other city allocates: I suggest you resign your position and look for another line of work.

To be a police officer requires complete dedication and the willingness to sacrifice unduly. I salute and respect all police officers from the East to the West Coast of the United States. We are truly all top cops who are sworn to be above the line of duty at all times.

To the citizens that have read this book, you have gotten an inside look of how it is to be a police officer out on the streets fighting crime. Chapters Sixteen, Seventeen, Eighteen, Nineteen will make your life a lot safer. If you listen and understand and grasp the advice that I have provided, someday one of the mistakes that other victims have made will save your life. Chapter Twenty will make you a safe driver.

The book I have completed has taken three years to write. As I completed Chapter Nineteen, I was haunted by the seven women who were killed by their estranged husband in June 1992. Hopefully when this book is released, the advice I have provided will save the women who are victims of domestic violence.

In Chapter Twenty I have provided advice to drivers who think going through a green light is free pass to proceed without the chance of an accident. In May 1992, a twenty-six year old mother of two children was tragically killed. The driver of a stolen car crossed the intersection of a red light at Broad and Market Street in Newark, New Jersey. Belleville police officers charged the driver with manslaughter.

Chapter Eighteen provided tenants with advice on how they can have window safety nets installed in high rise buildings. Hundreds of toddlers are killed every year.

I'm asking every police officer and their family members to take a stand.

On behalf of the 13,267 officers killed in the line of duty. On behalf of the 150 officers killed every year in the line of duty.

In the memory of Detective John Sczyrek Jr. and New York City Officer Edward Byrne of the one hundred third Precinct. Both officers were gunned down and assassinated in cold blood. Both were involved in drug-related hits.

Everyone who has read this book, I'm asking for your support. Write to your State Senators and Congressmen. Write to President Bill Clinton asking for a mandate. There has to be a death penalty imposed on killers of police officers.

I'm asking for the support from all New Jersey residents. We have to demand that Prosecutor Minor orders the death penalty to Al-Damanay Kamau and Tinesha James. They have to be injected with a lethal dose and put to death.

A message has to be sent out to the drug dealers and to cop hitmen and killers.

Newark as well as other towns and cities across the United States need the support of President Clinton.

Newark needs federal funds to strengthen our police force. Newark is undermanned by 400 police officers.

Mayor Sharpe James will lose the battle to save Newark if the President does not support our needs.

This is occurring despite the heroic efforts of Newark's finest. All police officers and their families, not to mention all citizens of this country, should and do support President Clinton's bill for an additional 100,000 officers.

Help us to make our streets safe.

Although my book was completed after twenty-one chapters, I added four chapters as a special dedication.

I know that Detective Sczyrek wanted me to do a chapter on the intangible dangers. We talked about combining the knowledge of probable cause and deadly force.

When John told me how important it is to the survival of an officer, I wrote Chapter Twenty-Two. It was intentionally written to save police officers' lives. Sczyrek was on the same wavelength as me. Officers can make a difference as you will see in Chapter Twenty-Three. Chapter Twenty-Four was written to ease the tension of the book. Chapter Twenty-Five should never have needed to be written.